The Editors

ROBERT W. SHAHAN is Chairman of the Department of Philosophy in the University of Oklahoma and editor of the *Southwestern Journal of Philosophy*. FRANCIS J. KOVACH, who also contributed to this book, is Professor of Philosophy in the University of Oklahoma. He is the author of, among other works, *Philosophy of Beauty*, also published by the University of Oklahoma Press.

D1327288

Bonaventure and Aquinas
Enduring Philosophers

University of Oklahoma Press : Norman

Bonaventure
& Aquinas

Enduring philosophers

Edited and with an Introduction by
Robert W. Shahan and Francis J. Kovach

By Robert W. Shahan

Bonaventure and Aquinas: Enduring Philosophers (coeditor; Norman, 1976)

By Francis J. Kovach

Die Aesthetik des Thomas von Aquin, eine genetische und systematische Analyse (Berlin, 1961)

Philosophy of Beauty (Norman, 1974)

Bonaventure and Aquinas: Enduring Philosophers (coeditor; Norman, 1976)

Library of Congress Cataloging in Publication Data
Main entry under title:

Bonaventure and Aquinas.

    Includes bibliographical references and index.
    1. Bonaventura, Saint, Cardinal, 1221–1274—Addresses, essays, lectures. 2. Thomas Aquinas, Saint, 1225?–1274—Addresses, essays, lectures.
I. Shahan, Robert W., 1935–   II. Kovach, Francis Joseph.
B765.B74B66   189'.4   75-40963

Introduction

There are enduring questions in philosophy—questions which, transcending historical periods, geographic limitations, and philosophic schools, have occupied the minds of thinkers throughout history. It is also true that there are enduring philosophers—philosophers who, transcending changes in philosophic attitudes, methods, and postulates, have influenced, challenged, or inspired other thinkers from their own lifetimes to the present.

Philosophia perennis is very much on the minds of American philosophers in the decade of the seventies. The United States Bicentennial Year has occasioned several national and one all-Americas conference at which the major figures of American philosophy and the major themes of that tradition have been studied and celebrated.[1] Not only does the decade of the seventies include the anniversary of the American Revolution, but also it includes the anniversaries of the deaths of five of the greatest philosophers who ever lived. The year 1979 will be the three-hundredth anniversary of the death of Thomas Hobbes; 1977 will be the three-hundredth anniversary of the death of Spinoza; 1976 is the two-hundredth anniversary of the death of David Hume[2] and 1974 was the septemcentennial anniversary of the deaths of both St. Thomas Aquinas (on March 7) and St. Bonaventure (on July 15). It is this double septemcentennial anniversary which has occasioned this anthology.

1. *American Philosophy: Edwards to Quine,* based on the proceedings of the Sixth Annual Oklahoma Conference on Philosophy, is available from the University of Oklahoma Press (Norman, 1977). The contributors are, in addition to Quine, A. Robert Caponigri (on Thoreau and Emerson), Roland A. Delattre (on Edwards), Max H. Fisch (on Peirce and Pragmatism), Peter Fuss (on Royce), and Frederick A. Olafson (on Santayana).

2. A commemorative volume devoted to Hume, *David Hume: Many-sided Genius,* is available from the University of Oklahoma Press (Norman, 1977). The volume contains articles by R. F. Atkinson, Ralph Cohen, William Davie, Kenneth R. Merrill, James Noxon, Terrance Penelhum, Richard H. Popkin, and Eugene Rotwein, as well as the first English translation of Adolf Reinach's "Kants Auffassung des Humeschen Problems."

St. Bonaventure (1221–74) and St. Thomas Aquinas (1225–74) are unquestionably enduring philosophers. Bonaventure was the greatest Augustinian Platonist of the Middle Ages, if not the greatest Augustinian thinker of all time, and also one of the most outstanding mystic thinkers and authors in history. Thomas Aquinas, on the other hand, was a boldly innovative analytic genius, especially in metaphysics; the most outstanding and successful synthesizer of Platonism and Aristotelianism; and an impressively consistent, zealous, and precedence-setting advocate of the purity of philosophy by strictly distinguishing between faith and reason, theology and philosophy. For these and other reasons, he is unquestionably the most influential of all the schoolmen.

Literally scores of commemorative conferences were held in 1974 upon the septemcentennial anniversary of the deaths of both Thomas and Bonaventure. This collection of essays, which we regard as a kind of treasure-trove of significant and refreshing reflections upon Bonaventure and Aquinas, was conceived as a part of a worldwide tribute.

The articles in this anthology are thematically arranged in three different groups. Three articles deal exclusively with Bonaventure (those by Cousins, Quinn, and Brady), two deal exclusively with Thomas (those by Owens and Kreyche), and three compare these two philosophers either from the historical point of view or from both the historical and logical points of view (those by McInerny, Sweeney, and Kovach). The early pages of Cousins' article at the same time properly serve as a kind of historical setting for all the other papers.

All these articles except one originally appeared in the July, 1974, issue of the *Southwestern Journal of Philosophy*. Cousins' paper was first published in the December, 1974, issue of the *International Philosophical Quarterly*.

The principles of order within each of the three named groups of essays are taken from the Aristotelian-Thomistic theory of sciences: theoretical sciences, like metaphysics and cosmology, are naturally prior to the practical science of ethics; theology, as the science of the principle of being, is naturally prior to metaphysics, the science of being; and science in the proper sense, like any other branch of philosophy, is naturally prior to science in the improper sense, like history.

In more contemporary or less tradition-bound terms the selected articles touch upon virtually all the important areas of systematic philosophy (epistemology, metaphysics, cosmology, moral philosophy) and the history of philosophy, by focusing on some specific problems in those areas.

We sincerely wish to thank each of the authors for his contribution to this commemorative anthology. The article of one of the eight contributors, Robert Kreyche, is his last published work. Thus we can thank him here only posthumously—with sadness and warm memories. We wish also to acknowledge our appreciation and gratitude to Norris Clark, S.J., editor of the *International Philosophical Quarterly*, for kindly granting us permission to reprint Cousins' article from the December, 1974, issue of that journal. We would be remiss if we did not express our thanks also to some others: Edward Shaw, Director of the University of Oklahoma Press, and the many other fine persons at the Press in the editorial, production, design, and sales divisions, with whom we have enjoyed working; Ms. Susan Taylor, our indispensable secretary, who managed the numerous details associated with this publication from its conception; and Mrs. Jeanne Crabtree, our conscientious and careful copy editor.

With this anthology the essayists and the editors wish to pay homage to *doctor seraphicus* and *doctor angelicus*—two memorable mediaeval monks who, together with such philosophic geniuses as Plato, Aristotle, St. Augustine, Duns Scotus, Descartes, Hume, Kant, and Hegel, represent the most enduring figures in the history of philosophy and are two of the most outstanding representatives of *philosophia perennis*.
Norman, Oklahoma
May 25, 1976

ROBERT W. SHAHAN
FRANCIS J. KOVACH

Contents

Bonaventure and Aquinas
Enduring Philosophers

Fra Angelico, *St. Bonaventure* (1445–55)
Vatican, Nicholas V. Chapel
Detail

Carlo Crivelli, *St. Thomas Aquinas* (1746)
The Demidoff Altarpiece
Detail

CHAPTER 1.

St. Bonaventure, St. Thomas, and the Movement of Thought in the 13th Century

EWERT H. COUSINS

The centenary year 1974, commemorating the seven hundredth anniversary of the death of Thomas Aquinas and Bonaventure, provides a special vantage point for looking back on the thirteenth century. For we stand at a point where we can examine a vast amount of historical data and at a time when we can view these data from changing perspectives. Such moments offer great possibilities for creative insight, for old issues can suddenly be seen in a new light; horizons can expand, revealing deeper levels of complexity and more intricate relations among apparently disparate elements. The following study attempts to tap the creativity of this moment by viewing the historical data from fresh perspectives. I will examine three areas: knowledge through subjectivity, God as dynamic, and the Islamic problematic. By viewing these from fresh points of view, we can broaden our horizons of interpretation, casting new light on the thought of Thomas and Bonaventure, on the complex issues of the thirteenth century, and on the relation of this formative period to the development of Western thought.

In looking back at the thirteenth century in the year 1974, we are heirs to a vast amount of research on the thought of Thomas and Bonaventure and on the thirteenth century. The past hundred years have witnessed the neo-scholastic revival, which led to the editing of critical texts: the Leonine edition of Thomas and the Quaracchi edition of Bonaventure. These formed the basis for countless studies of their thought: articles, monographs, dissertations, major works by specialists. During this period neo-Thomism emerged as one of the living philosophical schools of the twentieth century, with roots in the thirteenth century, but deeply immersed in the philosophical issues of our age.

From the standpoint of interpreting the thirteenth century, the rise of neo-Thomism as a contemporary philosophical movement was, I believe, problematic. On the one hand, it enormously stimulated historical research, revealing the vitality of Thomas' thought and bringing

* Reprinted with permission from the *Intern. Phil. Quarterly*, Dec. 1974.

to life the drama of the intellectual ferment of the thirteenth century. But at the same time, it tended to provide a single perspective for viewing the thirteenth century and medieval thought as a whole. It is widely acknowledged that Thomas represents a shift of consciousness in the Middle Ages, whether this be interpreted as a significant break with the previous tradition or a transformation of that tradition into a new mode. If this is the case, then to view medieval thought from the Thomistic shift of consciousness is problematic since other perspectives may not be adequately explored. At this point in 1974, however, the impetus of neo-Thomism as a contemporary movement has waned, providing a climate for a re-evaluation of issues from other perspectives. I believe that the reappraisal of issues of the thirteenth century from multiple perspectives will enhance our understanding of Thomas' contribution at the same time that it will clarify Bonaventure's role and show their relation to larger currents of thought that converged in thirteenth century Europe.

Three Perspectives

I propose, then, to study three areas from three different perspectives: (1) knowledge through subjectivity, seen from the perspective of the Augustinian tradition and providing a background for interpreting Thomas on subjectivity; (2) God as dynamic, seen from the perspective of the Pseudo-Dionysian tradition—a perspective which can initiate a radical reappraisal of the God-question in the Middle Ages, for it self-consciously focused on the divine fecundity and God's relation to the world; (3) the third area I have called the Islamic problematic. Closely connected with the second, this deals with the tension between the Islamic sense of God's transcendence and the Greek notion of immanence, whether this be the immanence of reason enclosed within nature or the immanence of the divine reflected in the sphere of creation. This problematic emerged in Islam when the Muslim philosophers had to confront the revelation of the Koran. I believe that this problematic was imported to the West along with the texts of Aristotle and Muslim commentaries and that it underlies a number of the hotly-debated issues in thirteenth century Europe.

From a systematic standpoint, these represent three distinct but overlapping philosophical areas: human subjectivity, the divine dynamism, and God's relation to creation. From an historical-cultural standpoint, they represent three distinct strands, each emerging from a different area of our cultural past but all converging in a most dramatic way in thirteenth century Europe. The first emerges out of the West's

6

sense of the human subject in his interiority and historicity. This sense of subjectivity was given a classical expression in *The Confessions* of Augustine and has persisted through successive philosophical revolutions into the twentieth century. The second was developed in the theological ethos of the Greek Fathers and was transmitted to the Western Middle Ages through the Latin translations of the Pseudo-Dionysius. The third represents a Semitic heritage, with its sense of God's transcendence and the profound separation between God and creation. Rooted in the Hebraic past of Western culture, this consciousness was channelled in a new way into the West in the thirteenth century through Islamic sources. These three areas, then, represent three circles with ever-widening cultural horizons. The Augustinian sense of subjectivity emerges within the Latin West; the dynamic notion of God in the Greek East; and the sense of God's transcendence in the Semitic Middle East. Flowing from diverse geographic zones and through different historical periods, these strands converge in a striking way in the intellectual ferment of Western Europe in the thirteenth century.

As an avenue into these areas, I have chosen three groups of texts from Bonaventure: (1) his treatment of the knowledge of God in subjectivity, in the first of the *Quaestiones Disputatae de Mysterio Trinitatis* and in Chapter Three of the *Itinerarium*; (2) his discussion of the divine fecundity, in the first book of the *Commentary on the Sentences* and in Chapter Six of the *Itinerarium*; and (3) his criticism of Aristotle and the Muslims, in the sixth of the *Collationes in Hexaemeron*.[1] I have chosen Bonaventure because he offers an alternate perspective to that of Thomas, a perspective that has often been obscured during the ascendency of neo-Thomism. In his synthesis of the earlier medieval tradition, Bonaventure preserved the perspective of Augustinian subjectivity and the Pseudo-Dionysian doctrine of the divine fecundity. In his criticism of Aristotle he traced the disputes of his time over the eternity of the world and the immortality of the soul to what I have termed the Islamic problematic. Although I am drawing them from Bonaventure, these alternate perspectives are not unrelated to Thomas, for at times they converge with his and at other times they provide a

---

1. Bonaventure, *S. Bonaventurae Opera Omnia*, edita studio et cura pp. Collegii a S. Bonaventura, 10 vols. (Quaracchi, 1882–1902); on subjectivity: *Quaestiones Disputatae de Mysterio Trinitatis*, q. 1, a. 1 (V, 45–51) and *Itinerarium*, c. 3 (V, 303–306); on the divine fecundity, *I Sent.*, d. 2, a. un., q. 2 (I, 53); d. 27, p. 1, a. un., q. 2 (I, 468–474) and *Itinerarium*, c. 6, n. 2 (V, 310–311); on Aristotle and the Muslims, *In Hexaemeron*, VI, n. 1–6 (V, 360–361).

larger context for situating his position in controversies and for evaluating his contribution.

Knowledge Through Subjectivity

Our first area deals with knowledge through subjectivity, specifically knowledge of God through subjectivity. This approach flowed as a mainstream from Augustine through the Middle Ages and forms a background to the shift of consciousness that occurred in the thirteenth century. With the Aristotelian influx there was a shift from the inner way of subjectivity to the outer way of empiricism, with the point of departure taken from sense knowledge. Thomas' epistemology is clearly rooted in the sense world and proceeds through the Aristotelian doctrine of abstraction. How much of the Augustinian epistemology he retains is a complex question. The point I wish to make in this section is the following: In order to understand this shift of consciousness in the thirteenth century, we must be aware of the presence of a major medieval tradition that moved through subjectivity. It is necessary to call attention to this fact since the majority of scholarship on this period in the past century has been guided by the Thomistic perspective. In some cases, it has simply remained within the Thomistic epistemology; in others, where it took into account the counter-tradition, it tended to treat it in polemic terms. If we bring into focus this other tradition, we will be in a position to reassess the movement of thought in the thirteenth century; for this tradition forms the backdrop against which Thomas worked and, I believe, can serve as a major factor in determining precisely how he is situated in this shift of consciousness. For example, I believe that in the light of this tradition, there are strong historical grounds for supporting the "Transcendental Thomist" interpretation of Thomas' texts, according to which there is a significant dimension of subjectivity even within Thomas' position on abstraction from sense data.[2]

Our best way into the earlier medieval tradition, as this flowed into the thirteenth century, is through Bonaventure, since he produced its major synthesis in the high Middle Ages. He drew from Augustine on subjectivity and from the Greek Fathers via the Pseudo-Dionysius on the dynamic doctrine of God. These traditions he integrated with the emerging Aristotelianism and his own Franciscanism, with its awareness of the presence of God in creation and its focus on Christ the center. The Augustinian tradition of knowledge of God through sub-

2. On Transcendental Thomism, cf. note 19 below.

jectivity is developed throughout the corpus of his writings, from the early period at the University of Paris, through the middle period when as newly elected General of the Franciscan Order he turned to more mystical writings, and into the final period when he was engaged in heated controversies over the development of a heterodox Aristotelianism in the Faculty of Arts of the University of Paris.[3]

A revealing series of texts occurs in the first question of Bonaventure's *Quaestiones Disputatae de Mysterio Trinitatis*, delivered at the University of Paris during the early period of his career. He divides the question into two articles, the first dealing with the certitude with which God's existence is known and the second dealing with the faith by which the Trinity is believed.[4] In the first article, he does not set out to prove the existence of God in the way Thomas does in his *Summa Theologiae*.[5] Rather he follows a generic Augustinian approach, asking whether the existence of God is a truth which cannot be doubted. The very statement of the question situates the issue within the sphere of the mind with its subjective states of doubt and certitude. In order to establish his position, he moves in three directions: first within himself, then outside himself, and then above himself. Bonaventure claims that there is no rational basis for doubting God's existence, "Since if the intellect enters within itself or goes outside itself or gazes above itself, if it proceeds rationally, then it knows that God exists, with certitude and without doubt."[6] Although the posing of the question is from an Augustinian perspective, Bonaventure integrates into his perspective the Aristotelian proofs from act and potency based on the contingency of creatures. This is what he means by moving outside oneself. In the third division, in which the intellect gazes above itself, he integrates into the Augustinian perspective also Anselm's ontological argument. For when the intellect looks above itself to the notion of God as that than which no greater can be thought, it must realize that God necessarily exists.[7]

Although Bonaventure has subsumed all three approaches within an Augustinian perspective, it is the first approach which will command our attention here: namely, through our own subjectivity, since this is

3. In addition to the references in note 1 above, cf. *Quaestiones Disputatae de Scientia Christi*, q. 4 (V, 17–27); *Christus Unus Omnium Magister* (V, 567–574); *In Hexaemeron*, I, n. 13 (V, 331).

4. Bonaventure, *De Mysterio Trinitatis*, q. 1, a. 1 and 2 (V, 45–58).

5. Thomas, *Summa Theologiae*, I, q. 2, a. 3.

6. Bonaventure, *De Mysterio Trinitatis*, q. 1, a. 1, concl. (V, 49); unless otherwise indicated, the English translations of Bonaventure are my own.

7. *Ibid.*, q. 1, a. 1, n. 1–29 (V, 45–48).

9

most characteristically Augustinian. He begins this approach by stating that every truth impressed on all minds is a truth that cannot be doubted. But he contends: "Both by authorities and by reasons it is shown that God's existence is impressed on all rational minds."[8] He cites John Damascene as saying: "Knowledge of God's existence is naturally inserted in us." He next quotes from Hugh of St. Victor: "God so regulated knowledge of himself in man that just as what he is can never be totally comprehended, so his existence can never be completely unknown." Next he quotes Boethius: "There is inserted in the minds of men a desire for truth and goodness." Bonaventure then reasons that desire presupposes knowledge; hence there is impressed on the minds of men knowledge of truth and goodness and the desire of what is most desirable. But, Bonaventure says, this good is God. He then proceeds to draw from the *De Trinitate* of Augustine the notion of the soul as image of God. According to Augustine, the image consists in the mind, knowledge, and love. The soul, then, by its very nature is the image of God; hence it has knowledge of God inserted within itself. "But what is first known about God is that he exists; therefore this is naturally inserted in the human mind." Then drawing certain principles from Aristotle, Bonaventure interprets them in the same vein. He concludes the section gathering other material from Augustine and by reasoning on the soul's knowledge of itself. He brings his exploration to a climax by saying: "God is most present to the soul itself and through himself is knowable; therefore there is inserted in the soul knowledge of God himself."[9]

In each of the ten paragraphs where he developed these themes, Bonaventure has moved through the path of subjectivity to knowledge of God. In the process, he has gathered a number of quotations from the tradition to bolster his position. Citing several authorities, he draws most heavily from Augustine, especially his notion of the soul as image of God, which is developed extensively in the *De Trinitate*.[10] In the light of this Augustinian approach, Bonaventure can even bring Aristotle into the path of the inner way. Everything about the text indicates that Bonaventure is aware that he is not taking this path alone. The structure of the piece, Bonaventure's statement of the question, his own

8. *Ibid.* (V, 45).
9. *Ibid.*, n. 1–10 (V, 45–46); John Damascene, *De Fide Orthodoxa*, I, c. 3; Hugh of St. Victor, *De Sacram.* I, p. 3, c. 1; Boethius, *De Consol.*, III, prosa 2; Augustine, *De Trinitate*, VIII–XV; Aristotle, *Poster.*, II, c. 18; *Metaph.*, I, c. 1; Augustine, *De Civitate Dei*, XIX, c. 11–13.
10. Augustine, *De Trinitate*, VIII–XV.

reasoning, and especially his attitude towards his predecessors—all reveal that he feels he is moving within an established tradition. For him the path through subjectivity is not uncharted; the way has been traversed and marked by his predecessors, chief among whom is Augustine, who serves as his primary guide.

Subjectivity in the Itinerarium

A more extensive and systematic treatment of the same theme is found in the *Itinerarium Mentis in Deum,* written some fifteen years later, after Bonaventure had been chosen Minister General of the Franciscan Order.[11] Here the journey motif is made explicit as the unifying theme of the entire work. The path of the journey is basically the same as that outlined in the disputed question. Bonaventure contemplates God in the external world, within the soul and in God himself; however, the Franciscan contemplation is interwoven with characteristic Augustinian speculation and dialectical self-reflection.

After contemplating the reflection of God in the external world, Bonaventure turns to the soul in the third chapter of the *Itinerarium.* He says that we are "to re-enter into ourselves, that is, into our mind, where the divine image shines forth."[12] Using the image of entering into the tabernacle of Moses, he says that we are to leave the outer *atrium,* that is the external world, and enter into the inner realm of the tabernacle, that is into ourselves, where we will see God through a mirror, for the light of truth shines like a candelabrum in our minds. "Enter into yourself, therefore, and observe . . .," Bonaventure bids us as he leads us on an inner journey into the depths of our memory, understanding, and will, where we discover the reflection of God in the soul as image of the Trinity.[13]

Bonaventure first explores the memory, moving through its various levels until he comes to the reflection of God in its depths. On one level the memory retains and represents temporal things: "the past by remembrance, the present by reception, and the future by foresight."[14] On another level it retains basic mathematical notions such as the point. On a deeper level it retains the principles and axioms of the

11. Bonaventure, *Itinerarium,* c. 3 (V, 303–306).
12. *Ibid.,* n. 1 (V, 303); the English translation of passages from the *Itinerarium* is taken from *Works of Saint Bonaventure,* Vol. II: *Saint Bonaventure's Itinerarium Mentis in Deum,* translated by Philotheus Boehner, O.F.M., (Saint Bonaventure, N.Y.: The Franciscan Institute, 1956).
13. *Loc. cit.*
14. *Ibid.,* n. 2 (V, 303).

sciences in such a way that it cannot forget them as long as one uses reason. For when he hears them again, he assents to them, not as though he were perceiving them anew, but rather recognizing them as innate and familiar. On this third level the memory has present in itself a changeless light in which it remembers changeless truths. Bonaventure then concludes:

> And thus it is clear from the activities of the memory that the soul itself is an image of God and a similitude so present to itself and having Him so present to it that it actually grasps Him and potentially "is capable of possessing Him and of becoming a partaker in Him."[15]

In a similar way Bonaventure explores the intellect, analyzing our knowledge of terms and definitions and our awareness of being. We can know limited being only in the light of unlimited being, since the mind knows negations only in the light of something positive. Therefore our intellect does not arrive at a full analysis of any single created being unless it is aided by a knowledge of the eternal and absolute Being. For, Bonaventure asks, how could we perceive something as defective if we had no knowledge of the Being that is free from all defect? Also the intellect grasps certain truths as changeless and necessary; but this knowledge can be had only in the divine unchangeable light.[16]

Bonaventure next examines the will or elective faculty. When it inquires of two things which is better, it does so in view of the notion of the highest Good which must necessarily be impressed upon the soul. Furthermore, when we judge that something is right, we do so in the light of the divine law that transcends our minds but nevertheless is stamped on the mind. Finally, when we desire something, we desire it in the light of the highest Good, either because it leads to it or resembles it. After making this journey into the depths of subjectivity through the memory, understanding, and will, Bonaventure concludes: "See, therefore, how close the soul is to God, and how, through their activity, the memory leads us to eternity, the intelligence to Truth, and the elective faculty to the highest Good."[17]

For a full treatment of Bonaventure's approach through subjectivity we would have to examine many more texts and investigate the psychological, epistemological, and metaphysical aspects of his theory of

15. *Ibid.* (V, 304); the quotation within the text is from Augustine, *De Trinitate*, XIV, 8, 11.
16. Bonaventure, *Itinerarium*, c. 3, n. 3 (V, 304).
17. *Ibid.*, n. 4 (V, 305).

knowledge. We would have to study in detail his key text on knowledge in the fourth question of the *Quaestiones Disputatae de Scientia Christi*.[18] Here he analyzes the ontological ground of certitude and presents his subtle position on "contuition," in which the temporal and the eternal are grasped together. Furthermore, we would have to explore his position on sense knowledge, abstraction, and the agent and possible intellect. Bonaventure's epistemology is complex because it brings together both Aristotelian and Platonic elements; just how these elements are integrated in his system has been a matter of considerable discussion among his interpreters. Granted this complexity, the point I wish to make here is simply that the path to God through subjectivity is clearly a royal road for Bonaventure. It is indisputably present in major texts throughout his writings and it represents a mainstream tradition stemming from Augustine and flowing with full force into the thirteenth century.

What are the implications of this fact? First of all, it explodes one of the myths about the Middle Ages: namely, that medieval thinkers were concerned exclusively with objectivist modes of thought, supported by principles of reason and external authority, and that the discovery of subjectivity is a distinctly modern achievement. Of course, one must distinguish: the religious subjectivity of Augustine and Bonaventure is not coextensive with the subjectivity of Kant or Sartre. Yet Augustine and Bonaventure are centrally concerned with subjectivity. The difference is by excess rather than default, for they go more deeply into subjectivity than many moderns. Furthermore, as is clear from the texts cited, this medieval sense of subjectivity is by no means exclusively mystical; it is also self-consciously philosophical. It is true that Bonaventure embarks on a contemplative journey into God which culminates in mystical ecstasy. But en route he constantly employs speculative reason, with its self-reflective analyses and Augustinian dialectic. It would be totally inaccurate, then, to relegate his enterprise to the cloister of ineffable mystical consciousness and to recognize philosophical acumen only in modern modes of subjective analysis or in medieval objectivist thought. Bonaventure's exploration of subjectivity has every reason to be taken with philosophical seriousness.

If this is the case, then what are the implications for interpreting the movement of thought in the thirteenth century? In the shift of consciousness it was precisely this sense of subjectivity that receded into the background of philosophical concern, going underground, as it were,

18. Bonaventure, *Quaestiones Disputatae de Scientia Christi*, q. 4 (V, 17–27); on contuition, cf. *ibid.*, concl. (V, 22–24); cf. also references in note 3 above.

into spirituality and mysticism, appearing for example, with problematic brilliance in Meister Eckhart. But did it recede as much as is
sometimes thought? In the shift of consciousness brought about by
Aristotelian empiricism, did there linger more of a subjectivist dimension than is usually claimed? I would be inclined to answer in the
affirmative. I am referring here to the interpretation of Thomas by the
current known as Transcendental Thomism, represented by Joseph
Maréchal, Karl Rahner, and Bernard Lonergan. Over the past fifty
years all three men have engaged in major interpretations of texts of
Thomas.[19] Remaining within Thomas' generic Aristotelian-empirical
orientation, they nevertheless discovered a dimension of subjectivity
which opens up to the religious sphere. I am inclined to believe that
their interpretation has the support of the historical context. If the
awareness of subjectivity constituted so deep a current in medieval culture, as the evidence indicates, then there is reason to expect that a
dimension of subjectivity would be retained even with a shift of
consciousness.

To be sure, the transcendental analysis of Rahner is by no means
identical with the inner way of Augustine and Bonaventure. For Augustine, and even Bonaventure, who appropriated considerable amounts of
Aristotelianism, are not concerned primarily with the process of abstraction from sense knowledge. It is true that the interpretation of
Thomas by Transcendental Thomism has taken its point of departure
from the Kantian critique and therefore runs the risk of "reading in"
to the texts of Thomas a notion of subjectivity that is modern. However, one could take a medieval point of departure—from the Augustinian-Bonaventurian tradition—and arrive at the Transcendental
Thomist position. Such an approach would proceed from the Augustinian-Bonaventurian awareness of the reflection of the Absolute Good
within the human spirit as constantly drawing the latter towards the
Good through all finite goods and the presence of a transcendent dimension in all knowledge of truth. Open to this transcendent horizon, then,
the human spirit in its very quest for knowledge would be seen as involved in a dynamic process of self-transcending striving towards the
Good. And, of course, for this tradition the Good could not existen-

19. Cf. Joseph Maréchal, S.J., *Le Point de départ de la métaphysique:* 5 vols.
(1922–1947), especially, Cahier V: *Le Thomisme devant la philosophie critique*
(Brussels: Éditions Universelles, 1949); Karl Rahner, S.J., *Geist in Welt: Zur
Metaphysik der endlichen Erkenntnis bei Thomas von Aquin* (München: Kösel,
1957); Bernard Lonergan, S.J., *Verbum: Word and Idea in Aquinas* (London:
Darton, Longman and Todd, 1968).

14

tially draw a man's spirit towards It unless It were already present deep within him, though at first with a veiled, not yet recognized presence. This transcendent horizon of the spirit's drive towards being both as true and as good is the clearly recognizable ancestor of Transcendental Thomism's "dynamism of the spirit toward the Infinite" (Maréchal, Rahner, etc.) and the "unrestricted drive to know" (Lonergan).

The claim of the Transcendental Thomists to have discovered a subjective dimension in Thomas calls for a serious restudying of the role of subjectivity in the thirteenth century—against the background of the Augustinian-Bonaventurian tradition. There is work to be done in clarifying the precise relation of the alleged subjective dimension in Thomas with the subjectivity traditions that preceded him. This reassessment of the thirteenth century would call for a serious collaboration among intellectual historians, Transcendental Thomists, and Augustinian-Bonaventurian subjectivists. Perhaps this centenary year can be an impetus towards such a collaboration.

God as Dynamic

The next area that we will explore is the doctrine of God as dynamic, which flowed into the West through the Pseudo-Dionysius.[20] The prevalence of this tradition in the Middle Ages has been significantly obscured, for Thomas did not appropriate this strand in the way Bonaventure did. When one studies the God-question in the thirteenth century, he usually focuses on Thomas' proofs for God's existence, his doctrine of our knowledge of God's attributes and creation from nothing.[21] In all of these areas Thomas employs the Aristotelian notions of act and potency, viewing God as Pure Act. As has been forcefully pointed out by neo-Thomists, Thomas significantly transformed the Aristotelian notion of God in the light of his Christian faith and his metaphysical genius.

That there is an alternate tradition, which focuses on God's fecundity, is not widely known, although the basic historical research has been accomplished now for almost a hundred years by Théodore de Régnon. With his monumental work as a foundation, research has continued in important monographs but has not had a noticeable effect

20. For a longer exploration of this area, see my study entitled "God as Dynamic in Bonaventure and Contemporary Thought," to be published in the proceedings of the Forty-Eighth Annual Meeting of the American Catholic Philosophical Association, 1974.

21. Thomas, *Summa Theologiae*, I, q. 1–26; 44–45; *Summa Contra Gentiles*, I, and II, c. 1–38.

on the larger intellectual community.[22] Yet the fecundity tradition is still largely unknown. An example of this can be seen in Arthur Lovejoy's book *The Great Chain of Being*, which studies the tension throughout the history of Western thought between two notions of God: as self-sufficient absolute and as self-diffusive fecundity. When Lovejoy treats the Middle Ages, he does not cite the leading Western exponents of the divine fecundity, nor does he identify this medieval tradition as such.[23] The omission seems especially glaring since the medieval fecundity tradition was concerned with the central problematic of Lovejoy's book. Another indication that this tradition has been obscured is found in the critique of classical theism by the process school of Whitehead and Hartshorne. Process thinkers criticize the image of God as absolute perfection, the Unmoved Mover, transcendent and unrelated to the world; they propose in its stead their conception of a dynamic, related God who is enriched by the temporal process. One of their chief targets of criticism is Thomas' doctrine of God as Pure Act; but in their assessment of the classical theism they have not taken into account the fecundity tradition of the Middle Ages, which proposes an image of God as dynamic and related to the world, not wholly unlike theirs.[24]

Perhaps the chief reason why the medieval fecundity tradition was obscured is the fact that it is formulated through the doctrine of the Trinity. The Father in the Trinity is seen as the fecund source of the divine processions and of the dynamic inner life of the divinity. Since the neo-scholastic revival was chiefly concerned with philosophy, the doctrine of the divine fecundity was relegated to theology, where even there it tended to be supplanted by the alternate Trinitarian model of Augustine.[25] Yet the fecundity model has important philosophical dimensions which merit critical study. Furthermore, by bringing this

22. Cf. Théodore de Régnon, S.J., *Etudes de théologie positive sur la Sainte Trinité*, 4 vols. (Paris: Retaux, 1892–1898), especially Vol. II: *Théories scolastiques.*, 1892; among studies of Bonaventure's doctrine of God, cf. A. Stohr, *Die Trinitätslehre des Hl. Bonaventura* (Münster in Westfalen: Aschendorff, 1923); J.-M. Bissen, *L'exemplarisme divin selon Bonaventure* (Paris: Vrin, 1929).

23. Arthur O. Lovejoy, *The Great Chain of Being* (Cambridge: Harvard Univ. Press, 1936), especially Chapter III: "The Chain of Being and Some Internal Conflicts in Medieval Thought."

24. Cf. Alfred North Whitehead, *Process and Reality* (New York: Macmillan, 1929), pp. 519–533; Charles Hartshorne, *The Divine Relativity* (New Haven: Yale Univ. Press, 1948); *Man's Vision of God and the Logic of Theism* (Chicago: Willet, Clark 1941); (with William L. Reese) *Philosophers Speak of God* (Chicago: Univ. of Chicago Press, 1953).

25. Cf. note 34 below.

tradition to light we can better discern the currents of thought that flowed into the West from the Greek world. For this doctrine of fecundity, although found in some form throughout the history of Western thought, is chiefly a heritage from the Greek Fathers, through the Pseudo-Dionysius. Since the tradition was concerned with God's dynamism and his relatedness to the world, we can discern here the continuity of Western thought, for the Middle Ages were preoccupied with issues which have persisted into modern times, for example, in Hegel and twentieth century process thinkers. This means that the thirteenth century has a richer treatment of the God-question than has been often recognized. It has dealt extensively with the two strands of the problematic studied by Lovejoy: God as self-sufficient absolute developed by Thomas and God as self-diffusive fecundity developed by Bonaventure.

Bonaventure develops his notion of the divine fecundity by applying two philosophical principles absolutely to the Father in the Trinity and relatively to creation. These are the principles of fecund primordiality and the self-diffusion of the good. In the second distinction of the first book of the *Commentary on the Sentences* he states his principle of fecund primordiality: "The more primary a thing is, the more fecund it is and the principle of others."[26] Bonaventure applied the principle first to the divine essence as the fecund source of creatures and then to the Father as fecund source of the divine processions: "Just as the divine essence, because it is first, is the principle of other essences, so the person of the Father, since he is first, because from no one, is the principle and has fecundity in regard to the persons."[27] In distinction twenty-seven of the first book of the *Commentary* he again applies the principle to the Father, this time citing Aristotle as his source of the principle. In this context, he refers to the Father's *fontalis plenitudo* or fountain-fullness: because the Father is primary in the Trinity, because he is from no one, therefore he is the fecund source of the divine processions.[28]

Later in the *Itinerarium*, Bonaventure applies to the Trinity the Pseudo-Dionysian principle of the self-diffusion of the good. Drawing also from Anselm's logic of the *Proslogion*, Bonaventure writes:

26. Bonaventure, *I Sent.*, d. 2, a. un., q. 2 (I, 53).
27. *Loc. cit.*
28. Bonaventure, *I Sent.*, d. 27, p. 1, a. un., q. 2 (I, 468–474), especially ad 3 (I, 470–472); although Bonaventure cites Aristotle as his source, the Quaracchi editors indicate that he is, in fact, drawing from the *Liber de Causis*. This treatise was erroneously thought to have been written by Aristotle.

Behold, therefore, and observe that the highest good is unqualifiedly that in comparison with which a greater cannot be thought. And this good is such that it cannot rightly be thought of as non-existing, since to be is absolutely better than not to be. And this good exists in such a way that it cannot rightly be thought of unless it is thought of as triune and one. For good is said to be self-diffusive, and therefore the highest good is most self-diffusive.[29]

Where, then, is the highest self-diffusion to be found? In God's diffusion in creation? No, because "the diffusion that occurred in time in the creation of the world is no more than a pivot or point in comparison with the immense sweep of the eternal goodness."[30] This diffusion must be realized within the divine life, in the Trinitarian processions, for it is only there that the highest self-diffusion can be had, which Bonaventure claims must be "actual and intrinsic, substantial and hypostatic, natural and voluntary, free and necessary, unfailing and perfect."[31]

God Transcendent and Immanent

By placing absolute fecundity in the Trinity, Bonaventure has saved both God and the world. He has rescued the divine fecundity by freeing it from the limits of creation, and he has preserved the world by protecting it from God's overwhelming power. If the only way the divine fecundity could be actualized were in creation, then we would encounter the host of problems described by Lovejoy. This could produce a static world in which all possibles must be actualized or so enmesh God in the world for his own self-actualization that his transcendence would be swallowed up in creation. This problem has bedeviled philosophers through the centuries and is at the heart of the problematic character of the doctrine of God in Hegel and Whitehead. That a medieval tradition had something to say to the heart of this problem is significant, for it shows both the continuity of Western culture and the vitality of medieval thought.

Paradoxically the very principle that accounts for God's transcendence is the root of his immanence. Bonaventure had founded God's transcendence in his fecundity, which is so great that it cannot be exhausted within the world. However, when God expresses himself in creation, he does so out of the ultimate mystery of Trinitarian fecundity. When the Father generates the Son, he produces in the Son the archetypes of all he can make. As Bonaventure says: "The Father

29. Bonaventure, *Itinerarium*, c. 6, n. 2 (V, 310).
30. *Loc. cit.*
31. *Loc. cit.*

generated one similar to himself, namely the Word, co-eternal with himself; and he expressed his own likeness and as a consequence expressed all the things that he could make."[32] While remaining radically contingent, creation *ad extra* is an overflow of the Father's fecundity and always remains deeply grounded in the Word. The world, then, is like a mirror reflecting God. In his highly developed metaphysics of exemplarism, Bonaventure divides creatures into various levels of representing God: shadow, vestige, image, and similitude.[33] Bonaventure has used the Platonic metaphysics of exemplarism to give a philosophical grounding to the Franciscan sense of the presence of God in nature. In a most emphatic way for Bonaventure, God is in the world and the world in God. Since the immanence of God is a recurrent theme in Western thought, it is important to be aware of a major metaphysical statement of this theme in the Middle Ages.

What are the implications of this tradition for understanding the thirteenth century? It indicates a greater Greek influence than has generally been acknowledged—an influence coming not from Aristotle or Plato, but from the Greek Fathers and their Trinitarian theology. As we have pointed out, although the formulations are ultimately within the theological sphere of the Trinity, they have enormous philosophical implications for the problems of God's fecundity and immanence. Furthermore, this tradition can lead to a significant reclassification of positions. For example, in epistemology Bonaventure is usually classified as an Augustinian to distinguish him from Thomas the Aristotelian. Although in our first point I indicated how this might be nuanced, I believe it is basically accurate. However, on the doctrine of God, especially the relation of the One God and the Trinity, Thomas is much more Augustinian than Bonaventure. One could say that Thomas is more typically Western in his focus on the unity of the divine nature and Bonaventure more Eastern in his focus on the Trinity of Persons. Historians of thought have pointed out how Augustine in his polemic against the Arians in the *De Trinitate* made a methodological distinction between the divine nature and the three Persons, treating the three Persons under the transformed Aristotelian category of relation.[34] This distinction between the divine nature and the Persons, who are then studied as relations, is characteristic of much of Western

32. Bonaventure, *In Hexaemeron*, I, n. 13 (V, 331).
33. Bonaventure, *I Sent.*, d. 3, p. 1, a. un., q. 2, ad 4 (I, 72–74); *Itinerarium*, c. 1–4 (V, 296–308).
34. Augustine, *De Trinitate*, V–VII; cf. Harry Wolfson, *The Philosophy of the Church Fathers*, Vol. I (Cambridge: Harvard Univ. Press, 1964), 350–359; Paul Henry, S.J., *Saint Augustine on Personality* (New York: Macmillan, 1960).

medieval thought on God. It is this tradition that shaped the structure of Thomas' treatment of God in the *Summa Theologiae*, where he deals first with the divine nature and then with Trinity, bringing the Augustinian tradition to a brilliant culmination with his development of the interpretation of the divine Persons as subsistent relations.[35] In the East the Greek Fathers began, not with the single divine nature, but with the Father as dynamic source of the Trinitarian processions. It is this tradition that Bonaventure inherited.

More important than the question of influence and classification is that of the issues themselves. These two traditions represent alternate basic options; the strategic moves at the outset are foundational and establish alternate visions. Since I believe that these two visions are valid and that they can be reconciled, I see their very plurality manifesting the richness of medieval thought.[36] To become aware of this diversity is enriching not only for our understanding of the Middle Ages but for our own endeavors to deal with the same issues.

The Islamic Problematic

The first area we studied involved two distinctly Western traditions: Augustinianism and Thomism on the question of subjectivity. In the next area we enlarged our horizon to encompass the Greek Fathers and the Latin tradition on the doctrine of God. Now we will extend our horizons into the Near East and deal with what I have called the Islamic problematic. By this I mean the tension between the Semitic doctrine of God's transcendence and Greek immanence as this was confronted in the Latin West in the thirteenth century. The approach I am taking here involves both method and content. Methodologically it contends that the three monotheistic religions share a common core of doctrines and a common set of problems. It is advantageous to examine these problems within each monotheistic development. In terms of content, it implies that a basic issue in these religions was the confrontation between the Semitic notion of God's transcendence and what I have called Greek immanence, whether this be reason within nature or the participation of nature in God. At certain times in their history all three of these religions were caught up in this issue, and all three responded out of their own resources.

In the Middle Ages this problem emerged in a new way in Islam,

35. Thomas, *Summa Theologiae*, I, q. 2–26, on the divine nature: and q. 27–43, on the Trinity; on the divine persons as relations, cf. q. 28–29.

36. On how these two visions can be seen related by way of complementarity, cf. my article: "Models and the Future of Theology," *Continuum*, 7 (1969), 78–92.

which gives a uniquely forceful expression to the transcendence of God. This Islamic sense of transcendence, as embodied in the Koran, came in conflict with Greek philosophy, which in the hands of certain Muslim thinkers was used to rationalize their revelation in unorthodox ways. This problematic was introduced into the West through the importation of texts of Aristotle and Muslim commentaries. It would be enlightening to trace this issue as it emerges in Islam until it becomes the underlying intellectual crisis of thirteenth century Europe.[37] This would be a monumental task and far beyond the scope of the present study; yet I believe that the full impact of the controversies in Paris in the thirteenth century will not be grasped until they are seen through their roots in Islamic culture. All I can do here is merely to sketch the outlines of the problem and to suggest some concrete data for getting at the underlying issues.

One of the ways of seeing the problem in the Latin West is to investigate the specific controversies that were debated at the University of Paris: for example, the eternity of the world and the immortality of the soul. Another way is to plunge to a deeper level where we can touch the underlying issues. It is possible to take this second way by following Bonaventure, who analyzed the problems in precisely this way, reducing them to a single source: Aristotle's negation of exemplarism. In the *Collationes in Hexaemeron*, delivered in 1273, Bonaventure entered into the mounting controversies over a heterodox form of Aristotelianism taught by the Faculty of Arts of the University of Paris. This form of Aristotelianism, very much colored by Muslim interpretation, Bonaventure attacked with great force and incisiveness.

In the sixth lecture of the series, Bonaventure summarizes his objections to various positions of Aristotle, relating them all to a single principle: exemplarism. Because Aristotle rejected the ideas of Plato, he fell into a series of errors. Bonaventure's strong feelings on this matter are expressed in the term he uses, saying that Aristotle "cursed" (*execratur*) the ideas of Plato. Hence Aristotle claims that God knows only himself, that he has no need of the knowledge of anything else and that he moves creatures in so far as he is desired and loved. It follows, then, that God knows no particular thing.[38]

From this fundamental error two others follow: that God exercises

37. For an attempt to trace one phase of this movement, cf. my article "The Indirect Influence of the Koran on the Notion of Reason in the Christian Thought of the Thirteenth Century," to appear in the proceedings of the Fifth International Congress of Mediaeval Philosophy (Madrid, Córdoba, Granada, 1972).

38. Bonaventure, *In Hexaemeron*, VI, n. 2 (V, 360).

no providence nor judgment over the world. First, from the rejection of exemplarism, there follows another error, "that is, that God had neither foreknowledge nor providence, since he does not have within himself a rational justification of things by which he could know them." Since there are no truths about the future except what is necessary, it follows that all things come about by chance or by necessity. Because they reject chance, the Arabs "conclude to absolute necessity, that is, that these substances that move the globe are the necessary causes of all things." If all things are determined, there is no basis for reward and punishment in the afterlife. From Aristotle's basic cluster of errors there follows, Bonaventure claims, a threefold blindness or darkness: namely, that the world is eternal, that there is a single intellect, and that there is no personal immortality.[39]

Bonaventure's attack goes right to the heart of the central issue as he sees it. Aristotle has radically separated God and the world by eliminating the ontological basis of mediation between the two: namely, exemplarism. It should not be surprising that Bonaventure has pinpointed the problem in exemplarism; in his view the fundamental problem in the thirteenth century controversies is that of mediation. This is perfectly consonant with his Trinitarian vision, his emphasis on the divine fecundity and on God's immanence in the world. His logic is not that of separation but of the coincidence of opposites.[40] In his Christian response to the Islamic problematic he sides with orthodox Islam in subordinating Aristotle to revelation; but his strong affirmation of mediation would not be acceptable to classical Islam, which affirms a much greater separation between God and the world than would be allowed by Bonaventure's Trinitarian exemplarism or his cosmic Christocentricity. Bonaventure is responding to the deepest level of the Islamic problematic from a Christian immanentist perspective; in this he has much more affinity with the Sufi mystic than with the orthodox interpreter of the Koran.

Thomas, on the other hand, represents another Christian response to the Islamic problematic. Like Bonaventure and like the orthodox Muslims, he does not place Aristotle above revelation. But unlike Bona-

---

39. *Ibid.*, n. 3–4 (V, 361); English translations from *The Works of Bonaventure*, Vol. V: *Collations on the Six Days*, translated by José de Vinck (Paterson, N.J.: St. Anthony Guild Press, 1970).

40. On interpreting Bonaventure from the standpoint of the coincidence of opposites, cf. my articles: "The Coincidence of Opposites in the Christology of Saint Bonaventure," *Franciscan Studies*, 28 (1968), 27–45; "La 'Coincidentia Oppositorum' dans la théologie de Bonaventure," *Etudes franciscaines*, 18 (Supplément annuel, 1968), 15–31.

venture, Thomas is less of the Sufi and closer to the orthodox Islamic position in emphasizing the polarity between God and the world. In so doing, he makes a stronger affirmation of the Semitic sense of God's transcendence than Bonaventure does. I am, of course, not denying that there are significant dimensions of divine immanence clearly expressed in Thomas' thought. My point here is that, seen against the background of the Islamic problematic, the emphasis on transcendence in Thomas is drawn more sharply into focus. This emphasis is present in spite of Thomas' extended use of Aristotelian rational analysis. Paradoxically, he uses Aristotelian rational reflection to affirm God's transcendence, emphasizing the contingency of creatures and their dependence on God as Pure Act, carefully delineating the spheres of reason and revelation, of the natural and the supernatural. Once one penetrates through the rational structure of Thomas' thought, one can see a strong affirmation of God's transcendence and of the apophatic quality of our knowledge of God.[41] Seen thus against the background of the Islamic problematic, the contours of the thought of Thomas and Bonaventure become more sharply focused, as do the issues in the controveries of the thirteenth century.

By viewing the thirteenth century from different perspectives, we have attempted to clarify problems, to enlarge horizons and to pose new questions. This study has intended to open issues, not to close them. It has been merely able to sketch some areas for research and to present some textual evidence suggesting further investigation. Although application to concrete areas may be judged inadequate, perhaps its general method may prove valid. The method assumes that there is considerable pluralism within the fabric of medieval thought and that the approach through multiple perspectives is a fruitful technique to bring that pluralism to light. To encompass this pluralism, we must explore not merely different schools of thought within the West but enlarge our horizons into the Christian East and the Jewish and Islamic worlds. There is reason to think that medieval research will move increasingly into pluralistic perspectives as we advance towards the next centenary year.

41. For a recent study of the apophatic dimension of Thomas' treatment of God, seen from a linguistic perspective, cf. Victor Preller, *Divine Science and the Science of God* (Princeton: Princeton University Press, 1967).

CHAPTER 2.

The Moral Philosophy of St. Bonaventure

JOHN F. QUINN, C.S.B.

To grasp St. Bonaventure's understanding of moral philosophy, we must see first of all how he looks upon philosophy itself. Distinguishing four kinds of science, he speaks of human philosophy as a purely speculative science founded on the principles of reason and acquired from creatures. He speaks also of three practical sciences. The first is in the intellect as it is inclined by the will. Founded on the principles or articles of Christian faith, this is the acquired science of sacred Scripture, or of theology. The second is in the intellect, or human reason, as it inclines the will to do good work. Bonaventure refers here to the moral science of prudence acquired from the principles of natural law, which order man toward righteousness and probity of life. The third is in the intellect, not only as it inclines the will to do good work, but also as the intellect itself is inclined by Christian faith. This science, arising from grace and the principles of faith, is the gift of knowledge from the Holy Spirit.[1]

According to Bonaventure, then, the practical sciences of theology and of the gift of the Holy Spirit are distinct from the speculative science of philosophy and the moral science of prudence. Taking human science as a whole, however, he makes moral science the practical part of philosophy. Thus, dividing philosophy into theoretical and practical parts, he separates it from theology or the science of Scripture, which is wholly practical. Philosophy differentiates purely speculative truth from moral truth. Theology and Scripture are based on faith, which is the foundation of morals, justice or holiness, and the whole of right living. Consequently, sacred science does not differentiate between knowledge

1. III *Sent.*, d 35, un. 2, Resp. ". . . Spiritus Sancti." (III, 776; III, 781) The more standard abbreviations are used in referring to St. Bonaventure's texts. The first numbers in parentheses refer to his *Opera omnia* (Quaracchi, 1882–1902); the second refer to his *Opera theologica selecta* (Quaracchi, 1934–64). References to the works of ancient and medieval authors use the standard abbreviations: Aristotle's works show the numbers of the Bekker edition, *Aristotelis Opera* (Berlin: 1831–70); patristic and later writings show the volume and pagination of Migne's *Patrologia Graeca* (PG) or *Patrologia Latina* (PL). References to the books of Scripture use an adaptation of the now fairly common signs.

of morals and knowledge of things, or the objects of belief. The science is divided, rather, between the Old and the New Testaments.[2] Philosophy deals with the being and knowledge of natural things. Theology deals with the being and knowledge of things revealed by the Holy Spirit. Using philosophy, nonetheless, theology makes a substrate of philosophical knowledge and, taking what it needs from natural things, erects a ladder as it were with its feet touching the earth and its peak touching heaven. The whole of theology, therefore, is modeled after Christ, who is both human and divine and the middle person in the Trinity.[3]

The union of faith and philosophy in theology has both antecedents and consequences regarding the gift of the Holy Spirit. The antecedents are the innate *lumen* of reason and the infused *lumen* of faith. The innate *lumen,* coming from the light of the intellect, is a natural power of judgment given by God to the rational creature. The infused *lumen,* coming from the light of faith, is a gift of God to the rational creature by way of grace. The consequences are a clear knowledge of the Creator and a revealed knowledge of the Savior. The formation and development of theological knowledge, therefore, or the union of faith and philosophy, is the way to the science of the gift of the Holy Spirit. Hence, reconsidering the four kinds of science, Bonaventure redefines them. Philosophical science is certain knowledge of truth as it can be scrutinized. Theological science is devout knowledge of truth as it can be believed. The gift of science is holy knowledge of truth as it can be loved. The science of glory or of beatitude is everlasting knowledge of truth as it can be desired.[4]

We have seen now, first, that Bonaventure distinguishes philosophy from theology; second, that he also unites philosophy to faith in the science of theology. When using philosophy, and before uniting it to faith, he always seeks the truth of its objects according to the proper principles and methods of philosophical science. Our aim, however, is not to show him using or developing moral philosophy, a task beyond the limits of this short essay. We intend, rather, to see how he looks upon moral philosophy as a science of natural reason. To do this, we must go to his texts describing the objects, principles, and methods of the philosophical sciences. It will be necessary, then, to see also the ways in which he distinguishes the many sciences of philosophy. This

2. *Brevil.*, Prol., n 1 "Recte autem . . . speculatione considerato." (V, 203; V, 6, n. 2)

3. *Ibid.*, n 3 "Et hoc . . . Ecclesiam militantem." (V, 205; V, 9–10, n 2) *Cf.* p 1, c. 1 (V, 210; V, 19–20), p 2, c. 5 (V, 222–24; V, 41–44).

4. *De donis,* coll. 4, n 2, n 5 (V, 474); *cf. M. Trin.*, q 1, a 2, Resp. (V, 54–56).

presentation is divided into two parts corresponding to Bonaventure's early period (1254–59) and late period (1266–73). We shall start from his main texts on the philosophical sciences and then proceed to an explanation of his understanding of the science of moral philosophy by means of coordinate and parallel texts of the same period.[5]

Early Period

In the first of two main texts in this period, Bonaventure speaks of the *lumen* of philosophical knowledge as illumining the mind to scrutinize truths that it can understand. This is an interior *lumen* empowering the mind to inquire into the hidden causes of things by the principles of the sciences and of natural truth, principles that are implanted naturally in every man. The sciences are rational, natural, and moral philosophy. Rational philosophy considers the truths of words and of concepts, searches for the formal or exemplar cause, and arrives at God as the source of understanding. This science is subdivided into grammar, logic, and rhetoric. Grammar deals with the power of reason to apprehend truth and the ways that it can be expressed in suitable speech, or the manner in which a man can make truly known a concept of his mind. Logic deals with reason's power to judge truth and the ways that it can be taught to move a man more readily to believe. Rhetoric has to do with reason's power of motivation and the modes of ornate speech that move a man to love or to hate.

Thus, ruling the intellect's interpretation of truth, the *lumen* of rational philosophy illumines the mind to understand the truth of doctrine. Natural philosophy considers the truth of things and of being, searches for the efficient cause, and attains God as the origin of being. The science is subdivided into physics, mathematics, and metaphysics. Looking to the formal reasons of material things, physics considers their generation and corruption according to natural powers and seminal reasons. Dealing with intellectual reasons in the human soul, mathematics considers the forms that can be abstracted from material things according to intelligible principles. Turning to the ideal reasons of

5. By coordinate texts, we mean texts from the *same work* with the *main* text; by parallel texts, we mean texts from *other works* close in time to the work with the main text. For the chronology of Bonaventure's works see: *Introduction to the Works of Bonaventure*, trans. from the French of J. Guy Bougerol, O.F.M., by José de Vinck (Paterson, N.J.: 1963), pp. 88–134, 156–78; John F. Quinn, C.S.B., "Chronology of St. Bonaventure (1217–1257)," *Franciscan Studies* 32 (1972), pp. 168–86. As we proceed, we shall indicate in the notes, whenever necessary, the difference between Bonaventure's theological and philosophical understanding of moral problems.

divine wisdom, metaphysics has to do with knowledge of all beings, which it takes back to God as their first principle, for they emanate from God according to His ideal reasons inasmuch as He is their origin, end, and exemplar.

Hence, directing the intellect in its judgments, the *lumen* of natural philosophy illumines the mind to understand the truth of science. Moral or practical philosophy considers the truth of moral action and of life, searches for the final cause, and reaches God as the order and end of human life. The science is subdivided into monastic, economic, and political disciplines. They are concerned respectively with the moral life of the individual, the family, and the populace.

The intention of the whole of moral philosophy has to do chiefly with righteousness or general justice, which Anselm calls "rectitude of the will." To be right, or to have rectitude, human actions must attain the mean between extremes. To live rightly, or with rectitude, a man must order and direct his life according to the rules of divine or eternal law. Thus, living and acting righteously, a man is morally upright in his life and actions. Wherefore, governing the will, the *lumen* of moral philosophy illumines the mind to understand the truth of life and of action.[6]

The whole of philosophy, then, comes to rest in the truth of the causes of creatures. In the genus of efficient causes, or of origin, natural philosophy takes every mutable being back to the immutable being. Since everything that is moved is moved by something else, there can be rest only in the unmoved mover. In the genus of formal and exemplar causes, or of forms and beauty, rational philosophy takes the beautiful and the more beautiful back to the most beautiful. There can be rest here only in that form and exemplar which is essential beauty. In the genus of final causes, or of ends, moral philosophy takes the good and the better back to the best, for there is rest or repose only in the optimum good.[7]

We have here a brief description of the appropriate method for the philosophical sciences. Seeking their proper objects, or the truth of beings, forms, and moral goodness, the sciences proceed reductively from effect to cause until they attain the first cause of natural truth.

6. *Red. art.*, n 4 (V, 320–21; V, 219–20), nn 23–25 (V, 325; V, 227–28); St. Anselm, *De ver.*, 12 (PL 158.480). The association of the three sciences of philosophy with God respectively as the source of understanding, the origin of being, and the order or end of life is taken from St. Augustine, *De civ. Dei*, 8.4 (PL 41.228–29). The threefold division of natural philosophy is influenced by Aristotle, *Metaph.*, 6.1 (1026a7–32), 11.7 (1064a28–1064b13).

7. I *Sent.*, d 3, p 1, dub. 1, Resp. "In aliis . . ." (I, 78; I, 56).

Moral philosophy, in particular, proceeds from this or that particular good to arrive at the optimum good, which is the final cause or end of all moral goodness. Now, in Bonaventure's view, the sufficient end of the human soul can be only that good for which it is created. This is the supreme good, which is superior to the soul, and the infinite good, which is beyond the powers of the soul. The soul's natural knowledge is not restricted, however, because it can by nature know in some way all things. For this reason, the soul's knowledge is not completed by any kind of object, but only when it knows every object and that supreme object by which it knows all things. Likewise, the human will by its nature loves every good, so that no good suffices for its end except the supreme good, which is the good of every other good and all the good in all good things. This is also the infinite good, which is the end of the soul according to the necessity of estimation: no man would be happy unless he thinks that he is happy. Such an estimation goes beyond all that is finite, because a man can think of something greater than every finite thing. Since the range of the will extends to the range of estimation, the will necessarily goes beyond everything finite, and so only the infinite good is the sufficient end of the soul. Thus, as the supreme and infinite good, God alone suffices as the end of the human soul. God is also its end, moreover, because He alone gives perfect delight. Everything delighting the soul is good and beautiful: since God alone is essential goodness and beauty, only in God is there perfect delight for the soul. Where there is delight, furthermore, there is also a union of the object and the one delighted. Now God is united most perfectly to the soul: He is united to it both truly and intimately because of His supreme simplicity and spirituality; God is so truly present to the soul that He is more intimate to it than the soul is to itself. In short, the soul has a natural capacity to perceive the supreme and infinite good, which is God, in whom alone it ought to rest and to take delight or enjoyment.[8]

We know now what Bonaventure means when he says that moral philosophy, seeking the final cause, reaches God as the order and end of human life. The science attains a knowledge of God as the supreme and infinite good, or the only sufficient end in which the human soul can repose with enjoyment, and to which man is ordered through knowledge and love. Bonaventure, citing Aristotle, identifies 'end' with that for whose sake something is done. He then distinguishes the ultimate end, which is 'end' in the proper sense, from an end under an end, or a proximate end, which is only a terminus and does not include the

8. *Ibid.*, d 1, a 3, q 2, Resp. (I, 29–30; I, 40–41); *cf.* q 1, Resp. (I, 38; I, 27).

ultimate end.[9] Thus, in directing a man to the end of human life, moral philosophy is ordering him to God as the ultimate end. All creatures are good, moreover, because they tend and are ordered to God, who is the cause of their goodness. As the ultimate end, then, God is sought because of His goodness, for the nature of good coincides with that which has principally the nature of end.[10]

Bonaventure, again following Aristotle, holds the principle that it is the wise man who sets things in order. Now there is a twofold order, namely, of part to part within a whole and of means to an end. The first order looks principally to knowledge and the second chiefly to love, which inclines to an end.[11] Applying this to moral philosophy, we can see that as a science or mode of knowledge, it unites its three subsidiary sciences by ordering them to one another as parts within a whole. In that way, the knowledge of moral philosophy is united under its principal intention of righteousness or rectitude of the will. Under the same intention, the science also puts order into human actions, for they are the parts within the whole of moral life. Hence, governing the will through knowledge, moral philosophy orders man toward righteousness and probity of life, thus preparing the way for love, which inclines and orders the good, or proximate end, of human actions to their ultimate end. This end is known by an estimation of what it is that makes men happy or beatified. According to Boethius, a desire for the true and the good is implanted in the minds of men. Such a desire presupposes knowledge, Bonaventure adds, so that knowledge of the true good and a desire for the supreme delight are impressed on the minds of men. All men, then, have a natural capacity to know and to love God. Moreover, according to Augustine, every man has a natural desire for beatitude, so that no man can doubt the will of another to be happy. To Bonaventure, siding with Augustine, human beatitude consists in the supreme good, which is God, and so every man has some knowledge implanted in his soul that there is a supreme good.[12]

Citing Boethius a second time, Bonaventure insists that the true good of men's desire is the good that makes them truly happy. This is implied by Aristotle in saying "all things long for the good." They do not long for any sort of good, Bonaventure comments, but only for that good

9. *Ibid.*, d 1, dub. 15, Resp. ". . . dicit Magister." (I, 45; I, 34); Aristotle, *Phys.*, 2.3 (194b32–195a2).

10. II *Sent.*, d 1, p 1, a 2, q 2, sc 2 (II, 28; II, 21, sc b).

11. III *Sent.*, d 19, un. 2, ad 3 ". . . finem inclinare." (III, 639–40; III, 634–35); Aristotle, *Metaph.*, 1.1 (980b20–982a1).

12. *M. Trin.*, q 1, a 1, fa 3, 7 (V, 45, 46). Boethius, *De consol.*, 3, pr. 2 (*PL* 63.724); St. Augustine, *De Trin.*, 4.7 (*PL* 42.1018–19), 20.25 (*PL* 42.1034).

which suffices for their desire, and the true beatitude alone suffices for the desire of the human soul.[13] The human desire for beatitude is natural, not deliberative. If it were deliberative, a man could choose the opposite, or misery. Augustine has shown, however, that no one deliberatively chooses to be miserable. Since a natural desire is perpetual and common to all men, every man has the natural desire for the true beatitude. Consequently, having also a natural desire for perfection, every man naturally desires to be perfected by the true beatitude.[14] This desire is natural to men because the human soul, which is created in the image and likeness of God (*Gen.* 1:26), is capable of possessing the most sufficient good. But the soul is not sufficient unto itself, and so it needs the true good of beatitude, for which it has a natural desire.[15]

It is true, nonetheless, that some men do not know the true beatitude. Explaining this, Bonaventure first sets down a twofold relation of knowledge and love in all men: as their deliberative knowledge precedes deliberative love, so their natural knowledge precedes natural love. Then, stating that men have a twofold instinct for good, he distinguishes between a general and a specific desire for good. The instinct or dictate regarding good in general comes from natural knowledge, and no one errs in this regard. The instinct or dictate concerning a specific good does not come entirely from a natural disposition but from an assumption made by a deliberation of reason, and so men can err concerning that good. Likewise, having a desire for the true beatitude in general, all men know in general and believe that beatitude is the good sufficing for them and the one that everyone desires. When men assume that this is a specific good, however, their desire can be in error; for instance, if they desire as the true beatitude such goods as honor and riches. All men know the true beatitude in general, Bonaventure says, because knowledge of it is innate to the human soul. It is innate through the soul's awareness of its own need for and inclination toward

13. IV *Sent.*, d 49, p 1, un. 2, fa 1-2 (IV, 1002-03; IV, 987, fa a-b); Aristotle, *Ethica*, 1.1 (1094a3).

14. *Loc. cit.*, fa 3-4 (c-d); St. Augustine, *De lib. arb.*, 3.6-8 (PL 32.1279-82).

15. *Ibid.*, Resp. (V, 1003; V, 988). The image and likeness (or imitation) of God are natural to the human soul, according to Bonaventure, who maintains that the ancient philosophers knew these characteristics of the soul and, from them, came to know the attributes of God, i.e., the divine unity, truth, and goodness—a fact evident from the tripartite division of philosophy (by the philosophers themselves) into natural, rational, and moral science; but the philosophers, lacking Christian faith, did not know the perfect image (and likeness) of God in the soul, namely, that it reflected the essential unity of the three divine persons. I *Sent.*, d 3, p 1, un. 4 (I, 75-77; I, 54-55), p 2, a 2, q 3 (I, 92-93; I, 69-70); M. *Trin.*, q 1, a 1, ad 9 (V, 51).

the one good that suffices to fulfill its natural desire for beatitude. Knowledge of beatitude is innate as knowledge of the natural law is innate to all men. Although the human soul, when it comes into being, has no knowledge, even so, this is to be understood only of the similitudes and species that the soul must acquire through the senses. The innate knowledge of beatitude, however, and of natural law, does not depend on abstract species.[16]

Thus, by natural knowledge of beatitude, Bonaventure means innate knowledge of God as the supreme good. By deliberative knowledge, he means the assumption or estimation made by a deliberation of reason about some specific good to be ordered to beatitude. This good can direct a man away from beatitude if he ignores his innate or general knowledge of it. Again, by natural love, Bonaventure means the movement of the will following its instinctive desire for beatitude, or the dictate of nature inclining the will immutably and determinately to beatitude. By deliberative love, he means the movement of the will following a deliberation and judgment of reason regarding the order of this or of that good to beatitude. The order should be established according to the natural instinct or dictate of the will, which can be inclined toward opposite goods, so that it can be turned away from beatitude if a man errs in his judgment. These two movements of the will come from it respectively as it is 'natural' and 'deliberative'.[17]

A man erring in his moral judgments is at fault because he turns away from the supreme good to which he can order his actions. He is at fault by his failure, through his freedom of choice, to order his actions to God. As a rational creature, a man comes from God and, as an image of God, ought to have God as the principle, exemplar, and end of his actions. Imitating God, however, a man is good in his actions. As a creature, nevertheless, a man originates from nothing, and so he can fail to be good in his actions. This comes about when he loves himself too much and acts for his own sake in such a way that, not seeking God as the end, he does not act for the sake of God. Hence, although using

16. IV *Sent.*, d 49, p 1, un. 2, ad 1–3 (IV, 1003–04; IV, 988–99). Man's natural knowledge of the divine being (*esse divinum*) is innate to his soul because of the divine image, which is the reason why there is implanted in his soul a natural desire, knowledge, and memory in regard to God, to whom it naturally tends in order that it can be beatified in Him. *M. Trin.*, q 1, a 1, Resp. "Est enim . . . possit beatificari." (V, 49). To know God, although innately, a man must first be disposed formally by a knowledge of exterior things, then retire within his mind to find there God in His image. I *Sent.*, d 3, p 1, un. 3, ad 1–2 (I, 75; I, 54–55); q 1, ad 5 (I, 69–70; I, 50).

17. II *Sent.*, d 24, p 1, a 2, q 3, Resp., ad 2 (II, 566; II, 584); *cf.* fa 1–4 (II, 565–66; II, 583–84, fa a–d).

freedom of choice, a man can fail to be good in his actions by moving away from the right order to his ultimate end.[18]

We have seen, thus far, how Bonaventure understands the true object, appropriate method, and proper end of moral philosophy. It remains now to see what he means by saying that the principles of the philosophical sciences and of their truth are innate or implanted naturally in every man. With respect to moral philosophy, these are the principles of natural law and of moral truth, particularly beatitude, to which all men are inclined innately by an instinctive desire. All this involves man's freedom of choice, which has to do with the right means ordering human life to its ultimate end in accord with the rule and dictate of natural law. It is a dictate of natural law, for instance, that God is, and that God is good.[19] But natural law is itself a reflection of the eternal law, which is the ultimate rule of all human action and the principal source of the order of human life. What we must see, then, is how Bonaventure looks upon moral philosophy as the science directing man toward rectitude of the will, or general justice.[20]

18. *Regn. Dei*, n 43 "Cum autem . . ." (V, 551–53; V, 433–34). Bonaventure is speaking, in the texts that we have used, of man's instinctive desire for beatitude, which he can know in a general or innate way by his natural reason. It is thus that the ancient philosophers considered the final end of man and the means to attain it. In fact, the true beatitude is known explicitly only by Christian faith and cannot be desired or attained without divine grace. The philosophers desired beatitude only as they knew it by natural reason, and so they could neither desire nor attain beatitude as it is known by faith. II *Sent.*, d 28, a 2, q 1, ad 2–3 (II, 683; II, 705), cf. d 19, a 3, q 1, Resp. ". . . habebat completionem." (II, 469; II, 483–84): d 29, a 1, q 2, Resp. (II, 698–99; II, 720–21). Some philosophers, knowing God with a certain degree of love, tended toward God in a natural way, but could not thereby become truly beatified; it is more true to say that they were cast down, or despondent, than to say that they were tending toward God. III *Sent.*, d 24, a 3, q 2, arg. 7 (III, 527–28; III, 519), ad 7 (III, 529; III, 521). On the way that a Christian knows and desires beatitude, *see* II *Sent.*, d 38, dub. 1 (II, 894; II, 929). Some men now refuse to accept beatitude as it is known by Christian faith, thus ignoring the dictate of natural reason and violating the dictate of natural law, which they know innately by their conscience and according to which they will be judged. *Ibid.*, d 22, dub. 3 (II, 528; II, 546); *Comm. Lc.*, c 12, v 57, n 84 (VII, 334–35), c 19, v 21, n 34 (VII, 484): *cf.* c 20, v 25, n 32 (VII, 511); *De s. Dominico*, n II (IX, 564–65).

19. "Quaedam sunt . . . de dictamine iuris naturalis, sicut Deum esse, Deum esse bonum." III *Sent.*, d 24, dub. 3, in Resp. (III, 530; III, 523).

20. By general justice, Bonaventure means the unity of all the moral virtues; as a specific virtue, justice is one of the cardinal virtues. General justice, or righteousness and probity of life, is a sort of moral wisdom, as speculative wisdom is a general science unifying the other speculative sciences, from which it is distinct, nevertheless, as a specific knowledge of the highest causes of things. See III *Sent.*, d 35, dub. 1, Resp. (III, 787; III, 793–94); *cf.* Aristotle, *Metaph.*, 1.1 (981a13–982a1).

Bonaventure's understanding of our innate knowledge of natural law is contained in his texts on conscience. His understanding of our instinctive desire for the true good is found in his texts on synderesis. Consequently, we shall have to see how he considers conscience and synderesis, which have the primary principles of freedom of choice. He takes the name *conscience* to mean, first, the law of which we are conscious, as John Damascene says, "conscience is the law of our intellect," for it is the law that we know by our conscience. Second, the name means the habitus by which we are conscious of the law. Third, it means the conscious potency according as the natural law is said to be written on our conscience. Since the second is the more usual meaning, Bonaventure says, conscience is a habitus of the practical intellect, which differs from the speculative intellect only by extension, as Aristotle shows. Hence, inclining and moving the will, the practical intellect is perfected by conscience, which dictates the rules and principles of moral conduct, e.g., that God is to be honored.[21]

Asking whether conscience is innate or acquired, Bonaventure first gives reasons for both sides of the question. It is innate according to Scripture (*Rm.* 2:14–15) and to the teaching of Augustine, who puts in man a natural power of judgment which has conscience as a habitus. It is also innate according to human reason: nature teaches man the natural law which binds his will before the law is known; from naturally implanted knowledge—every man has an instinctive desire for beatitude and a natural inclination to honor his parents.[22] Conscience is acquired according to the teaching of Aristotle, who shows that the human soul originates without knowledge, which is acquired through the senses, as Augustine came to see in denying that the soul knows moral truth naturally or innately. Aristotle also shows that the conclusions of science come from principles, so that conscience is acquired from the principles of natural law. This is evident from reason: moral truths are more difficult to know than speculative truths, which are not innate; if conscience were innate, it would always be right and never vary, but it can be wrong and a man can acquire a new conscience.[23]

Bonaventure, reconciling the opposing positions, follows Aristotle and Augustine in rejecting the Platonic view that all habitual knowl-

21. II *Sent.*, d 39, a 1, q 1, Resp. (II, 899; II, 933–34); St. John Damascene, *De fide orth.*, 4.22 (PG 94.119); Aristotle, *De anima*, 3.9 (432b21–433a8).

22. *Loc. cit.*, q 2, fa 1–6 (II, 901; II, 935–36, fa a–f); *cf.* q 1, ad 2 (II, 900; II, 934–35); St. Augustine, *De lib. arb.*, 3.20.56 (PL 32.1298).

23. *Ibid.*, sc 1–6 (II, 901–02; II, 936–37). Aristotle, *De anima*, 3.4 (429b29–430a1); *Anal. post.*, 1.3 (72b18–33), 1.18 (81a37–38). St. Augustine, *Retract.*, 1.8.2 (PL 32.594).

edge is innate to the soul.[24] He then sets aside two other views: habitual knowledge is innate with respect to the agent intellect and acquired with respect to the possible intellect, a view contrary to Aristotle's teaching that the agent intellect, depending on the senses, makes things known to the mind, which becomes what is known by the possible intellect; habitual knowledge is innate regarding principles and acquired regarding conclusions, a view contrary not only to Aristotle but also to Augustine, who shows that we have no prior knowledge of principles, which are known in the spiritual light of the soul.[25]

Setting forth a third view, which he accepts, Bonaventure holds that a habitus is innate because of the natural *lumen* of the mind, or its natural power of judgment, to which Augustine refers. It is also acquired because of the species that Aristotle says must be obtained through the senses, as experience shows, for no one would know *whole* or *part*, nor *father* and *mother*, without receiving likenesses of them through the senses. As first speculative principles are most evident in the innate *lumen* of the mind, so are first moral truths, or principles of natural law, e.g., that God is to be obeyed, and never do to another what you would not have done to yourself (*cf. Tb* 4:16). The first moral principles are known innately, however, only after reception of species through the senses. Although the natural power of judgment suffices for the mind to know those principles from their own evidence and without any other persuasion, the mind's innate *lumen* does not suffice to draw evident conclusions from them apart from some persuasion or a new capacity for instruction about particular things that ought to be done. That capacity is conscience, which directs our judgments of particular moral actions. Thus, conscience is innate regarding the natural *lumen* of the intellect and the primary dictates of natural law, both of which suffice for a man to be conscious that he should honor his parents and not harm his neighbors.

Conscience is also acquired, however, regarding additional knowledge received through the senses, for no one has innate species of his parents or of his neighbors. With respect to things knowable through the senses, therefore, conscience is at once innate and acquired: it is acquired because of the species of its particular objects; it is innate because of an intellectual *lumen* that manifests what is universally good, and thus conscience is the seedbed of other habitual dispositions or moral virtues

24. Aristotle, *Anal. prior.*, 2.21 (67a20–25); *Anal. post.*, 1.1 (71a25–71b8); *Ethica*, 2.1 (1103a14–25). St. Augustine, *De Trin.*, 12.15.24 (PL 42.1011); *De Gen. ad litt.*, 7.11.16 (PL 34.361).

25. Aristotle, *De anima*, 3.5 (430a14–16); *Anal. post.*, 2.19 (99b20–100a14). St. Augustine, *De Trin.*, 12.15.24 (PL 42.1011).

to be acquired. With respect to things not knowable through the senses, but by their essence, such as 'loving God' and 'fearing God', conscience is a simply innate habitus. We know *love* and *fear* by their essence, for they are essentially in the will. We know God, as Augustine says, because knowledge of God is implanted naturally in us. We do not, therefore, get all our knowledge through the senses. Whenever Aristotle says that what is in our intellect must first be in the senses and that all our knowledge arises from the senses, he is to be understood only of those things that have to be known by abstract likenesses. He says, very notably, that nothing is inscribed originally on the soul, not because it has no knowledge, but because it has no abstract likeness. Augustine says the same thing: God gave us a natural power of judgment by which we know light and darkness, or good and evil, in the "book of light," for truth is implanted naturally in the hearts of men.[26]

Man was created originally, Bonaventure says, with a twofold rectitude of nature. The one, rectitude of conscience, was for judging rightly; the other, the instinct of synderesis, was for willing rightly. These two principles of moral action are so related that conscience stirs the will by means of synderesis, which stimulates the will to do good and to repel evil. This is why synderesis is sometimes called the 'spark of conscience'.[27]

26. II *Sent.*, d 39, a 1, q 2, Resp. (II, 902–04; II, 937–39). Aristotle, *De anima*, 3.4–8 (429a10–432a13); *De sen. et sens.*, 6 (445b17–20). St. Augustine, *De civ. Dei*, 11.27.2 (*PL* 41.341). *See above*, n 16. As any man knows innately *rectitude* and *love*, so a Christian knows innately that charity is *rectitude of love*; thus, according to Augustine, charity is known by its likeness in the intellect and in the eternal truth, not because no species come to-be in the intellect, but because it has no pure species, and because the eternal truth impresses on it a cognitive likeness of charity. I *Sent.*, d 17, p 1, un. 4, Resp., (I, 301–02; I, 244); St. Augustine, *De Trin.*, 9.6.9 (*PL* 42.965–66), 8.9.13 (*PL* 42.959–60), 8.6.9 (*PL* 42.953–56). Bonaventure speaks, then, of innate principles which are known in a general way. He never speaks of *innate ideas*, although he does refer to an innate habitus of species (universal knowledge) in Adam and Christ. II *Sent.*, d 23, a 2, q 1, Resp. (II, 538; II, 556–57); III *Sent.*, d 14, a 3, q 1 (III, 318–20; III, 312–14) *Brevil.*, p 4,c 6. (V, 246–47; V, 87–89). Because of original sin, we do not have such a habitus, but must abstract species to form a habitus, which Adam did not do: he judged by his innate species what he perceived by his senses. Aristotle's view of all knowledge arising from the senses is true only of the state of fallen nature. III *Sent.*, d 14, a 3, q 2, ad 3–4 (III, 322; III, 316); Aristotle, *Metaph.*, 1.1 (980b25–981a12). If we had innate species, we would know singular things as Adam knew them, or as an angel now knows them. II *Sent.*, d 3, p 2, a 2, q 1, ad 4 "Ponatur etiam . . ." (II, 121; II, 112).

27. *Brevil.*, p 2, c 11 "Et quoniam . . . ad bonum" (V, 229; V, 55, n 6); II *Sent.*, d 39, div. text. (II, 897b; II, 932); a 1, q 1, ad 4 (II, 900; II, 935); a 2, q 1, ad 3 (II, 910; II, 945).

Bonaventure considers three ways of understanding synderesis. The first identifies it with the higher part of human reason, i.e., as it is turned toward God and is always right. Directed by conscience, the higher part rules the lower part according to natural law. In this respect the higher part is not always right, for the lower part of human reason is turned toward the sense appetites. Bonaventure rejects the opinion because the act of synderesis is always right, observes the natural law, and looks to both God and neighbor. The second way subjects the deliberative movements of reason and will to free choice, which sometimes inclines them toward evil, and subjects their natural movements to conscience, synderesis, and natural law, which are identical and always incline reason and will toward good. By way of appropriation, synderesis is the one potency of reason and will, conscience is their one habitus, and natural law their one object. Regarding good and evil, synderesis is taken as a habitus of universal knowledge, conscience of particular knowledge, and natural law as indifferent to either habitus. Bonaventure rejects this opinion because conscience is a habitus of the intellect and synderesis a principle of the will. Considering the third way, which he endorses, Bonaventure holds that conscience moves the intellect toward moral truth, and synderesis moves the will toward the noble good, which is a moral good. Thus, corresponding to the innate part of conscience, synderesis is a natural habitus of the will and the principle stimulating it continually to desire the good.[28]

Conscience and synderesis have a common relation to natural law. As a habitus, natural law enfolds conscience and synderesis, for it is the means of instructing man in moral truth and ordering him rightly to the good. Taken properly, however, natural law is a collection of precepts, and so it is the object of conscience and synderesis, the one dictating and the other inclining toward the good. Thus, properly considered, synderesis is the will's natural ability to desire and to tend toward the good as dictated by conscience and made known by natural law. Given a wider significance, synderesis refers to the will and to the sense appetites as they are moved naturally and rightly, but not deliberatively. As habituated by synderesis, whose movement is always

28. II *Sent.*, d 39, a 2, q 1, Resp., ad 1 (II, 909–10; II, 944–45). By the noble good (*bonum honestum*), Bonaventure means primarily the divine and supreme good, which is the beatifying good, and secondarily, created although spiritual goods, particularly moral goods, such as the virtues both natural and infused. I *Sent.*, d 1, a 3, q 2, con. 4 (I, 40; I, 29), ad 4 (I, 41–42; I, 30); III *Sent.*, d 28, un. 5 (III, 629–31; III, 625–27): d 33, un. 3, fm 5 (III, 716; III, 718, fm e). *See* Cicero, *De invent.*, 2.52; St. Augustine, *De div. quaest.*, 30 (PL 40.19–20); *De civ. Dei*, 19.25 (PL 41.656).

right, the will is never involved in, but rather corrects, the erroneous actions of the sense appetites.[29]

Looking to universal truth, which is known in a simple manner, an innate judgment of conscience is never erroneous and so cannot lead synderesis astray. Regarding a particular truth which is known by a discourse of reason, a deliberative judgment of conscience can be erroneous, and thus synderesis can be led astray by a faulty deliberation of reason. It is the deliberative judgment of conscience, then, and the deliberative movement of the will that are subject to free choice and not the natural instinct of synderesis or the innate judgment of conscience.[30] As an innate habitus, conscience originates from man's intellective nature and attains perfection inasmuch as his intellect attains perfection. As an acquired habitus, conscience has its origin from man's free choice, which can be used only when his intellect has achieved an adequate degree of perfection. A virtuous act, however, does not require a perfect virtue. The act need flow only from a deliberation of reason in accord with the natural rectitude of the will. Thus, using free choice, a man must act rightly from a true judgment of his conscience along with the natural inclination of synderesis in his will.[31]

Bonaventure distinguishes the practical science of the mechanical arts, which has to do with productive work such as carpentry, from the practical science of moral philosophy, which is concerned with the work of free will or free choice.[32] Explaining free choice, he says that the appetite of the will is directed toward an object according to natural instinct or according to deliberation and choice. The will is properly called *elective* from its act of election, which is indifferent to each side of a choice, and so the act is said to come from free choice. Since the indifference arises from a preceding deliberation in conjunction with the will, free choice is a faculty of reason and will involving all the powers of the soul, as Augustine says, "When we speak of free choice, we do not speak of a part of the soul, but to be sure of the whole soul." Thus, according to Bonaventure, an integral freedom concerning the choice of

29. II *Sent.*, d 39, a 2, q 1, ad 4 "Ex praedictis . . ." (II, 911; II, 945-46). On the rectitude and inerrancy of synderesis, which is naturally inseparable from the will and whose act, according to Augustine, can never be lost, although a man can move against its dictate regarding his proper good, and so fall into sin and evil, *see ibid.*, q 2, sc 3, Resp. (II, 912; II, 947-48, sc c); q 3, sc 3, Resp. (II, 914; II, 949-50, sc c): St. Augustine, *De civ. Dei*, 19.12.2 (*PL* 41.638-39).

30. II *Sent.*, d 39, a 2, q 3, ad 4, 6 (II, 915; II, 950-51).

31. IV *Sent.*, d 4, p 2, a 2, q 2, Resp. "Huiusmodi autem . . ." (IV, 114; IV, 105); III *Sent.*, d 33, un. 5, ad 5 (III, 724; III, 727).

32. III *Sent.*, d 14, a 3, q 3, ad 5 ". . . practicam fabricandi." (III, 325; III, 319); *cf. Red. art.*, nn 1-2 (V, 319-20; V, 217-18).

good or of evil arises from a concourse of reason and will, reason acting self-reflectively in concomitance with the will.[33]

Man has free choice because, by nature, he is a rational creature with both reason and will. His other powers move in obedience to reason by which he discerns the just and the unjust. Judging things completely by his reason, he can know the supreme justice, which is the measure of every right. Man can also know himself and reflect upon himself because matter does not limit his reason, and so he can judge what is his own and what belongs to another. As a natural image of God, then, man has the power to comprehend what is right and just. Moreover, his will is free because of its full dominion over its objects and its own acts. His will is able to seek every good, to avoid all evil, and to move him in regard to his body and soul, so that he has a natural capacity to love and to hate. Consequently, from his complete judgment of reason and full dominion of will, man has free choice concerning his due and proper good, which is the noble good.[34] Reason and will have free choice rather than free judgment, Bonaventure maintains, for choice regulates reason by a command of the will, but judgment regulates it by the rule of truth, or the eternal law. A judge is one who decides a case according to law, but an arbiter is one who decides it by his own will. The faculty of freedom, therefore, is named properly from choice, because the decisions of free choice, properly considered, are made more according to will than according to precept of law.[35]

33. *Brevil.*, p 2, c 9 "Postremo, quoniam . . ." (V, 227; V, 51, n 8): the citation is from pseudo-Augustine, *Hypognosticon*, 3.5.7 (*PL* 45.1624); cf. II *Sent.*, d 25, p 1, un. 3 (II, 597–600; II, 615–19). On free choice as a 'faculty' of reason and will see *loc. cit.*, q 2 (II, 595–96; II, 613–15).

34. II *Sent.*, d 25, p 1, un. 1, Resp., ad 1–4 (II, 593–94; II, 611–13).

35. *Loc. cit.*, dub. 1, Resp. ". . . nomen iudicii." (II, 607; II, 626). The philosophers see free choice as the principle of moral actions subject to the natural law, but the theologians see it as the principle of meritorious works assisted by grace, which is necessary to please God and to merit beatitude; under natural law, free choice looks to good deeds ordered to the ultimate end, such as honoring parents, but those deeds cannot be actually ordered to that end without grace, which is also necessary to combat the effects of original sin. *Ibid.*, p 1, dub. 3, Resp. "Ad illud . . ." (II, 607; II, 626); d 29, a 1, q 2, Resp., ad 4 (II, 698–99; II, 720–22); d 28, a 2, q 3, Resp. (II, 689–90; II, 711–13): cf. *Brevil.*, p 2, c 12 (V, 230; V, 55–57). Since the philosophers did not know of original sin, they thought that man was made in his present state of misery; the theologians think that, even according to the certain evidence of reason, man was not made in that condition. II *Sent.*, d 30, a 1, q 1, Resp. "Attendendum est . . ." (II, 716; II, 737). The philosophers were unaware of the rebellion of sensuality against reason, so that they considered as unreasonable many things such as complete continence, that are reasonable to Christians. *Ibid.*, d 24, p 2, dub. 3, Resp. "Ad illud . . ." (II, 588; II, 609); III *Sent.*, d 23, a 1, q 1, ad 3–4 (III, 472; III, 463). A Christian sometimes acts contrary to the natural

It is by a right use of free choice that a man, to have moral rectitude, must order and direct his life according to the rules of the eternal law. He consults this law by his superior reason, which observes the immutability of God's power and equity, thus bringing about an understanding of His will. When considering the good of his body and sense appetites, he uses his inferior reason, which is ruled by his superior reason. Hence, in deliberating about moral goods, a man regulates and commands his sense powers by his superior reason, which includes his inferior reason, although the consideration of spiritual goods is the principal act of human reason.[36]

When judging according to the eternal law, human reason does not err, for this is the noblest act of the superior reason. It can err by deviating from that law and attending inordinately to the good of the soul, or by allowing the inferior reason to seek inordinately the good of the sense appetites by ignoring the natural instinct of synderesis. Human reason is always right in its moral judgments only when consulting the eternal law from which it receives the rules or first principles of moral truth, i.e., of natural law. In applying those rules to particular actions, reason needs the direction of moral virtue. When Aristotle says that the intellect is always right, this is to be understood of man's natural conscience, which is his intellect as it is moved by synderesis and not by the deliberation of free choice.[37]

---

dictate of reason, but he acts virtuously because of his conformity to divine law, which is supreme and superior to natural law. III *Sent.*, d 18, a 1, q 3, ad 4 (III, 386; III, 379); II *Sent.*, d 39, a 1, q 3, ad fa 2–3 (II, 907; II, 941, ad fa b–c).

36. The superior and inferior reasons are not diverse powers, but different dispositions giving rise to diverse functions of reason in the deliberations of free choice: II *Sent.*, d 24, p 1, a 2, q 2, Resp. (II, 564; II, 582); III *Sent.*, d 16, a 2, q 2, ad 6 (I, 357; III, 351). Bonaventure, following Augustine literally, holds that even an unjust man knows with certitude the immutable rules of justice in the eternal law or the "book of light" which is truth; to know a thing with such certitude is to know it according to its eternal rule, or truth, which is essentially the thing's rectitude. *Sc. Chr.*, q 4, fa 8, 26 (V, 17–18, 20). St. Augustine, *De Trin.*, 14.15.21 (*PL* 42.1052); 8.6.9 (*PL* 42.954); *Retract.*, 1.4.4 (*PL* 32.590), 1.8.2 (*PL* 32.594).

37. II *Sent.*, d 24, p 2, a 1, q 1, Resp., ad 2–5 (II, 574–75; II, 594–95): d 5, a 3, q 1, ad 2 (II, 155; II, 149); III Sent., d 33, un. 3, ad 5 (III, 718; III, 720–21): Aristotle, *De anima*, 3.10 (433a21–433b5). Because of original sin, all men are afflicted with blindness in the practical intellect, whose judgment is impeded by a disorder in the sense appetites; error in a practical judgment, which pertains to free choice, can be a moral fault. II *Sent.*, d 7, p 2, a 1, q 1, Resp., ad 3 (II, 191; II, 183–84); d 23, a 2, q 2, ad 1 "Aliter potest . . ." (II, 541; II, 560): cf d 22, a 2, q 1, Resp., ad 2–4 (II, 522–23; II, 539–40). Since a man can now learn very little about moral truth, the Holy Spirit reveals in Scripture more about faith and morals than about natural things; ignorance of moral truth is culpable only when accompanied

The goodness of the will is grounded in its natural instinct or appetite of synderesis but is completed in its deliberative appetite, which follows free choice. The will is both good and right only in moving toward the same object both naturally and deliberatively. To be completely good and right, a man must first proceed from his natural will and, perfecting his action virtuously, then will the object rightly and deliberatively. The human will must ultimately be conformed to the divine will with regard both to act and to object. What God wills, He wills lovingly and freely or justly. Likewise, what a man wills, he ought to will from love and freedom or justice. Thus, as God wills for the right end, so ought a man to will for the same end.[38]

A man is right when his reason and will are rightly conformed to God. Human reason is right when a man's intelligence is adequated to the supreme truth, for truth is rectitude perceptible by the mind alone, as Anselm says.[39] A human intellect adequated to truth is necessarily rectified, provided the intellect is actually turned toward truth, because truth in act is an adequation of a thing and an intellect. A man judging rightly looks to truth (*Lk.* 7:43); so, without truth, no man judges rightly, as Augustine teaches.[40] The human will is right when it is con-

by a deliberate and disordered will, although grace is necessary to overcome the effects of original sin. *Ibid.*, d 23, dub. 3 (II, 548–49; II, 568); d 30, a 2, q 2, Resp. (II, 725–26; II, 747); d 22, a 2, q 2, Resp., ad 4–5 (II, 524–25; II, 541–42): cf. III *Sent.*, d 29, un. 4, ad 4 (III, 647; III, 642–43); *Coll. Jn.*, coll. 37, c 39, vv 1–5 (VI, 578–79). The human intellect, however, has a sufficient illumination to know the natural law and to acquire all the philosophical sciences, which a man can use erroneously, although they are good because they come from God: I *Sent.*, Prol., dub. 5, Resp. "Licet autem ..." (I, 24; I, 15); *Epiph.* 3 "De primo ..." (IX, 159); 3 *Adv.* 1 "Secundo nescitur ..." (IX, 59); *ibid.* 2 "Et quando? ..." (IX, 60): cf. *Comm. Eccl.*, c 5, vv 17–19, q 4 (VI, 49); c 1, v 13 (VI, 18).

38. II *Sent.*, d 39, dub. 3 (II, 917; II, 953–54); I *Sent.*, d 48, a 1, q 1, Resp. (I, 852; I, 676–77): q 2, fa 3–4, Resp. (I, 853–54; I, 677–78, fa c–d). The good or evil of human actions follows a man's intention, which is the rule of his rational appetite, or the light of reason inclining him toward God and directing him to choose the right good ordering him to beatitude; but this appetite is moved freely or deliberatively, so that a man does not always desire the better in his actions, as nature does by moving the appetite of other creatures in a determinate way. II *Sent.*, d 38, a 2, q 1, Resp. (II, 890–91; II, 925); d 34, a 1, q 3, Resp. (II, 809; II, 837). For Bonaventure's view of the evil, particularly of sin, resulting from a defect of the will, which has a natural defectibility strengthened by original sin, although this does not destroy the will's natural power to preserve rectitude of justice, because a man can will the good with equity by his free choice, see *ibid.*, d 34, a 1, q 2, Resp. (II, 806–07; II, 834–36); d 31, a 2, q 2, sc 5 (II, 752; II, 776, sc e); d 35, a 1, q 1, ad 5–6 (II, 823–24); II, 852); d 25, p 2, un. 3, Resp. (II, 614; II, 634); cf. d 24, p 1, dub. 3 (II, 572; II, 628).

39. *De ver.*, 12 (PL 158.480).
40. *De vera relig.*, 31.57 (PL 34.147).

formed to the supreme goodness, which is the supreme equity or justice. A man is the better as he is just, for justice is rectitude of the will, as Anselm also says.[41] A man's will is necessarily rectified, therefore, when it is conformed to the supreme goodness and equity, thus turning toward God with love, for a man loving God is right.[42]

This account of Bonaventure's view of conscience, synderesis, and free choice completes our presentation of his understanding of moral philosophy as he explains it in the first main text of his early period. In the second such text, his division of the philosophical sciences follows much the same pattern as before. Having shown how the sciences assist in a speculation of the truth of the Trinity, he says that all the philosophical sciences have certain and infallible rules descending into our mind, so to speak, as *lumina* or rays of truth from the eternal law of God. Our mind is so illumined by the splendor of those rays that it can be led by them, unless it is blind, to contemplate God's eternal light.[43] This is the light of truth and the one infallible rule containing the laws by which we judge whatever we know by our senses. Making an indelible impression on our memory, those laws are the infallible and indubitable source of the invariable principles and axioms of the philosophical sciences, both speculative and practical.

With regard to the practical sciences of moral philosophy, Bonaventure gives a very brief and condensed description of their mode of operation under the headings of counsel, judgment, and desire. Counsel consists in inquiring whether this or that good is the better, and the better good is known from its greater assimilation to the supreme good, which is known necessarily from its natural impression on the human mind. Judgment is certain when made according to a law that is right and superior to the human mind, which cannot judge that law. This is the eternal law imprinted on the mind by God, who alone is superior to

41. *De lib. arb.*, 3 (PL 158.494).

42. II *Sent.*, Prooem. "Primo igitur . . . rectus est." (II, 4; II, 5). For Bonaventure's view of our natural love of God, which he contrasts with our love of God from charity, see II *Sent.*, d 3, p 2, a 3, q 1, ad 3 (II, 126; II, 117–18); d 5, a 3, q 1, ad 4 (II, 155; II, 149): cf. d 1, p 2, a 2, q 1, ad 1–2 (II, 44; II, 36). *See also* III *Sent.*, d 26, a 2, q 3, ad 3 (III, 574; III, 568); d 29, un. 3, ad 1 (III, 644-45; III, 640). Not knowing original sin, the philosophers were nescient of the true rectitude and justice of man and how he ought to be ordered to God. A man is properly ordered to God when his spirit is under God and his sensitive nature obeys the command of his spirit; a man is perverse when his soul and sense powers preside over his rational spirit: this is a truth known plainly not only according to Christian faith, but also according to moral philosophy. II *Sent.*, d 30, a 1, q 2, Resp. "Praedominantia concupiscentiae . . . etiam culpabiliter." (II, 719; II, 741).

43. *Itin.*, c 3, nn 6–7 ". . . lucem aeternam." (V, 305; V, 198–99).

the human mind, which can know His eternal law by judging things completely. Desire has to do chiefly with that which moves a man to love the good and to seek beatitude, or the supreme good, which is his final end. What a man desires, he ought to desire because it is the supreme good or because it directs him to the supreme good. So great is its power, Bonaventure remarks, that nothing can be loved by a creature except through a desire for the supreme good. A man is deceived and errs when he accepts an image or false likeness for the truth of the supreme good.[44]

Late Period

There are three main texts in this period when Bonaventure opposed the falsification, in his judgment, of the truth of philosophy by the Averroists, notably Siger of Brabant. The first text divides the philosophical sciences in a way similar to the early texts, but here Bonaventure attributes to Solomon a knowledge of these sciences. Bonaventure then describes them very briefly, showing in particular that moral philosophy directs man to his end or final good. The science seeks moral truth, or the rectitude of human life, in accordance with the dictate of natural law, which measures rectitude. Next, grading the moral sciences under prudence, he says that great prudence is needed for self-control, greater still to rule a family, and greatest of all to rule over a city. If a man is disordered in himself, he cannot have order in his family, and so he cannot rule well over a city. It is impossible, then, for any man lacking self-control to rule over his neighbor.[45]

Thus, stressing again the fundamental role of natural law, Bonaventure understands moral philosophy to come partly from a dictate of nature, from a frequency of experience, and from an illumination by God. The dictate of nature arises from the natural *lumen* of the in-

44. *Ibid.*, c 2, n 9 (V, 301-02; V, 191-92); c 3, nn 2-4 (V, 303-05; V, 194-98). Bonaventure's notion of the natural impressions of the eternal law and the supreme good on the human mind depend on St. Augustine; *De lib. arb.*, 2.12.34 (*PL* 32.1259); *De vera relig.*, 31.58 (*PL* 34.148); *De Trin.*, 8.3.4 (*PL* 42.949). Since Bonaventure says no more than what we have presented on the three subsidiary sciences concerning the individual, the family, and the political community, it is not possible to show how he would have applied his general understanding of moral philosophy to them. He does, however, make copious references to and applications of both natural law and human laws in his treatments of the sacrament of matrimony. IV *Sent.*, dd 26-42 (IV, 661-880; IV, 650-870); *Perf. ev.*, q 3 (V, 166-79). He also frequently invokes natural law in his treatments of the Old and New Law of Sacred Scripture and of religious obedience. III *Sent.*, d 40 (III, 884-96; III, 896-910); *Perf. ev.*, q 4 (V, 179-98).

45. *De donis*, coll. 4, nn 6-10 (V, 474-75): esp., nn 7 & 10.

tellect, which is able to know the first principles, as Aristotle shows. He shows also that sense knowledge gives rise to memory and this to experience, so that, from a frequency of experience, there comes to be universal knowledge, which is the principle of art and science. No matter how good a natural power of judgment, however, or a frequency of experience any man may have, he still needs an illumination from God to know truth with certitude. Bonaventure refers here to the natural illumination of human reason, or the influence on the intellect of the eternal light, which is needed to see the true laws of justice according to which even a wicked man judges rightly, as Augustine shows.[46]

The second and third main texts are somewhat different. In the second text, Bonaventure speaks of the metaphysician, physicist, mathematician, logician, ethician, and politician. Describing their individual sciences, and opposing the errors of the Averroists, he points out theologically how Christ is the medium of all the philosophical sciences.[47] The ethician considers the medium of moderation, or the mean of virtue, especially in moral choice as the mean is determined by right reason. Bonaventure follows with a short description of a progression from political virtues to purgative virtues, and then to the virtues of a soul already cleansed and capable of contemplating the exemplar virtues in God. This leads to the politician or jurist, who deals with the mean of justice, i.e., the judicial determination of retribution and awards pertaining to juridical science.[48]

Bonaventure prefaces his third text with the statement that the ancient philosophers gave us nine sciences and promised us a tenth of contemplation. Some philosophers, however, fell into error because of pride, but others were one, under natural law, with the patriarchs and prophets, who were sons of light. Elaborating on this, Bonaventure

46. *Ibid.*, coll. 8, nn 12–15 ". . . relinquit' etc." (V, 496–97). Aristotle, *Anal. post.*, 1.3 (72b18–24); 1.10 (76a30–76b21); 2.19 (99b15–100a8). St. Augustine, *De Trin.*, 14.15.21 (PL 42.1052); *see above* n 36. Bonaventure, for his own part, holds that the natural law is given to us according to an impression of the eternal law; the ten commandments given to Moses are a specification of the natural law in regard to justice, commandments 1–3 looking to God and 4–10 looking to our neighbor: *Decem praec.*, coll. 2, nn 2–3 (V, 511); *cf.* coll. 1, nn 20–24 (V, 509–10).

47. *Hexaëm.*, coll. 1, nn 11–30 (V, 331–34; D, 5–15). The second references in parentheses to this work indicate *Collationes in Hexaëmeron*, ed., F. M. Delorme (Quaracchi, 1934).

48. Bonaventure, keeping to his principal theme, describes how Christ is the medium of these natural virtues and of juridical or judicial justice: *loc. cit.*, nn 31–36 (V, 334–35; D, 15–18). The doctrine on the mean of virtue as determined by right reason is taken from Aristotle, *Ethica* 2.6 (1106b8–1107a8).

44

says that the light of the soul is truth and it emits three primary rays making known the three main sciences of natural, rational, and moral philosophy. The sciences were not discovered by the philosophers, but became known to them when they adverted to the principles of truth present in the human soul, as Augustine indicates.[49]

Bonaventure then considers the truth of the three sciences in relation to God as its principle of origin, to the soul as its receiving subject, and to the object as the terminus of philosophical truth. This truth shows that the human mind is borne naturally to God as the cause of being, the source of understanding, and the order of life. The threefold ray of truth in the soul, therefore, illumines the mind to know God as the cause of all things.[50]

There follows a very long account of the three subsidiary sciences, first, of natural philosophy and second, of rational philosophy. Bonaventure, in the course of his presentation, discusses the many errors that he finds in the philosophers. Although he examines these six sciences in greater detail than before, his understanding of them remains essentially the same.[51]

There is a significant change in regard to moral philosophy. Instead of three subsidiary sciences, Bonaventure speaks of three kinds of virtue: common, intellectual, and judicial. The first looks to moderation, the next to acquiring diligence, and the last to exercising justice according to political laws. Regarding the common virtues, Bonaventure notes that Aristotle posits twelve, but he himself will select the six principal ones for his consideration, although he manages to include four of the

49. *Ibid.*, coll. 4, nn 1–2 (V, 349; D, 48–50); St. Augustine, *De civ. Dei*, 11.25 (*PL* 41.338–39). Bonaventure reaffirms his position that the human mind is illumined by the immutable rules of divine wisdom, so that a man knows and judges with certitude that, e.g., according to natural law, he must venerate the supreme principle in the highest way, he must believe and assent to the supreme truth, and he must both desire and love the supreme good above every other good. Thus, manifesting God's wisdom, His infallible and indubitable rules are so certain that we do not judge them, but judge other things by them, as Augustine says, for we cannot contradict them except by an error in our own reasoning, as Aristotle has shown. These eternal rules or laws are rooted in the eternal light: they draw the human mind to that light, which illumines every man, although no man can see it in itself. *Ibid.*, coll. 2, nn 9–10 (V, 337–38; D, 9–10). St. Augustine, *De lib. arb.*, 2.12.34 (PL 32.1259); Aristotle, *Anal. post.*, 1.10 (76a30–76b21). *See above* n 46.

50. Bonaventure remarks here that, with the aid of faith, it is easier to know God, so that the cause of being is attributed to the Father, the source of understanding to the Son, and the order of life to the Holy Spirit. *Loc. cit.*, nn 3–5 (V, 349; D, 50–51); *see above* n 6.

51. *Ibid.*, nn 6–25 (V, 349–53; D, 51–72); nn 21–24 in the Delorme version, which lacks n 25, are greatly expanded by the auditor who composed the text.

other six. Starting with temperance, which removes the vices of gluttony and lust, he puts down this virtue as necessary before all the others, because a man is drawn at birth immediately to the delight of taste and, when a boy, to the greater pleasure of touch. Both passions remain in him up to old age and can give rise to the vices of concupiscence and greed. The two extremes of concupiscence are taking delight in bodily pleasures as the final end and spurning them altogether as profane. Regulating the appetite of the soul, temperance is the mean by which a man conquers concupiscence in moderating his bodily appetites with due regard for his own welfare and that of others.

The vice of greed, or of avarice and rapacity, is conquered by the virtue of munificence, which includes the virtue of liberality and of magnificence. Bonaventure calls munificence a fontal virtue: a fount does not retain but distributes its abundance of waters. According to Aristotle, it is difficult to possess the virtue perfectly, because a man can be so generous that he thinks himself to be great in his own eyes and in the eyes of other men. Thus, according to Bonaventure, it is necessary to establish the mean of moderation to avoid the other extreme of presumption, or grasping for renown.

The third virtue is courage, which overcomes cowardice, sloth, and indolence. Setting the mean between fear and audacity, courage is necessary for a man that he not be timid or rash, but ready to sustain fearful things and prepared even to die. Courage makes a man noble, but it can also make him scornful of other men.

A courageous man, then, also needs the fourth virtue of good temper or mildness to subdue rage, hatred, and impatience. Controlling irascibility and wrath, mildness moves a man to be angry only when and where he ought.

The fifth virtue is benignity, including the virtue of friendship, which is to stand in the way of no man and to aid the progress of any man. Benignity removes envy and malignity according to the dictate of reason, which directs a man to be of good will toward other men. Although Aristotle says that we should do good to our friends and evil to our enemies, Christ teaches us to love all men, to do good to every man, and not to harm any man.

The sixth virtue is magnanimity, which suppresses pride, arrogance, vanity, and ostentation. The virtue sets the mean of moderation between evaluating great things and despising vile things. This is really humility, which despises seemingly great things and puts a true value on things apparently of little worth. Although Aristotle says that a magnanimous man desires honor, he says what is true only when the honor looks to eternal things. Thus, including the virtue of truth, which moderates speech, Bonaventure points to the man who values greatly the most vile praise of other men when the truth makes known to his own mind that, in fact, he is an evil man unworthy of honor, and yet he is all puffed up with praise! In conclusion, Bonaventure states that reason is placed beneath the truth of faith in these common virtues.[52]

To understand his attitude here toward Aristotle, which is one more of correction than of criticism, and his reference to Christ's teaching, which is given philosophical rather than theological implications, it is necessary to return briefly to Bonaventure's early period. He referred then to the ignorance or nescience of the philosophers about sin as an offense against God and how it weakened man's ability to be virtuous by his free choice. They thought that a man could become just by acting justly, as he becomes unjust by departing from right reason. Aristotle thought, then, that an evil man, overcoming his vice, could make great advances toward virtue and even become virtuous. Theologians, knowing what sin is and its consequences, maintain that no man can overcome vice or its effects without grace.[53] The teaching of Christ in regard to our neighbor is an explication of natural law that Bonaventure finds summed up in the text, to which he often refers: ". . . never do to another what you would not have done to yourself." (*Tb.* 4:16) Christ teaches the same thing: ". . . treat others as you would like them to treat you; this is the meaning of the Law and the Prophets." (*Mt.* 7:12; *cf.* 5:3–12) Thus, for Bonaventure, the whole of the Law and the Prophets consists in love of God and of neighbor (*Mt.* 22:40); this is also true of the whole wisdom of philosophy, as Augustine says.[54] As a man, Christ gave us the most perfect example of observing the moral law by subjecting himself in worship to his Creator, in truth to his teachers, and in piety to his parents. Christ is the master or teacher of morals and of the whole of moral philosophy: He would direct us to order every good to the supreme and essential good.[55]

Bonaventure, in his late period, thus maintains that, according to the philosophers, men are good because they do good. But Christian wisdom teaches that without grace no man's goodness has merit. According to nature, men are good if they do good. According to Christian

52. *Ibid.*, coll. 5, nn 1–11 (V, 353–56; D, 73–78); Aristotle, *Ethica*, 2.7 (1107a27–1108b10), 3.6–4.9 (1115a7–1128b35); *Topica*, 2.7 (112b30–113a19): the two virtues not considered by Bonaventure are love (or nobility) of honor [*philotimia*] and readiness of wit [*eutrapelia*].

53. II *Sent.*, d 28, a 1, q 1, Resp. (II, 675–76; II, 696–97); Aristotle, *Ethica*, 2.1 (1103a14–1103b25).

54. *Comm. Lc.*, c 12, v 12, n 20 (VII, 316); *cf. De s. Dominico*, "Prima est . . . in terra," (IX, 565): St. Augustine, *Epist.*, 137.5.17 (PL 33.524).

55. *Ibid.*, c 2, vv 39–52, nn 91–111 (VII, 65–69); c 18, v 79, n 37 (VII, 462).

47

wisdom, if men are good, then they do good, because good acts flow from virtue informed by grace.[56]

Turning to the intellectual virtues, Bonaventure associates them with speculation. He distinguishes speculation in itself, which pertains more to logic than to moral philosophy, from speculation in the practical order, where it concerns affects d and effects. The one virtue concerning affects or love is wisdom, which is knowledge of the highest causes and of things as they are known through those causes. The first virtue concerning effects is art, which unites knowing and making, although by a preceding love and through the medium of choice, which is of the will and is ordered to the work to be done. Because a man loves what he chooses, he chooses to do the work that he loves, and so he has the virtue of prudence, which is the medium between wisdom and art. He uses the virtue of intelligence when moving up from prudence to wisdom, which is the knowledge of principles and of the rules having certitude. He uses the virtue of science in moving down from prudence to art, as a physician uses science to find the right rules in his art of medicine. Now the essence of every virtue is in the rational part of the soul. The common virtues are there essentially. The intellectual virtues of wisdom, intelligence, and science are in the rational part according as it is speculative, although in the practical order. Art and prudence are in the same part inasmuch as it controls the soul's sensitive powers.[57]

Introducing the judicial virtues, or moral justice according to the dictate of political laws, Bonaventure says that he speaks as a philosopher, not as a theologian or as a jurist. These virtues have to do with four things not given by the philosophers, but which can be drawn from their writings. The first is the rite of worship. All the true philosophers worshipped one God, especially Socrates, who was executed for not sacrificing to Apollo. He rejected the plea to flee by Plato, who was so ashamed of his action that he was absent when Socrates died. Now, according to Cicero, piety consists in worship of the gods. His reference to *gods*, however, is displeasing to the Christian, who worships the one God in praise and sacrifice. After a short description of sacrifice in

56. *De s. Stephano* 1, coll. "Sapientia christiana . . . et prodigiosa." (IX, 482); cf. 17 *Pent.* 1, "Secundo ista . . ." (IX, 419).

57. *Hexaëm.*, coll. 5, nn 12–13 (V, 356; D, 79–80). Bonaventure relies here on Aristotle, *Ethica*, 6.1–8 (1138b17–1141b23); this reliance includes the distinction of the rational from the sensitive (irrational) part of the soul. *Ibid.*, 1.13 (1102b13–1103a10); cf. III *Sent.*, d 33, un. 3 (III, 715–18; III, 717–21). The main difference between the common and intellectual virtues is that the former order a man toward the means to an end, but the latter, particularly wisdom and intelligence, order him to the end itself. III *Sent.*, d 23, a 1, q 1, sc 2, ad 2 (III, 470–71, 472; III, 461, 462–63); Aristotle, *ibid.*, 2.6 (1106b28), 2.1 (1103a14–20).

48

Scripture, Bonaventure then notes that, according to all the philosophers, the dictate of natural reason and of natural law obliges men to give God sacrifice of praise. In particular, Aristotle says that men are bound to honor their parents and to venerate God.[58]

Bonaventure's view of the natural rite of worship, or the virtue of religion, is simply a more explicit observation than the one that he had taken in his early period. He noted then that, before the coming of Christ, there had always been men famous for worshipping God, thus giving an example to other men. Although the natural law and the written law (i.e., of the Old Testament) could not take a man to salvation without grace, even so, natural law could dictate from human misery and a knowledge of divine justice and mercy that men needed a redeemer whom God in His goodness was disposed to provide. The need for a redeemer could also have been known from divine inspiration, which God offered to every man seeking Him with humility. It is indubitably true, therefore, that the ancient philosophers could have had some knowledge of the Savior, although they were not obliged to have an explicit knowledge because they did not have divine revelation.[59] Now the virtue of religion is a form of piety, both natural and Christian. The piety of Christian religion, according to Augustine, consists properly in worship of God or the true wisdom of faith, hope, and charity. Christian piety is also a gift of the Holy Spirit, and thus Augustine and Gregory say that it consists in works of mercy. (Cf. 1 Tim. 4:8) Augustine calls natural piety a duty toward parents, which conforms to the saying of Cicero, "piety is benevolence toward parents." Natural piety, for Bonaventure, is subsidiary to the virtue of justice because this piety is governed by the rule of natural law and the obligation to relieve parents in their need.[60]

Natural piety looks first to God, whom man ought to worship and to serve chiefly because he is made in the likeness of God, the first principle of man's being and creation. Second, natural piety looks to parents, whose image their children bear and from whom they take their origin. As a gift of the Holy Spirit, Christian piety looks to the image of God

58. *Hexaëm.*, coll. 5, nn 14–17 (V, 356–57; D, 80–81); for the many sources in regard to Socrates and Plato *see Op. omn.*, V, 356, note 6; Delorme, 80, note 1. For the rest consult: Cicero, *De nat. deorum*, 1.41: cf *De officiis*, 2.3; Aristotle, *Topica*, 1.11 (105a3–9); *cf.* 2.11 (115b11–35).

59. III *Sent.*, d 25, a 1, q 2, ad 5–6 (III, 541; III, 533–34); *cf. Comm. Lc.*, c 18, v 35, n 58 (VI, 470).

60. *Ibid.*, d 35, un. 6, sc 1–4, Resp. ". . . nomen doni." (III, 785–56; III, 791–92, sc a–d); *cf.* I *Sent.*, d 46, dub. 5 (I, 835; I, 663). St. Augustine, *De doct. chris.*, 2.7.9 (PL 34.39); *De civ. Dei*, 10.1.3 (PL 41.279); *Enchir.*, 2–3 (PL 40.231); St. Gregory, *Moral.*, 1.32.44 (PL 75.547); Cicero, *Rhetor.*, 2.5.4.

in every man, and so benevolence and beneficence are due to each man. These three forms of piety are related in an analogical way, so that the worship of God is the first and principal form to which the other two forms are posterior.[61]

Bonaventure's late texts on piety and religion follow the same lines. He accuses some of the philosophers of idolatry, however, and the Averroists, in going beyond the due bounds of reason in their philosophical investigations.[62]

The second object of judicial virtue is the form of social life, which falls under the natural dictate of eternal law: "What you would not have done to yourself, you ought not to do to another." (*Tb.* 4:16; cf. *Lk.* 6:31) This dictate of natural law is the source of the laws, canons, and decrees protecting the state from the harm of wrongdoers. The third object is the norm of government or the mutual relation that ought to exist between the ruler and the people. Coming from God as the first truth, the true norm requires the people to assist their ruler, who ought to promote their welfare and not, as a tyrant, to seek his own gain. Bonaventure then adverts to the evil in his own day of hereditary rulers who should not be governors unless, having the art of governing, they know how to rule. Although the Romans did not always have good rulers, even so, their rulers were elected and some of them were wise. But the Roman norm of government deteriorated and the state fell into ruin when the rulers came through succession and not by election. The fourth object of judicial virtue is the office of judgment. This also has its source from God as the first truth. It is by the divine truth that a man knows with certitude what is to be judged, whether in regard to persons, things, or human actions.[63]

61. *Loc. cit.*, ad 1–4 ". . . cuiusdam analogiae." (III, 786; III, 792–93); d 9, a 1, q 2, ad 3 (III, 214; III, 206); *cf. M. Trin.*, q 1, a 2, Resp. "Et hoc . . . et equitate." (V, 55–56). *See above* nn 54–55. It belongs to the virtue of justice to give what is due to God and to our neighbor; honor and reverence are due principally to God, so that the beginning of all justice is to honor and to worship God, and thus humility is the root and foundation of justice. *Perf. ev.*, q 1, Resp. "Est etiam . . . est humilitas." (V, 121)

62. *De donis*, coll. 3, nn 5–19 (V, 469–73); *Decem praec.*, coll. 2, nn 17–29 (V, 513–15). Aristotle's error on the eternity of the world is noted very specifically (n 28), but Bonaventure associates idolatry with Aristotle's followers (who make an idol of him) rather than with Aristotle himself. *See also Decem praec.*, coll. 5 (V, 522–25); *Hexaëm.*, coll. 9, nn 24–29 (V, 376; D, 123–25). Bonaventure refers (n 24) to the natural piety of Plato, who recommended his soul to his maker, and to the Christian piety of St. Peter, who recommended his soul to his Creator.

63. *Hexaëm.*, coll. 5, nn 18–20 (V, 356–57; D, 81–83). The reference to the tyrant depends on Aristotle, *Ethica*, 8.10 (1160a35–1160b22). On the divine origin of human government or civil power, which has coercive force because of original sin

Bonaventure concludes his account of the philosophical sciences, first, with a synopsis of the errors of the philosophers, second, with a brief summary of the subsidiary sciences and the three kinds of moral virtue. With regard to moral philosophy, he says that the art of morals (i.e., ethics) had the least occasion for errors because it does not rest in speculation alone. The science of law (i.e., politics) had many occasions because of the lust for money. It seems, then, that the common and the intellectual virtues pertain to ethics and the judicial virtues to politics, so that ethics is the moral science of the individual, and politics the moral and juridical science of the state, with both sciences holding a common ground in the family, which involves the individual and the state.[64]

The philosophers gave us all these sciences, which they had through an illumination from God. Drawn by truth, they wanted to be wise, and so they promised to give their disciples wisdom or beatitude, which was an achieved understanding or contemplation. Bonaventure proceeds to show how the philosophers tried to achieve wisdom, which they could have done, if they had not fallen into error. They could have known, ultimately, that the first being (*primum esse*) is the essential good through which all men are beatified and, therefore, that it is supremely desirable, so that, offering men repose, it ought to be supremely desired. The philosophers, knowing that so lofty a wisdom could not be attained without moral virtues, took it upon themselves to teach moral virtues. Socrates, for instance, was renowned for his teaching, which he undertook because he realized that it was not possible to attain contemplation unless the soul was cleansed by virtue.[65]

Bonaventure speaks next of metaphysical exemplarity. He finds Aristotle in error for not putting the ideas of all things in God, an error

and not from natural law, see II *Sent.*, d 44, a 2, qq 1–2 (II, 1005–09; II, 1046–51); *Comm. Lc.*, c 16, v 1, n 2 (VII, 403): cf. *Apol. paup.*, c 11 nn 9–11 (VIII, 313–14). Because God is the origin of human government, the decrees of civil rulers are to be obeyed and not spurned. *Comm. Lc.*, c 2, v 5, n 8 (VII, 46); cf. II *Sent.*, d 44, a 3, q 1 (II, 1009–12; II, 1051–54). Civil justice requires one supreme judge to give final decisions in juridical cases and one principal leader or ruler to propose the law. *Perf. ev.*, q 4, a 3, Resp. "Civilis etiam . . . litigium terminetur." (V, 194); cf. *Apol. paup.*, c 10, n 15 (VIII, 309).

64. *Hexaëm.*, coll. 5, nn 21–22 ". . . virtus iustitialis." (V, 357; D, 83–85). We should note that Bonaventure attributes error only to the philosopher, or to the man, and never to his science, which cannot be in error because this is contrary to the nature of science, just as an error in Christian faith is in the heretic and not in the virtue of faith. III *Sent.*, d 23, a 1, q 5, arg 4 (III, 481; III, 471), ad 4 (III, 482; III, 472–73).

65. *Ibid.*, nn 22–23 "Has novem . . ." (V, 357–59; D, 85–90); for the reference to Socrates, see St. Augustine, *De civ. Dei*, 8.3 (PL 41.226).

resulting from his rejection of Plato's doctrine of ideas. This error was the cause of Aristotle's other errors, particularly on the divine fore-knowledge, the eternity of the world, and the denial of eternal beatitude. His errors were amplified by Arabian commentators, notably Averroes: although illumined by God, they failed to dispel the darkness of ignorance, so that their errors put out the light shining through the sciences that they had achieved.[66]

Considering moral exemplarity, Bonaventure states that the eternal light is the exemplar of all things, that it raises the mind to God as it elevated the minds of the noble among the ancient philosophers, especially Plotinus and Philo. It is in the eternal light that they saw the divine exemplars of the virtues. Philo spoke of prudence, fortitude, justice, and temperance or sobriety. They are imprinted on the soul by the eternal light, Bonaventure comments, thus giving the soul serenity, stability, sweetness, and sincerity. They are, then, the four cardinal virtues whose exemplars are in God and of which the whole of Scripture treats. They are also taught by the noble and ancient philosophers, but not by Aristotle, who says nothing about them.[67]

Bonaventure presents the cardinal virtues from three points of view. They are, first, the ways of acquiring all the moral virtues. According to Aristotle, moral virtue consists in moderation or in the mean between two extremes as it is set by a wise man. According to Augustine, moral virtue is the mode of life established by prudence, which directs the virtues and guides human actions toward the center and away from all excess. Thus, set by prudence, the true mode of life and of action is

66. *Ibid.*, coll. 6, nn 1–5 (V, 360–61; D, 90–92). Note the considerable difference in the two versions regarding Aristotle: "... licet enim magna lux videretur in eis praecedentibus scientiis, tamen omnis extinguitur per errores praedictos. Et alii videntes, quod tantus fuit Aristoteles in aliis et ita veritatem, credere non possunt, quin in istis dixerit verum." *Op. omn.*, n 5 (V, 361). "Cautius ergo est dicere quod Aristoteles non senserit mundum aeternum . . . quia tamen fuit quod omnes ipsum sequerentur et assererentur idem dicere; sic omnis lux determinata in praecedentibus extingueretur. Sequamur autem nos eum in quibus bene dixit, non in eis in quibus fuit tenebrosus, quae nescivit vel celavit." Delorme, n 5 (p. 92). For Bonaventure sources on the questions at issue in Aristotle, *see Metaph.*, 12.7 (1072a18–1073a12), 12.9 1074b15–1075a11), 1.9 (990b1–992b13), 7.13–14 (1038b1–1039b19), 12.3 (1070a9–30), 13.4–5 (1078b7–1080a11); *Ethica*, 1.6 (1096a11–1096b7); *Periherm.*, 9 (18a28–19b4); *Phys.*, 8.1 (251b16–27); *De caelo*, 1.10 (280a23–35).

67. *Loc. cit.*, nn 6–10 (V, 361–62; D, 92–93). For Bonaventure's sources in Philo, *see Op. omn.*, note 8 (V, 361). The Delorme version does not mention Philo nor Aristotle in regard to the cardinal virtues: "De iis virtutibus loquitur sacra Scriptura." Delorme, n 11 (p. 93); "Hae sunt quatuor virtutes exemplares, de quibus tota sacra Scriptura agit; et Aristoteles nihil de his sensit, sed antiqui et nobiles philosophi." *Op. omn.*, n 10 (V, 362).

guarded by temperance, duly distributed by justice, and defended against adversities by fortitude.[68] The cardinal virtues are, secondly, the principal ground of the integration or interconnection of the moral virtues. In this regard, Bonaventure takes moral virtue as strength of mind for doing good and avoiding evil. The moral virtues are integrated, then, or interconnected, according to the acts of the cardinal virtues. Temperance modifies the moral virtues through the apposition of circumstances. Prudence rectifies them, for it belongs to right reason, taking account of all laws, to lead to the end. Justice puts the virtues in order, and fortitude gives them stability. Third, the cardinal virtues regulate and direct the whole of moral life according to the rule of reason. From this point of view, temperance gives sincerity to moral life, prudence gives clarity and serenity, fortitude gives constance or stability, and justice gives sweetness. Bonaventure illustrates his point of view with citations from Cicero on each of the cardinal virtues. Thus, according to Cicero, temperance moderates the sense appetites, prudence is knowledge of good and evil, fortitude overcomes danger and sustains hardship, and justice preserves the common utility while giving to each man his due. Bonaventure breaks down each one of the virtues into three different parts. He attributes piety to justice, for instance, which has to do with laws and retributions and whose end is not severity, but benignity. Summing up, he says that a man lacking the cardinal virtues lacks the true moral life of wisdom, no matter how learned he may be in the speculative sciences.[69]

The above consideration has to do with the cardinal virtues inasmuch as they are political and as they cleanse the soul for contemplation. Bonaventure goes on to consider them as they are in a soul already cleansed and prepared for contemplation. This consideration proceeds according as the virtues correspond to the influences of a fourfold light, the properties of the four elements, the effects of the four causes, and the four qualities of life. With regard to light, for instance, temperance purges, prudence illuminates, justice perfects, and fortitude strengthens the soul. Again, temperance corresponds to the material cause, prudence to the formal cause, justice to the final cause, and fortitude to the efficient cause. All four virtues flow into the soul from the eternal light and, taking the soul back to its origin, make it apt for contemplation, or beatitude. In sum, the cardinal virtues are political virtues looking to action, purgative virtues preparing the soul for contemplation, and

68. *Ibid.*, nn 11–12 (v, 362; D, 93–94). Aristotle, *Ethica*, 2.6 (1106a24–1106b27); St. Augustine, *De morib. Eccl.*, 19.35 (*PL* 321–326).
69. *Ibid.*, nn 13–19 (V, 362–63; D, 94–96); Cicero, *De invent.*, 2.54–55.

virtues of the soul already purged and disposed to see the divine exemplarity in the eternal light.[70]

Conclusion

Although a man and a theologian of the thirteenth century, St. Bonaventure had an appreciation of moral philosophy that can contribute immensely to our understanding of the science today. The central point of his appreciation is rectitude of the will, or probity of life, as the whole intention of moral philosophy. This intention is realized in the perfection acquired by the moral virtues, especially the cardinal virtues, and consummated in sapiential knowledge of God, who is desired with deliberation as the supreme and the infinite good. St. Bonaventure, then, attributes to natural reason the capacity to know God as the true good of man and to human will a natural ability to seek this good in every good thing that a man rightly desires and loves. The whole intention of moral philosophy, therefore, is gathered up in love of God and love of neighbor. Revolving around that intention, the moral actions and life of man consist in an unremitting search for beatitude, or happiness, founded on a general knowledge or innate awareness of the principles of natural law and on a natural or instinctive desire for the one and only good that can satisfy man's proper longing for spiritual fulfillment. Under natural law, his search is governed by conscience and synderesis, which ought to control his free and deliberative choice of action ordering each particular good to the noble good of beatitude.

70. Bonaventure closes with the statement that the cardinal virtues, as he has described them, are found in Scripture and were known to the noble philosophers of old, a fact that he shows by a long citation from Macrobius, speaking of Plotinus on these virtues: *ibid.*, nn 20–32 (V, 363–64; D, 96–98). The Delorme version has only a brief summary of the text of Macrobius, *Commentarium in Somnium Scipionis*, 1.8 (Willis, 2.39); trans. by W. H. Stahl, *Commentary on the Dream of Scipio* (New York, 1952), 121.8. *Cf.* Plotinus, *Enneads*, 1.2.1, 6–7. Bonaventure completes his consideration of the sciences and wisdom of philosophy by restating the errors of the philosophers in order to excuse Aristotle, except for his error on the divine ideas, and then by showing that the noble philosophers (Plotinus and Cicero) erred in thinking that their natural virtues could bring them beatitude, which they did not really know because they did not have Christian faith: excusing their errors because of this nescience, Bonaventure ends his account of the moral virtues by indicating how the theological virtues perfect them, thus disposing the soul to know and, through grace, to attain the true beatitude; coll. 7 (V, 365–68; D, 98–108). He dealt with the cardinal virtues in his early period mainly as theological perfections. He did, however, take the position that, as political virtues, they disposed a man for good moral action and, as such, were rooted by nature in the soul, but were completed either by frequent and steadfast good works, or by the influence of grace, or by both natural works and grace. See III *Sent.*, d 33, un. 5 (III, 721–24; 724–27).

St. Bonaventure's most significant contribution lies perhaps in his view of natural law as the object of conscience and synderesis and their consequent relation to free choice. Containing the first principles of natural law, conscience grows in perfection through the acquisition of experience and moral instruction. As a consequence, a man's knowledge of natural law, which is a reflection of God's eternal law, advances in proportion to his right use of free choice, which ought always to conform to the natural stimulus of synderesis toward the noble good. Thus, making considerable room for experience and moral instruction, St. Bonaventure's notion of conscience permits a wide variety of applications of natural law to moral situations, provided always that such applications are grounded solidly in the basic principles governing man's proper relations to God and neighbor: God ought always to be obeyed, honored, and worshipped; our neighbor should be treated on every occasion as we ourselves would like our neighbor to treat us. It was the fidelity to those principles of natural law that moved St. Bonaventure to praise the noble philosophers of olden times, especially for their true understanding of the cardinal virtues, which Aristotle did not know.

St. Bonaventure's attitude toward the moral doctrine of Aristotle is certainly not one of condemnation nor of outright criticism. On the contrary, he has a great respect for the philosopher and uses his doctrine whenever and wherever possible. St. Bonaventure departs from Aristotle simply because of a different view of man's moral life and of his ultimate destiny. This destiny can be known truly and perfectly only by Christian faith, although it can be known in a limited way by natural reason, as St. Bonaventure himself has shown time and again. Using Christian faith in an extrinsic manner, he corrects some of Aristotle's views; but this correction is made strictly according to the proper principles, method, and object of moral philosophy. It is the nescience of Aristotle, and also of the noble philosophers, in regard to original sin and its consequences that, in the final analysis, accounts for their erroneous views of the moral life and perfection of man. St. Bonaventure's preference for the doctrine of St. Augustine results primarily from their common and philosophical view of man's moral life, conduct, and dignity. There is no doubt that St. Bonaventure has a decided preference for the teaching of St. Augustine on many points. This does not, however, make St. Bonaventure an Augustinian thinker any more than he is an Aristotelian thinker because of his other preferences for the teaching of Aristotle. St. Bonaventure's view of moral philosophy is a truly original one, even though it manifests the influences of Aristotle and St. Augustine, each predominating in a given instance, while both share an equal influence in some instances. There are many other sources influencing the formation of St. Bonaventure's appreciation of moral philosophy. Not the least of them are Cicero concerning the cardinal virtues and St. Anselm with regard to moral rectitude. St. Bonaventure's preference for the philosophical doctrine of St. Augustine is due ultimately to the fact of the latter having already and admirably accommodated his philosophical thought to the truth of Christian revelation. In short, St. Augustine makes known to St. Bonaventure the best way to allow Christian faith to exercise an extrinsic control on the philosophical thinking of a theologian.[71]

71. St. Bonaventure tells us this himself: "For no one has described better than Augustine the nature of time and of matter in the *Confessiones* . . . the coming forth of forms and the propagation of things in *Genesis ad litteram* . . . questions on the soul and on God in *De Trinitate* . . . the nature of the creation of the world in *De civitate Dei* . . . the Masters have put in their writings few or no things which were not found in the books of Augustine. Read Augustine on Christian doctrine [*De doctrina christiana*], where he shows that Sacred Scripture cannot be understood without skill in the other sciences; he shows also that, as the sons of Israel took for themselves the vessels of the Egyptians, so the teachers and theologians [take for themselves] philosophical doctrine. Wherefore, we learn from the Fathers [*Sancti*] many things that we do not learn from the philosophers and the sayings of philosophy." *Trib. quaest.*, n 12 (VIII, 335–36). Bonaventure's attitude toward Aristotle and St. Augustine is best summed up in his own words; about Aristotle: "the more excellent among the philosophers," II *Sent.*, d 1, p 1, a 1, q 2, in Resp. (II, 22; II, 15); about St. Augustine: "a most profound metaphysician," *ibid.*, d 3, p 1, a 1, q 2, in Resp. (II, 98; II, 87). As an original doctrine, the philosophical thought of St. Bonaventure is properly *Bonaventurean*, just as the original and philosophical thought of St. Thomas Aquinas is properly *Thomist*.

CHAPTER 3.

St. Bonaventure's Doctrine of Illumination: Reactions Medieval and Modern

IGNATIUS BRADY, O.F.M.

It is to the credit of the Quaracchi editors of the works of St. Bona-venture that they discovered and published Questions, sermons, and treatises long forgotten but of utmost value for the new insights they provide into the doctrines of this great scholastic (d. 1274).[1] Not least among such findings are those which center on Bonaventure's so-called theory of illumination. (This is perhaps not the most apt title for what in reality is a metaphysical analysis of human certitude, but it will no doubt continue to be used, if only because on occasion Bonaventure himself adopts it, and his disciples do so even more frequently.)

Basic to Bonaventure's own thought, the theory enjoyed consider-able vogue throughout the thirteenth century, both within and without the Franciscan School (although unacceptable as such to Thomas Aquinas). Toward the end of the century, however, owing perhaps to the extreme interpretation given by Master Henry of Ghent, a reaction set in with the vigorous criticism addressed to Henry by the Franciscan John Duns Scotus. Thereafter the theory seems to have faded into oblivion and the Questions of Bonaventure and of his followers were lost in the dust of the centuries. When, in more recent times, after the Renaissance, the Friars themselves, particularly among the Capuchin Franciscans, sought to return to the teachings of Bonaventure, their sources were severely limited; at best, they possessed his Commentary on the *Sentences*, the *Itinerarium mentis in Deum*, the so-called con-ferences *In Hexaëmeron*, as well as the numerous spurious works which crowded the old editions of the Seraphic Doctor.[2]

1. Cf. *Doctoris Seraphici S. Bonaventurae S.R.E. Episcopi Cardinalis Opera Omnia*, 10 vols. and indices, Ad Claras Aquas (Quaracchi) prope Florentiam, 1882–1902.

2. *See*, for example, the Capuchin Bartholomaeus de Barberis (or de Castelvetro), *Flores et Fructus Philosophici ex Seraphico Paradiso excerpti seu Cursus Philoso-phici ad Mentem Sancti Bonaventurae Seraphici Doctoris*, pars III, Lyons 1677, pp. 403–56 (on Bonaventure's theory of knowledge); or the much later (1855) work of Amédée de Margerie, *Essai sur la philosophie de saint Bonaventure. Thèse presentée à la faculté des lettres de Paris*, Paris, 1855, especially pp. 197–200, based

How deep this void was can be judged from the reaction, not to say enthusiasm, which followed the partial publication in 1874 of the Disputed Question of Bonaventure on certitudinal knowledge: "Whether whatever is known by us with certitude is known in the Eternal Reasons themselves."[3] The complete Question, together with much cognate material from thirteenth-century followers of Bonaventure, provided in 1883 by the Bonaventure editors,[4] provoked even greater interest, although scholars had still to await the fifth tome of the *Opera Omnia* (1891) to study the Question in the full context of the Disputed Questions *De scientia Christi*. Since then, the horizon has been considerably widened as the Questions of Bonaventure's contemporaries and successors, in critical editions, have added to our knowledge of the problematic involved. The full history remains to be written, with some of the unexpected turns it has taken. Here, at best, we can but indicate some of its elements, beginning with Bonaventure himself and the thirteenth-century reactions, and ending with nineteenth-century reactions to the discovery and publication of a host of medieval texts.

The Writings of Bonaventure

It becomes increasingly evident how necessary it is to follow chronologically the development of Bonaventure's thought and to discover the *Sitz im Leben* of each work. The earliest of his writings, for example, issue from a university context, when, as Bachelor in Theology, he commented on the Lombard's *Book of Sentences*,[5] orally first and then in written form (c. 1252–53) and composed (and preached?) a series of Sunday sermons.[6] In neither the *Sentences* nor the sermons is there anything beyond an occasional hint of a theory of illumination: the principles are there, one might say, but in scattered form.[7] Only after

---

on the *Sentences* and the *Itinerarium*, totally unconscious of the real riches of Bonaventure's theory.

3. Edited in two forms by Fr. Fidelis a Fanna, whose indefatigable research provided the background to the new edition: first, in his *Ratio novae collectionis operum omnium sive editorum sive anecdotorum seraphici ecclesiae doctoris S. Bonaventurae* (Torino: 1874), pp. 229–46; then, in a separate edition with a new introduction: *De ratione cognoscendi seu Utrum quidquid certitudinaliter cognoscitur a nobis cognoscatur in rationibus aeternis* (Torino: 1874), 32 pp.

4. *De humanae cognitionis ratione anecdota quaedam Seraphici Doctoris S. Bonaventurae et nonnullorum ipsius discipulorum,* (Quaracchi: 1883), xxiv–252 pp.

5. Found in the *Opera omnia,* tomes I–IV (Quaracchi: 1882–89).

6. *Cf.* Tome IX, pp. 23–461. These, unfortunately, are not published as a unit, but mixed with others of later date throughout the liturgical year. They are, however, the first under each Sunday or feast.

7. Given the compass of questions asked in mid-thirteenth-century commen-

Bonaventure became a Master (sometime in 1255) and was charged with "reading" sacred Scripture, "disputing" theological Questions, and "preaching" before the university body,[8] did he weld his previous thinking into a coherent whole in the fourth Question of the series *De scientia Christi* (probably in the spring of 1256),[9] which is reflected in a concurrent (or later?) sermon *De Christo unico magistro*.[10] Both pieces, we should note, had been forgotten for centuries.

---

taries on the *Sentences*, Bonaventure would have had little opportunity to discuss illumination in any one question (if he had already developed his theory). Yet some elements are there in scattered form: God has in Himself the exemplars (*rationes*) of all things (*In I Sent*. dist. 35, art. unic., q. 1; tom. I, 601 a); God is, as it were, the highest light, which can shine upon our mind (*In I Sent*., dist. 3, art. unic., q. 1; tom. I, 69 a); God has a role in every action of creatures (*In II Sent*., dist. 37, a. 1, q. 1; tom. II, 862f); but has given to each its own power of acting and to man the possible and agent intellect, which is open to and needs divine illumination (*In II Sent*., dist. 17, a. 1, q. 1, ad 6; tom. II, 412f; and dist. 24, part 1, a. 2, q. 4; tome II, 568); God alone can illumine the superior part of man's reason (*In II Sent*., *passim*; tome II, 266 a, 412–13, 563–64, 575, 689–90, 716 a, 909f); the analysis achieved by the intellect is sometimes incomplete, at others complete, i.e., the distinction of an intellect *resolvens semiplene* and one *resolvens perfecte* (*In I Sent*., dist. 28, dubium 1; tome I, 504). The Sermon for the twenty-second Sunday after Pentecost, on the other hand, is the first clear adumbration of the theory: for perfect knowledge, unchangeableness is required on the part of the thing known and certitude on the part of the knower. Such are the conditions laid down by Aristotle for scientific knowledge. Yet, the object known is in itself subject to change, and the human intellect is open to error; therefore, the presence and influence of Eternal Truth is required to support the object known and the activity of the knowing subject (Tome IX, 441 b–442 a). See the reiteration of this in Bonaventure's *Postill on Ecclesiastes*, c. 1 (Tome VI, 11 b), which may be dated early in his teaching career.

8. See the famous words of Peter the Chanter (1191–92) on the threefold office of a master: "In tribus consistit exercitium sacrae Scripturae: circa lectionem, disputationem et praedicationem" (*Verbum abbreviatum*, cap. 1; *Patrol. Latina*, tom. 205, 25 A).

9. The seven Questions *De scientia Christi* (in Tome V, 3–43) investigate divine knowledge (of Christ as eternal Word) in the first three questions, the wisdom possessed by the soul of Christ in the last three, and in the fourth question the source of certitude in all human knowledge. See the remarkable "Note sur la consideration de l'infini dans les *Quaestiones Disputatae de scientia Christi*," of the eminent French philosopher, Paul Vignaux, in *S. Bonaventura 1274–1974*, tom. 3 (Grottaferrata: 1973), pp. 107–30. A complete translation of Question 4 is given by E. R. Fairweather, *A Scholastic Miscellany: Anselm to Ockham* (Phila.: 1956), pp. 379–400; the *Respondeo* is Englished in J. F. Wippel and A. B. Wolter, *Medieval Philosophy from St. Augustine to Nicholas of Cusa* (New York: 1969), pp. 314–17.

10. In Tome V, 567–574; English translation by R. E. Hasselbach, in *The Cord* 23 (1973), pp. 205–16. Since it is closely connected with Question IV, yet presents

Elected General of the Franciscans in February, 1257, Bonaventure had occasion in September–October, 1259, to visit La Verna, the friary in the mountains above Arezzo, where Francis of Assisi had experienced the vision of the Crucified Seraph in 1224. In quiet and solitude, Bonaventure seems to have undergone a deeply spiritual experience wherein he obtained an insight into the mystery of the Stigmatization of St. Francis and came to a deeper understanding of the way the mind of man can ascend in six stages from the contemplation of creatures to the very mystery of God. He was later to describe such an ascent in the *Itinerarium mentis in Deum*.[11] All that he had taught at Paris on man's knowledge of being, on God, the First Being, on the light of Truth, and on the sources of certitude, is made to serve the mind in its search for the heights of contemplation.[12]

Years later Bonaventure returned to the theme of illumination in the Lenten Conferences of 1268, on the gifts of the Holy Spirit, without perhaps adding any new facet of doctrine, except to attack three errors current in the Arts faculty at Paris.[13] Five years later, in the spring of 1273, faced with the rationalism rampant in the same faculty, Bonaventure delivered a long series of 23 conferences or evening sermons, which have come down to us as the *Collationes in Hexaëmeron* or as the

---

the conditions of certitudinal knowledge with much greater clarity, the sermon can rightly be considered somewhat later than the Questions. Related to it in doctrine is an undated sermon on St. Dominic (Tome IX, 562–65), which enables us to see that for Bonaventure illumination is either natural (or common), which helps us understand the truth of the works of creation as considered by philosophy, or spiritual and beyond human reason, as in the truths of salvation considered in theology (pp. 563 b–64 a); a distinction that is basic, yet not always observed in interpreting Bonaventure's wisdom-philosophy. Bonaventure does not seem to have found occasion to discuss such knowledge in the postills he gave as master in Scripture (in tomes VI–VII; the *In Sapientiam* does not belong to him).

11. Tome V, 295–313. The Latin text was published at least nine times, and translated into Italian and German before the Quaracchi edition. Several modern English translations may be consulted, e.g., P. Boehner, O.F.M., *Saint Bonaventure's Itinerarium Mentis in Deum. With an Introduction, Translation and Commentary* (St. Bonaventure, N.Y.: 1956), with parallel Latin text; J. de Vinck, *The Works of Bonaventure*, Vol. I (Paterson, N.J.: 1960), pp. 1–58. *See* A. C. Pegis, "St. Bonaventure, St. Francis and Philosophy," *Mediaeval Studies*, XV (1953), pp. 1–13.

12. Of particular importance in the light of later developments, are ch. 3, nn. 3–7 and ch. 5. It would sometimes be forgotten, unfortunately, that Bonaventure was writing of mystical contemplation, where nature and grace merge, and not a purely philosophical, rational treatise.

13. *Cf. Collationes de Donis Spiritus Sancti*, VIII, nn. 12–16 (Tome V, 496–98). The text is that taken down by a scribe; hence, it reflects the spoken word. The conferences were published in their entirety only in the Quaracchi edition.

Illuminationes Ecclesiae.[14] Running throughout is a call to return to Christian wisdom and the need to acknowledge that ultimately all and any certitude is achieved through the light shed on our minds by Eternal Wisdom.[15]

We can only conclude that the *loci classici* of Bonaventure's theory of illumination are to be found primarily in the fourth of the Questions *De scientia Christi* and in the *Sermon on Christ the Teacher*, with some help from the *Itinerarium*. This is borne out by developments of the theme in the Franciscans of the later thirteenth century.

The Followers of St. Bonaventure

There is no explicit documentation of any immediate reactions to Bonaventure's series, *De scientia Christi*. At most, we may suppose that Thomas Aquinas had Questions IV–VIII (on knowledge in the eternal reasons and the knowledge possessed by the soul of Christ) in mind when he engaged in the long series of Questions on Truth (*De veritate*, Paris 1256–59), wherein, without any manifest polemic, he insists that the light of human reason with which God has endowed man is itself a likeness of uncreated Truth and is capable of knowing first principles from whence arises the certitude of our knowledge.[16] The last Question of the series, Q. 20: *De scientia animae Christi,* very plainly has a relation to the seventh Question of Bonaventure.[17] Later (Rome, 1268), in the First Part of his *Summa Theologiae,* Thomas reiterates the position of the *De veritate*: the light of our intellect is a certain impression (or imprint) of the First Truth and thus needs no added illumination in the act of knowing.[18]

Such a position is in net contrast to what we know of the Franciscan masters at Paris after Bonaventure,[19] since most of them are inclined to

14. Tome V, 329–449. This text was previously published in the Bonaventure edition of 1495 (Strasbourg), 1504 and 1564 (Venice), and 1588 (Vatican), which latter was reprinted elsewhere more than once. Hence, the work was well known. For an English translation, *cf.* J. de Vinck, *The Works of Bonaventure*, Vol. 5 (Paterson, N.J.: 1969). Another reportation is that published by Fr. Delorme in the *Bibliotheca Franciscana Scholastica*, tom. VIII (Quaracchi: 1934) pp. 1–275.

15. *See especially, Coll.* XII, nn. 2–13 (Tome V, 385–86; de Vinck, 173–79).

16. *De veritate*, q. 11 (*De magistro*), art. 1 (ed. Leonina, tom. XXII [Rome: 1972], 351 b, 353 b); *see also*, q. 8, a. 7, ad 13 (p. 244–45).

17. *De veritate,* q. 20, art. 4 (*ed. cit.*, 574–85); Bonaventure, Tome V, 37–43.

18. *Summa theol.* I, q. 12, art. 11, ad 3; q. 84, art. 5 (directly on our problem).

19. Owing to lack of documentation, it is somewhat difficult to establish both the exact succession of masters in the Franciscan Studium and the writings to be attributed to them.

see illumination as concurring with our particular acts of knowledge, especially in judgments which are certain and unshakable. The first we can cite is Walter of Bruges, regent probably in 1267–68 (after William of Baglione, 1266–67, who does not touch the problem in his known works.)[20] In his Commentary on the Lombard (c. 1264), Book 1, distinction 3, Walter introduces a comparison between the eye, which needs exterior light of some kind to be able to function, and the intellect, which cannot know without the light infused or irradiated on our mind by God, who is, as Augustine says, in some way the cause (*ratio*) of our knowing all things. Yet, he concludes, this does not mean that this light is known or seen in itself.[21] Nor would he posit such a light for every species of certain knowledge, since the light of reason suffices for certainty in the lower sciences.[22] Walter's successor, Eustace of Arras (master, September, 1268–December, 1269), adds little or nothing to this position in the one brief question he devotes to illumination.[23]

Much more attention is given to the problem by succeeding masters: John Pecham, regent January, 1270–June (?) 1273; Matthew of Aquasparta, in his Questions *De fide* (1277–78) and *De cognitione* (1278–79); and Roger Marston at Oxford in his Questions *De anima* (1281–82). Pecham addresses himself to the theory in his Commentary on the *Sentences* (c. 1266–68), Book I, distinction 3, question 3,[24] arguing against an unnamed opponent (likely Thomas Aquinas, in his *De spiritualibus creaturis*, art. 10) and defending the interpretation of Bonaventure, however briefly and with no new insights. Later, as master, he repeats much of the same material, but with greater clarity

20. *Cf.* I. Brady, "Questions at Paris c. 1260–1270," *Archivum Franciscanum Historicum*, 61 (1968), pp. 434–61.

21. *Cf.* E. Longpré, "Questions inédites du Commentaire sur les Sentences de Gauthier de Bruges," *Archives d'histoire doctrinale et littéraire du moyen âge*, 7 (1933), 263, text and note 2.

22. So we gather from the third question on the Prologue of the *Sentences* whether theology is a science. *See* J. Brunner, "Die vier Ursachen der Theologie nach dem unedierten Sentenzenkommentar des Walter von Brügge," *Franz. Studien*, 40 (1958), pp. 377f.

23. Published in *De hum. cognitionis ratione* (see note 4), 183–87, from his Quodlibet III, q. 12 (dated December 1269). *But see also*, his Questions *De angelis*, q. 2, so far unpublished (*cf.* I. Brady, "Questions at Paris c. 1260–1270," *Arch. Franc. Hist.* 62 [1969], p. 373, n. 44).

24. Edited by G. Melani, as Appendix I in *Tractatus de anima Ioannis Pecham* (Firenze: 1948), pp. 131–38. The text stands in need of some amelioration. See the author's study of Pecham's defense of the Augustinian theory of knowledge, *ibid.* pp. 100–15.

of exposition, in his *Questions De Anima*, q. 5.[25] His Quodlibetal Questions add nothing of importance.[26]

In contrast to Pecham, who seems to argue more in a purely Augustinian framework, Aquasparta, while much his own man, is clearly a follower of Bonaventure: he is at home with the latter's writings, the Questions *De scientia Christi*, the Sermon on Christ the Teacher, the *Itinerarium*, and seems cognizant of intervening developments.[27] The theory of knowledge in the eternal reasons, or the so-called illumination doctrine, is examined twice, with more dependence on Bonaventure than the editors (myself included) managed to indicate in the notes. In both instances, Matthew displays his usual clarity of thought and wealth of knowledge, developing and deepening the theory without departing radically from the position of Bonaventure.[28]

The English master at Oxford, Roger Marston, seems to know the doctrine of Bonaventure primarily through the Questions of Aquasparta. As a student at Paris, he had perhaps assisted at the *Collationes in Hexaëmeron*, from which he borrows in his Questions on the Trinity (*De emanatione aeterna*).[29] But in the Questions *De anima*, qq. 3–4, 8–9, we can trace only the influence of Pecham and Aquasparta, as well as Henry of Ghent.[30] One question merits attention, since it testifies to

25. Ed. Hieron. Spettmann, *Johannis Pechami Quaestiones tractantes de Anima*, in *Beiträge zur Geschichte der Philosophie [und Theologie] des Mittelalters*, XIX, Heft 5–6 (Münster: 1918), pp. 59–71.

26. Of the *Quodlibetum Florentinum* (so-called because it is found only in a Florence manuscript), qq. 2–3, 5–6, are edited by Melani, *op. cit.*, 145–53; parallel questions in a newly found *Quodlibet* are published by V. Doucet, in *Antonianum*, 8 (1933), pp. 455–59; the fourth question of the *Quodlibetum Romanum* (i.e., disputed in the Roman curia about 1278), in *De humanae cognitionis ratione*, pp. 179–82, and more recently by F. Delorme (Rome: 1939). It is based quite literally on the questions of the I *Sent.*, d. 3, q. 3, and offers nothing new save a few arguments. The *Tractatus de Anima*, in chapters 3–5, pp. 9–21 is a straightforward, nonpolemical exposition.

27. This is evident in his third question *De cognitione*, where he cites the *Sapientiale* of Thomas of York, and refers to the writings of Pecham (*cf.* his *Questiones disputatae De fide et cognitione*, ed. 2 [Quaracchi: 1957], 257, 259).

28. See the *Qq. De fide* (dated 1277–1278), q. 1: *Utrum aliquid possit certitudinaliter sciri*, in the new edition, pp. 37–56 (with unnoted dependence, p. 44, on Bonaventure's sermon); and *De cognitione* (1278–1279), q. 2, pp. 222–48 (the Editors fail to indicate his use of Bonaventure on pp. 231, 233, 240). He criticizes the position of St. Thomas, pp. 231–32.

29. *Cf.* R. *Marston Quaestiones disputatae* (Quaracchi: 1932), pp. 78–82, 88–89. His *Quodlibeta Quatuor* were published by G. Etzkorn and myself (Quaracchi: 1968); in one question, on the Stigmata of Saint Francis (p. 443), he cites "Friar Bonaventure of happy memory."

30. *Quaest. disp.*, pp. 245–305, and 376–429. The Editors' references to Richard of Mediavilla must be discounted since he is later than Marston.

the author's perplexity. Asking in question 9 whether the species by which the soul understands things come to the intellect from external things or are found by the soul itself (a basic question in the whole problem), he admits he is somewhat disturbed to find that nowhere does Augustine touch on the formation of the *species intelligibiles*, while those who think to find an explanation in his writings end up in vagaries.[31] Throughout, Roger is fairly critical of several interpretations given Augustine in the past, a portent of the severe censure launched a few years later by Richard of Mediavilla (master at Paris 1284–87)[32] and Olivi (c. 1290).[33]

The controversy, as we have suggested, is climaxed by the extreme position held by the secular master at Paris, Henry of Ghent (regent 1276–92),[34] whose interpretation was examined and demolished by the Franciscan John Duns Scotus, first in his *Lectura* on the first book of the *Sentences* at Oxford about 1298–99, and in final form in his *Ordinatio*.[35] Scotus' attack, while not directed against Bonaventure, for all practical purposes marks the end of the discussion that had occupied the preceding 40 or 50 years. Bonaventure's Questions ceased to be copied, and his Sermon survived to our day in only one manuscript.

Nineteenth-century Reactions

The biographer of Fidelis a Fanna remarks that the publication in 1874 of the Question IV stirred up a hornet's nest. Partisans of onto-

31. *Quaest. disp.*, pp. 412–20. Cf. E. Gilson, "Sur quelques difficultés de l'illumination augustinienne," in *Revue néoscolastique de philosophie*, 36 (1934), pp. 321–31.

32. *See* text in *De humanae cognitionis ratione*, pp. 221–45, and summary in E. Gilson, *History of Christian Philosophy in the Middle Ages*, p. 696, n. 47. A detailed study is found in P. Rucker, O.F.M., *Der Ursprung unserer Begriffe nach Richard von Mediavilla* (*Beiträge zur Geschichte der Phil. und Theologie des Mittelalters*, XXXI, Heft 1, [Münster: 1934]), pp. 54–104.

33. Text in part in *De humanae cognitionis ratione*, pp. 245–48; in full, in B. Iansen (ed.), *Fr. Petrus Iohannis Olivi, O.F.M., Quaestiones in II Librum Sent.*, Appendix, tom. III (Quaracchi: 1926), pp. 455–517.

34. The precise date of his *Summa theologiae* (publ. Paris: 1520; reprint, St. Bonaventure, N.Y.; 1953) does not seem to be established. Part I, art. 1, deals with the question of knowledge, its possibility (q. 1) and the way we know (q. 2). It is in the second question he claims no certain and sincere truth can be known save in the light of eternal truth.

35. Cf. *Lectura Oxoniensis*, I, d. 3, p. 1, q. 3 (*Opera omnia*, ed. Vaticana, tom. XVI, 1960, pp. 281–309); *Ordinatio*, I, d. 3, p. 1, q. 4 (*ed. cit.*, tom. III, 1954, pp. 123–72); Latin text of the latter, with facing English translation, in A. Wolter, O.F.M., *Duns Scotus: Philosophical Writings* (Nelson: 1962), pp. 96–133. *See also*, E. Gilson, *Jean Duns Scot* (Paris: 1952), pp. 556–73.

logism and psychologism (=Cartesianism) engaged in a free-for-all,[36] as each party saw in the new-found text a vindication for their position. For long, for example, the Ontologists of the early nineteenth century had claimed that the doctrine of Malebranche was the fruit of a long tradition which went back to Bonaventure, to Augustine, to the Alexandrines (that is, the Greek Fathers and perhaps Plotinus), and thence to Plato. Of these, Augustine and Bonaventure were hailed as the principal authorities.[37] Vincenzo Gioberti, who perhaps originated such a claim (in 1839) in his *Introduzione allo studio della filosofia*,[38] cites at length the *Itinerarium*, chapters 3 and 5, without any commentary or attempt to twist the words of Bonaventure.[39]

More extreme was Professor G. C. Ubaghs, of Louvain, who in 1859 had undertaken to show at length that Bonaventure was truly the source of ontologism. But like others after him, he knew how to manipulate the texts of Bonaventure—and omit those which proved the opposite of his thesis.[40] These are but two examples of the trend of thought widespread in the Catholic schools of Europe about 1860 and later, despite certain interventions of the Holy See.

Conscious of such currents in France and Belgium and of the Rosminian theories in Italy, Fidelis had expected a reaction to the newly published text. Very pointedly, in fact, he had prepared the separate edition, *De ratione cognoscendi*, that devotees of philosophy might find in it the true mind of Bonaventure and the key toward interpreting his other works[41] and not be forced to wait until the fifth volume of the *Opera omnia*.

An early and positive response on the part of a writer who appreciated the value of the new document is the booklet of G. Ortoleva, Franciscan of Mistretta (Sicily), who is perhaps the first to present the "new" Bonaventure in the full context of the *Sentences*, the newly found Ques-

36. V. Meneghin, *Il Padre Fedele da Fanna dei Frati Minori 1838–1881* (Vicenza: 1940), 117.

37. See the detailed article of A. Fonck, "Ontologisme," in *Dictionnaire de Théologie Catholique*, XI (Paris: 1931), pp. 1002f, 1008f.

38. Tome I, ed. 2 (Capolago: 1849), p. 140; in the French translation of the first edition (Paris: 1847), p. 137.

39. *Introduzione*, t. II (ed. 1849) nota xxxix, pp. 374–79.

40. G. C. Ubaghs, *De mente S. Bonaventurae circa modum quo Deus ab homine cognoscitur* (Louvain: 1859), and his *Essai d'idéologie ontologique* (Louvain: 1860). He was answered a few years later by J. Krause in his *Dissertatio inauguralis* at Münster: *S. Bonaventurae de origine et via cognitionis intellectualis doctrina ab Ontologismi nota defensa* (Münster: 1868), which likely went unnoticed. Ubaghs by then was affected by a decree of the Holy Office, March 2, 1866.

41. *Cf.* the *Monitum* prefixed to the *De ratione cognoscendi*, pp. 3–4, and remarks in the preface, pp. 7ff.

tion, the *Itinerarium*, and the *In Hexaëmeron*.[42] Perhaps an indirect effect was an anonymous article in the *Civiltà Cattolica* rescuing the *Itinerarium* from the ontologists.[43]

But the blind remained blind, as their eyes were closed to anything new. Even after the publication of the first tome of the *Opera omnia* (1882) and of the whole text of Bonaventure's Question and cognate Questions (1883), we have the strange case of Fr. Sebastiano Casara, provost of the Rosmini Schools of Charity at Venice, who could not conceal his chagrin at not finding new arguments for his ontologism.[44] Earlier (1879), he had written a considerable pamphlet to show that the teachings of Thomas Aquinas conformed to those of Rosmini.[45] In an appendix, prepared especially for this third edition, Casara gives his version of the doctrine of Bonaventure, a version which ignores the text published by Fidelis and completely distorts or manipulates the texts he uses, omitting what would militate against his own views, drawing conclusions on Bonaventure's teaching without benefit of any text, citing words of Augustine without Bonaventure's comment: *Iste autem modus dicendi nihil est ad propositum*. Casara may also be the anonymous author who two years later published a volume on the light of the intellect according to Augustine, Bonaventure, and Thomas Aquinas.[46] Then, as Fr. Meneghin relates, when the *De humanae cognitionis ratione* appeared (1883), Casara obtained permission from the Franciscan General to make an Italian translation of the Question of Bonaventure (to which he added his own comments).[47] From a note of Fr. Ignatius Jeiler (successor of Fidelis as editor-in-chief) to the General, we may conclude that even here Casara could not refrain from

42. *L'Ontologismo e la Questione già inedita del serafico Dottore San Bonaventura su la cognizione certitudinale della verità* (Acireale: 1876).

43. "*L'Itinerarium Mentis in Deum di San Bonaventura bistrattato dagli Ontologisti,*" in series X, v. 6 (1878), pp. 653–72.

44. *Cf.* V. Meneghin, *Il Padre Fedele,* p. 117, n. 27.

45. S. Casara, *La luce dell' occhio corporale e quella dell' intelletto parallelo illustrata con dottrine del S. Dottore Aquinate a cui son dimostrate conformi quelle dell'illustre abate Antonio Rosmini.* Terza edizione riveduta ed accresciuta di qualche nota e di Appendice con dottrine del santo dottore di Bagnorea (Parabiago: 1879), 100 pp. (The second ed. was in 1857).

46. *Del lume dell'Intelletto secondo la dottrina dei Ss. Dottori Agostino, Bonaventura e Tommaso d'Aquino* (Modena: 1881). More probably, however, since Casara elsewhere praises the work, it was written by someone (a bishop?) of the School of Rosmini who preferred or needed anonymity.

47. *La questione "De cognitionis humanae suprema ratione" del Serafico Dottore tradotta ed annotata per Sebastiano Casara* (Modena: 1883). Though Jeiler had the book in hand (see following note), it is not to be found in the library of the College of Quaracchi (now at Grottaferrata).

repeating his old ideas: the translation is accurate, but in the notes he adjoins to the text one finds the same old unproven observations and outright equivocations. Fr. Meneghin concludes his note by remarking that the actions of Casara reveal how tenaciously the ontologists tried to make Bonaventure say what he did not say in order to shore up their system with the authority of a great Scholastic.[48]

Casara received his due and more in the lengthy refutation directed against him in 1890 by Dr. Emmanuele Zorzoli.[49] Step by step he takes Casara and the ontologists through Bonaventure's doctrine in the *Sentences,* then through a careful analysis of the *Respondeo* of the Question (although one may disagree with him on a few details), and finally through the arguments *pro* and *contra,* rebutting the interpretations Casara had given and offering the reader a fairly accurate interpretation and translation of the Question. Zorzoli's book reveals, one may say, how carefully one must read the Question; so succinct is the text (quite manifestly the work of Bonaventure himself and not a reportation), that every word counts.

Finally, to close this over-long survey, we cannot omit the Scholion which Jeiler appended to the *Itinerarium* in the critical edition of 1890.[50] Although polemic and therefore dated, it gives the death blow to the ontologists' claim to make Bonaventure their father and guide.

What twentieth-century studies of Bonaventure make of the doctrine of illumination is a story that still awaits its own historian.

48. *Cf.* V. Meneghin, *Il Padre Fedele,* p. 117, n. 27.
49. *La Questione di S. Bonaventura "De cognitionis humanae suprema ratione" commentata e difesa contro le rosminiane interpretazioni di S. Casara* (Torino: 1890).
50. *S. Bonaventurae Opera Omnia,* tom. V (Quaracchi: 1890), pp. 313–16.

CHAPTER 4.

Aquinas—"Darkness of Ignorance" in the Most Refined Notion of God

JOSEPH OWENS, C.Ss.R.

I

Ever since the time of Parmenides, Western philosophical thought has been conscious of difficulties in the notion of being. Parmenides had shown that the stable way of being is the way required by thought itself. He emphasized that outside being there is only not-being, a way that can yield no knowledge at all. A mixture of the two ways was forbidden him, since this results in unstable and deceptive appearance, not truth. In following the sole way permissible for philosophic thinking, Parmenides claimed that he had left the dwellings of night and had been guided to light.[1] There he could contemplate being as a luminous object. He could deduce conclusions from its nature just as from any object open to penetration by human thought. The conclusions, irrefutable in the Eleatic context, made impossible any genuine differentiation or plurality or change.

In their extreme form, these conclusions were unacceptable to subsequent philosophers. By some, being was retained as indestructible, yet as differentiated in elements or atoms. By Plato, its true nature was placed in differentiated Ideas outside perceptible things. By Aristotle, being was regarded as multisignificant and consequently as a plurality. It was given secondary status after a primal one by Plotinus. It was denied by Gorgias as nonexistent and unknowable and inexpressible. In numerous currents of modern thought it has been set aside as an empty or meaningless concept, a surd or a blank. On the other hand, being in its own nature was identified with God in patristic and Scholastic tradition. In fact, the formula "God is the being of all things" was, with appropriate qualifications, defended in medieval times.[2]

1. *Fr.* 1.9–10 (DK, 28 B). *Cf. Frs.* 6 and 9.
2. *See* Aquinas, *In I Sent.*, d. 8, q. 1, a. 2 (ed. Mandonnet, I, 197–198); *cf. SCG*, I, 26. Besides Dionysius and Bernard, as cited by Aquinas, the Boethian tradition likewise gave expression to this tenet. *See* Gilbert of Poitiers, *In I de Trin.*, 52, ed. Nikolaus Häring (Toronto: Pontifical Institute of Mediaeval Studies, 1966), p. 89.5–6, Thierry of Chartres, *In Boeth. de Trin.*, II, 56, ed. Häring (Toronto: PIMS,

In the thirteenth century this problem of being was faced by Thomas Aquinas against a proximate background of patristic speculation and a remote background of Neo-Platonic, Aristotelian, and Parmenidean thought. In solidarity with the patristic understanding of a verse in *Exodus* (III, 14), the first and characteristic name of God was for Aquinas "he who is."[3] For him, in spite of a reservation drawn from a comment by John Damascene, "being" was regarded in the context as signifying what God is, namely God's quiddity or nature.[4] Yet for Aquinas, being did not confront the mind in Parmenidean fashion as a luminous object. Rather, in accord with the background in *Exodus* (XIX, 9; XX, 21), it was enshrined in dense darkness (*caligo*). The notion, in its application to God, could be best attained through the gradual removal of all ordinarily understood aspects, even of the "is":

> The reply to the fourth is that all other names mean being under some other determinate aspect. For instance, "wise" means being something. But this name "he who is" means being that is absolute, i.e., not made determinate by anything added. Therefore Damascene says that it does not signify what God is—rather, it signifies an infinite (as though not determinate) ocean of substance. Hence when we proceed to God by "the way of removal," we first deny to him corporeal aspects; and secondly, also intellectual aspects such as goodness and wisdom, in the way they are found in creatures. Just "that (he) is" remains then in our understanding, and nothing more— hence it is, as it were, in a state of confusion. Lastly we remove from him even this very being itself, as present in creatures—and then it remains in a darkness of ignorance. In that ignorance, as far as the wayfaring state is concerned, we are best joined to God; and this is a dense darkness, in which God is said to dwell.[5]

1971), p. 173.44, and *In De Hebd.*, ed. Häring (Toronto: PIMS, 1971), 24, p. 409.48–49. A discussion of the metaphysical issues involved in the tenet may be found in Gerald B. Phelan, "The Being of Creatures," *Proceedings of the American Catholic Philosophical Association*, 31 (1957), pp. 118–25.

3. *In I Sent.*, d. 8, q. 1, aa. 1 and 3; I, 194–95; 199–201.

4. "But in God his very being is his quiddity; and therefore the name that is taken from being properly denominates him, and is his proper name, just as the proper name of man is that which is taken from his quiddity." *In I Sent.*, d. 8, q. 1, a. 1, Solut.; I, 195. Translations, unless otherwise noted, are mine. In Aquinas, no distinction is made between essential being and existential being. Accordingly, in a context like the present, *esse* and *est* may be translated in terms either of being or of existence, in the way English idiom requires; *cf.* "Unde per suum esse absolutum non tantum est, sed aliquid est" ("Hence by his own absolute being he not only exists, but is something")—*In I Sent.*, d. 8, q. 4, a. 1, ad 2m; I, 220.

5. "Ad quartam dicendum, quod alia omnia nomina dicunt esse secundum aliam

In this passage two overall considerations stand out. The first is that on the metaphysical level God is reached in terms of being. The second is that here the notion of being is not luminous, but rather is in a kind of darkness, a darkness resulting from ignorance. The passage is found in the earliest major writing of Aquinas, the *Scriptum super Libros Sententiarum Magistri Petri Lombardi*. It is meant to answer an argument taken from John Damascene.[6] Damascene, in accord with patristic tradition,[7] listed the first name of God as "he who is," in the sense of "an infinite ocean of being." As what is infinite is incomprehensible

rationem determinatam; sicut sapiens dicit aliquid esse; sed hoc nomen, 'qui est' dicit esse absolutum et non determinatum per aliquid additum; et ideo dicit Damascenus, quod non significat quid est Deus, sed significat quoddam pelagus substantiae infinitum, quasi non determinatum. Unde quando in Deum procedimus per viam remotionis, primo negamus ab eo corporalia; et secundo etiam intellectualia, secundum quod inveniuntur in creaturis, ut bonitas et sapientia; et tunc remanet tantum in intellectu nostro, quia est, et nihil amplius: unde est sicut in quadam confusione. Ad ultimum autem etiam hoc ipsum esse, secundum quod est in creaturis, ab ipso removemus; et tunc remanet in quadam tenebra ignorantiae, secundum quam ignorantiam, quantum ad statum viae pertinet, optime Deo conjungimur, ut dicit Dionysius, et haec est quaedam caligo, in qua Deus habitare dicitur"—*In I Sent.*, d. 8, q. 1, a. 1, ad 4m; I, 196–97. Although "aliquam" might be expected for the "aliam" in the opening sentence, the "aliam" gives an acceptable sense, for being has a determination proper to itself, e.g.: "Ita etiam divinum esse est determinatum in se et ab omnibus aliis divisum"—*In I Sent.*, d. 8, q. 4, a. 1, ad 1m; I, 219. "Intellectus" is used regularly in the context in the objective sense of "notion"; *see ibid.* (p. 219) and "non est de intellectu ipsius quidditatis," Exp. Iae partis textus, p. 209. The "wayfaring state" was a customary theological designation for man's life on earth. On this metaphor and its history through medieval times, *see* Gerhart B. Ladner, "*Homo Viator*: Medieval Ideas on Alienation and Order," *Speculum*, XLII (1967), pp. 233–59.

With the passage as a whole, one may compare Radhakrishnan's presentation of Buddha's teaching: "The primary reality is an unconditional existence beyond all potentiality of adequate expression by thought or description by symbol, in which the word 'existence' itself loses its meaning and the symbol of nirvāna alone seems to be justified." Sarvepalli Radhakrishnan, *An Idealist View of Life* (London: George Allen & Unwin Ltd., 1932), p. 100.

6. *De Fid. Orth.*, I, 9, 1–2 (*PG*, 94, 836); Burgundio trans., ed. Eligius M. Buytaert (Louvain: E. Nauwelaerts, 1955), p. 48. On the medieval translations of Damascene, *see* Buytaert's Preface, p. v., and Introduction, pp. ix–xx.

7. A survey of the patristic tradition may be found in C. J. De Vogel, " 'Ego sum qui sum' et sa signification pour une philosophie chrétienne," *Revue des sciences religieuses*, 35 (1961), pp. 346–53. The description, "an infinite and indeterminate ocean of being," has its source in Gregory Nazianzenus, *Orat.* 38, 7, and 45, 3 (*PG*, 36, 317B and 625C). On the meanings of "infinite" and "indeterminate" in this phrase, *see* L. Sweeney, "John Damascene's 'Infinite Sea of Essence,' " *Studia Patristica VI*, ed. F. L. Cross, in *Texte und Untersuchungen zur Geschichte der altchristlichen Literatur*, 81 (1962), pp. 248–63.

and therefore unknowable—so the argument is made to run—"he who is" cannot stand as a name for God. In replying to this argument, Aquinas claims that, for Damascene, "he who is" did not express God's nature but only an indeterminate ocean of substance. Even though all determination by corporeal and intelligible aspects had been removed, the residue still is not immediately capable of signifying the divine nature. The notion of being that remains in it, even though freed from quidditative limitations, manifests only the imperfect being that is known in creatures. Yet, with the removal of this final restriction, the last glimmer of light seems to die. The first and most characteristic name of God has been attained, but what it signifies is englobed in some sort of darkness.

What is the situation here? Damascene had meant that the dominantly significant and first name of God is "he who is." In this context the name "God" holds only second place. Damascene does not say in so many words that "he who is" does not signify what God is, but rather an ocean of substance. Yet Aquinas seems justified in interpreting the meaning of his statement just that way, since Damascene had made the general assertion that all designations of God fail to signify what God is in substance and then had listed "he who is" as the first of these designations. But what background does Aquinas use for the inference? Damascene had commenced his discussion by emphasizing the simplicity of the divine nature and the lack of any composition in it, in contrast to whatever consists of multiple and differing components. No characterization of God, accordingly, implies substantial differences in him, and from that viewpoint does not express anything in the order of substance.[8] For Aquinas this was sufficient to allow the conclusion that anything implying composition could not signify what God is. The reason had just been given in the reply to the immediately preceding argument: ". . . since the being of a creature imperfectly represents the divine being, also the name 'he who is' signifies it imperfectly, because it signifies in the manner of a concrete union and synthesis." Concrete being, in fact, in itself expresses imperfection, "as in this name 'he who is.' "[9] The being immediately known to the human mind is in that way regarded by Aquinas as involving composition and therefore imper-

8. "Oportet igitur singulum eorum, quae in Deo dicuntur, non quid secundum substantiam est significare estimare"—Damascene, *De Fid. Orth.*, I, 9, 1; Burgundio trans., p. 48.8–10. *Cf.* ". . . non ipsam substantiam comprehendimus, sed ea quae circa substantiam"—*ibid.*, I, 10, 2; p. 51.10–11.

9. ". . . cum esse creaturae imperfecte repraesentet divinum esse, et hoc nomen 'qui est' imperfecte significat ipsum, quia significat per modum cujusdam concretionis et compositionis; . . . sicut in hoc nomine 'qui est' "—*In I Sent.*, d. 8, q. 1, a. 1, ad 3m; I, 196.

fection. It is apparently considered by him as still luminous for the human intellect, since there is as yet no mention of darkness. But it is not sufficient to signify the divine nature.

Against that background the steps outlined for progress in knowledge of God may be examined, as they are sketched in the passage in question. The first step is to reject corporeal attributes from the notion "he who is." This is fully in accord with the basic Aristotelian tenet that only sensible things are immediately apparent to human cognition. They are the only starting point for philosophical procedure to God. From them the human mind has to reason to their primary cause and has to show that the primary cause cannot be a body. The procedure required had already been sketched in an earlier article in the Commentary on the *Sentences*: "But from the seeing of perceptible things, we reach God only through a reasoning process, insofar as those things are caused and everything caused is from an agent cause and the primary agent cannot be a body."[10]

What is the process by which corporeal attributes are removed from the original conception? The basic human conception of anything that is, is that of a perceptible existent. Such was the pre-Socratic notion of things,[11] and such is the notion of reality that is most readily acceptable in ordinary human discourse. In fact, to express anything other than the corporeal, one has to use negative notions. Incorporeal, immaterial, inextended, nonquantitative, are the notions employed. They presuppose what is corporeal and quantitative, and then negate the characteristically corporeal aspects. How is this possible? It cannot be achieved by a simple process of abstraction, in the way the notion "man" is abstracted from John and Dick and Harry and the other observable individuals. The abstraction merely leaves out of consideration the individual characteristics observed in each man and focuses upon what is common in them all, the notion "man." "Man" is an object already seen in each and now focused on in isolation from the individual traits. The same holds as in ascending scale the generic natures of animal, living thing, and body are isolated. These specific and generic natures are objects that confront the intellect in the individuals observed.

But can one go further and see within the notion "body" a still wider notion that would have "corporeal" and "incorporeal" as its differentiae? The schematizing in the traditional Porphyrian tree would seem to give that impression. From individuals, "man" is abstracted, from

10. "Sed visis sensibilibus, non devenimus in Deum nisi procedendo, secundum quod ista causata sunt et quod omne causatum est ab aliqua causa agente et quod primum agens non potest esse corpus"—*In I Sent.*, d. 3, q. 1, a. 2, Solut.; I, 94.

11. *See* Zeno, *Fr.* 1 (DK, 29 B); Aristotle, *Metaph.*, Gamma 5,1010a22–3.

man and brute, "animal," from animals and plants, "living thing," from animate and inanimate, "body," and allegedly from bodies and spirits, "substance." But is that what has actually happened at the last step? In all the other steps the different instances were observable before one's intellectual gaze. But were the instances "bodies and spirits" equally observable? No. There were no instances of spirits before one's direct gaze from which one could abstract a notion common also to bodies, as "man" was seen in Dick and Harry and "animal" in man and brute. Even the word "spirit" betrays its corporeal origin. Etymologically it means "breath," and as denoting something invisible it has lent itself to signifying an incorporeal substance. But it does not present any simple concept beyond the corporeal order, nor does it offer positively a new differentia comparable to life, sensation, or rationality.

Yet, the human mind is able to distinguish between the corporeal and the substantial in the instances of body that it immediately encounters. Body is originally conceived as able to have the three dimensions of length, breadth, and thickness. But the same thing can also be conceived as capable of existing or ceasing to exist. A table is made and destroyed, a tree grows and decays, an animal is born and dies. The two ways of conceiving the same thing can readily be distinguished. Conceived in relation to its being or to its existence, a body is known as a substance. In fact, the original designation of the Aristotelian category was in terms of being. It was *ousia* and meant a being in the primary sense of the notion. To say that a body is a substance was merely to say that it was a being in the basic sense of the term "being."

With Aquinas, already at the time of the first book of his Commentary on the *Sentences*, the quiddity or nature of a thing and the being of the thing were regarded as known through two different, although always concomitant, activities of the intellect.[12] As regards its nature,

12. ". . . since there is a double operation of the intellect, of which one . . . consists in the apprehension of simple quiddity, . . . the other . . . in the composition or division of a proposition, the first operation regards the quiddity of the thing, the second regards its being"—*In I Sent.*, d. 19, q. 5, a. 1, ad 7m; I, 489. Cf. d. 38, q. 1, a. 3, Solut.; I, 903. The Latin infinitive *esse* that signifies the actuality originally grasped in the second operation of the mind, may be translated in this context by either "being" or "existence," without any change in the meaning of the term (*see supra*, n. 4). The reason why being as encountered in sensible things is known through a synthesizing type of cognition, is that this being *consists* in a synthesis of form with matter or of accident with subject: ". . . consistit in quadam compositione formae ad materiam, vel accidentis ad subjectum"—d. 38, q. 1, a. 3, Solut.; I, 903. This immediate knowledge of being is intuition, in a contrast to inference and to conceptualization. It is in the form of a judgment, as in the ordinary intuition that something is so, or in the philosophic sense that something is true. A recent use of 'intuition' to describe the grasp of being through judgment may be seen in

the thing was known through simple conceptualization that could be expressed in language by a single word, such as gold, mountain, man, or phoenix. As regards its being, it was known through a synthesizing act of judgment that required a proposition and a sentence for its expression. In relation to what was known about it in the latter way, the thing was regarded as a being. Accordingly, the ground for the distinction between body and substance in the same thing is clear-cut. As a result of the highest type of simple conceptualization and abstraction in the first traditional category, the object is known as a body. As a result of reference to the actuality grasped through judgment, it is known as a substance.

But this recognized distinction allows for the play of further judgments in regard to the notions involved. The notion of something able to exist or to be is open to separation from the notion that originally accompanied it, the notion of body. Through a judgment one can negate the notion of body and retain the notion of existent. There is no question of leaving out the corporeal aspect as would be the case in simple abstraction. It is not left out by abstraction but it is negated by judgment. The object still appears corporeal but is judged to be incorporeal. The judgment is one of separation.[13]

Two instances in which this judgment is made in the metaphysics of Aquinas are the subsistent existence that is reached as the primary efficient cause of all perceptible things and the human soul that functions as the substantial principle of intellectual activity.[14] These are shown to be existents through reasoning processes in which the conclusion is drawn that they transcend the corporeal order. They are accordingly judged to be spiritual substances. To the extent the corporeal has been negated in them by judgment, the formation of a composite concept "incorporeal existent" follows. There is no simple abstraction from the corporeal, but its deliberate negation by judgment and the formation of the subsequent negatively expressed composite concept.

Maritain's posthumous work *Approches sans entraves* (Paris: Fayard, 1973), pp. 264-68.

13. Discussion of this topic may be found in my articles, "The Universality of the Sensible in the Aristotelian Noetic," in *Essays in Ancient Greek Philosophy*, ed. John P. Anton with George L. Kustas (Albany: State University of New York Press, 1971), pp. 462-77, and "Metaphysical Separation in Aquinas," *Mediaeval Studies*, 34 (1972), pp. 287-306.

14. "But the most perfect of forms, that is, the human soul, . . . has an operation entirely rising above matter . . . Insofar therefore as it exceeds the being of corporeal matter, being able to subsist and operate by itself, the human soul is a spiritual substance"—*De Spiritualibus Creaturis*, a. 2, c. Cf. *De Pot.*, III, 11, c; *ST*, I, 75, 2; *Q. de An.*, aa. 1 and 14.

The basic notion of an existent is retained from perceptible objects, and the negation of corporeality is joined to it.

Is this what has been taking place in the passage under consideration? Its wording is: "Hence when we proceed to God by 'the way of removal,' we first deny to him corporeal aspects."[15] "He who is" had been proposed as the first name for God. The object brought before the mind by the expression "he who is," is prima facie a perceptible existent, a man. This object has to be purified if it is to stand for the divine nature. The way designated is a way already dealt with in the Commentary. It consists in taking something that is imperfect and then removing the imperfections in order to reach something perfect.[16] In the present case the corporeal attributes are removed from the object "he who is," and the process is that of negation—"negamus ab eo corporalia." This is quite obviously the judgment of separation.

The first step in "the way of removal," accordingly, frees the notion "he who is" from the imperfections involved in corporeality. Basically, the object still appears as corporeal. But the corporeal characteristics in it have been explicitly negated by judgment and in this way removed from the conception. In this whole process no mention is made of any darkness. What is retained in the object is still treated of as luminous. In it the notions of "substance" and "existence" keep their full meaning. Although all sensible characteristics are deliberately set aside, the specifically intelligible traits seem to preserve their luminosity in entirely undiminished fashion. The conception, by and large, is now that of ordinary instructed Christians, who believe that God has no body while still regarding him as good and wise in the manner familiar to them, although raised to an infinite degree.

II

The second step in the procedure to God rejects from the notion "he who is" even intellectual attributes as they are found in creatures. The designation "intellectual" means obviously enough the kind that cannot be distinguished by the senses but only by the intelligence. The examples given are goodness and wisdom. The two seem rather disparate, but together they may illustrate an important facet of the reasoning in this passage. For Aquinas, goodness is a transcendental

15. See text supra, n. 5.
16. "Secunda ratio sumitur per viam remotionis, et est talis. Ultra omne imperfectum oportet esse aliquod perfectum, cui nulla imperfectio admisceatur." In I Sent., d. 3, div. lae partis textus; I, 88.

property of being.[17] It follows upon being and is present wherever being is found. Since no creature is identified with its being, still less can it be identified with its goodness. Accordingly, goodness as different from the thing's nature is removed from the notion "he who is."

Since goodness is meant to serve as an example, it would indicate that the other transcendental properties of being, such as truth and beauty, are being negated in the sense in which they are different from the subject that possesses them. But in the context the intelligible attributes negated have to be restricted to transcendentals that are properties. The basic notion from which they are being removed has to remain. It is that of something existent, "he who is." The transcendental subject of being, namely "thing," and its first actuation as "a being," are transcendentals that remain for the third step in the procedure. In a word, only the intelligible attributes that *follow* upon an existent nature are in question in the second step.

The other example given is wisdom. This is a different kind of attribute, not common to all creatures, and following upon a definite type of nature rather than upon existence. It had just been used to illustrate the way being can be determined under a definite aspect, for it "means to be something,"[18] namely, to be wise. It had also been given as an example of a divine name that in its meaning designated the source of God's activity in the created world and as an instance of a notion that in creatures implied imperfection.[19] In creatures, of course, wisdom belongs to the category of quality and has the imperfection of an accident.[20] What it is meant to illustrate in the context is a determination or limitation of being. All natures other than being itself come under

17. On the transcendentals in this context, *see In I Sent.*, d. 8, q. 1, a. 3, Solut.; I, 199–200. On the medieval background, *see* H. Pouillon, "Le premier traité des propriétés transcendantales," Revue neoscolastique *de philosophie*, 42 (1939), pp. 40–77. A recent coverage of the transcendentals is given by Karl Bärthlein, *Die Transzendentalienlehre der alten Ontologie*, I. Teil (Berlin: Walter de Gruyter, 1972), but, unlike Aquinas, it does not accept goodness and truth as properties of being.

Goodness and wisdom were used together by Peter Lombard as examples of the attributes of God in the text upon which Aquinas (*In I Sent.*, d. 8; I, 190) was commenting.

18. ". . . sicut sapiens dicit aliquid esse"—*In I Sent.*, d. 8, q. 1, a. 1, ad 4m; I, 196.

19. *Ibid.*, ad 2m; I, 196. Cf. *In I Sent.*, d. 2, q. 1, aa. 2–3 (I, 61–72), where goodness and wisdom are likewise the examples used.

20. ". . . sicut quod hoc nomen 'sapientia' imponitur cuidam qualitati, et hoc nomen 'essentia' cuidam rei quae non subsistit: et haec longe a Deo sunt"—*In I Sent.*, d. 2, q. 1, a. 3, Solut.; I, 69.

this designation—"all other names mean being under some other determinate aspect."[21] The attribute "male," implied by the Greek masculine article and participle and by the masculine relative pronoun in Latin, is no exception.

The general situation, as it is at this stage, seems described clearly enough in the text. The notion from which the start had been made found expression in the words "he who is." To have this notion stand for the divine nature, bodily aspects are first negated in it. Second, transcendental properties and definite natures, as these are known in creatures, are removed from it. What remains now in the original notion? Its content is described as only "that [he] is (*quia est*) . . . and nothing more."

How should the *quia est* be translated? It is reminiscent of the Parmenidean route of being, namely *hoti estin*, and presents the same barrier to exact translation. No subject is expressed, yet English requires the insertion of a subject term. The translation will read "that it is." In Parmenides this would imply a subject other than being, although there cannot be anything other than being for the Eleatic when traveling the way of truth. Further, in the thirteenth-century background, "that a thing is" was an expression that stood in contrast to "what a thing is." It designated the existence of the thing in contrast to the thing's nature, and it was for Aquinas what the act of judgment attained.[22] Here it is meant to signify "being itself, as present in creatures"—"ipsum esse, secundum quod est in creaturis." It is the existential actuality that confronts the mind whenever something is known to exist.

But what is this "being itself, as present in creatures," when taken just alone? It is the synthesizing actuality known through judgment, and expressed in proposition and sentence. However, all quidditative determinations have been removed from it in this second stage. From that standpoint it is entirely indeterminate. "Existing" is all that can be left in the object. That is, of course, wide enough to extend to everything. Yet, as known to the human intellect, it remains an actuality making something else exist. It has to imply, besides itself, an indefinite "something" that does the existing. The notion accordingly is "that which is" in the all-embracing universality to which existing can extend.

21. ". . . alia omnia nomina dicunt esse secundum aliam rationem determinatam" —*In I Sent.*, d. 8, q. 1, a. 1, ad 4m; I, 196. *Cf.*: "Praeterea, quidquid est in genere, habet esse suum determinatum ad illud genus. Sed esse divinum nullo modo determinatum est ad aliquod genus; quinimo comprehendit in se nobilitates ominum generum, . . . "—*In I Sent.*, d. 8, q. 4, a. 2, Contra; I, 221.

22. See *supra*, n. 12.

It means something that exists without limits—quite in accord with the simile of a boundless ocean.

There need be little wonder, then, that the description of this second stage concludes with the assertion, "Hence it is, as it were, in a state of confusion." There is no reference to a Greek source for that notion. Elsewhere the term *confusio* is found used by Aquinas in its various ordinary senses. It is directly opposed to *distinctio*, and in the concrete may signify a mingling in which each component keeps its own identity and yet is known in a way that does not distinguish it from the others.[23] In the present context it bears on the patristic description of God as "an infinite ocean of being." Aquinas is facing the interpretation that this does not signify what God is, in the sense that it does not express the divine nature. Yet, it does name God in terms of being only, and being is the nature of God. Why, then, does not "he who is," in the meaning of an infinite ocean of being, signify the divine nature? What is meant by saying that the notion is in a state of confusion that does not as yet permit it to signify what it intends?

Since no Greek source is indicated, the answer has to be sought in Aquinas' understanding of being. For him, being is the primary actuality of anything whatsoever.[24] Its range is accordingly unlimited. Where

23. Cf. "Distinctioni autem opponitur confusio"—*ST*, I, 66, 1, contra 2. There, and in the reply to the argument, *confusio* was used for the *chaos* of the ancients. *See also In IV Phys.*, lect. 1, Angeli-Pirotta no. 800. In the *Summa of Theology*, "sub quadam confusione" describes the instances under the universal as well as the parts in an integral whole: ". . . scientia imperfecta, per quam sciuntur res indistincte *sub quadam confusione* . . . Manifestum est autem quod cognoscere aliquid in quo plura continentur, sine hoc quod habeatur propria notitia uniuscuiusque eorum quae continentur in illo, est cognoscere aliquid *sub confusione quadam*. Sic autem potest cognosci tam totum universale, in quo partes continentur in potentia, quam etiam totum integrale; utrumque enim totum potest cognosci *in quadam confusione,* sine hoc quod partes distincte cognoscantur"—*ST*, I, 85, 3, c. Cf. ". . . in quadam communitate et confusione"—89, 1, c. *See also* 117, 1, ad 4m. In the Commentary on the *Sentences*, the opposition was described through contrast to arrangement of parts in place: ". . . confusio opponitur ordini partium qui pertinet ad rationem situs"—*In IV Sent.*, d. 10, a. 3, q. 3, ad 2m; ed. Moos, IV, 418 (no. 87). The overall meaning is that the components of something are not distinguished from one another. The adjective "indeterminate" in the text of Damascene seems to have been what suggested Aquinas' use of the term "confusion" in his explanation of the passage. So the ocean metaphor is explained at *De Pot.*, VIII, 5, c: "significat esse indeterminate."

24. Being (*esse*) is presented in this sense as "the actuality of essence" (*actus essentiae*)—*In I Sent.*, d. 33, q. 1, a. 1, ad 1m; I, 766. In later works the universal range is made explicit: ". . . the actuality of all acts, and on this account it is the perfection of all perfections"—*De Pot.* VII, 2, ad 9m; ". . . being is the actuality of every form or nature"—*ST*, I, 3, 4, c. Cf. *In I Periherm.*, lect. 5, Leonine no. 22.

it subsists, it will actualize every aspect of reality. In this way it may be regarded as an indeterminate ocean of being, containing the totality of being in a way that leaves each aspect indistinct from every other. But is the notion so formed as facile as it appears at immediate encounter? Why should any problem at all arise about distinction within it, if it satisfactorily subsumes everything under the one characteristic of being?

First, there is the question of how being is originally grasped by the human intellect. For Aquinas, being is originally known through the synthesizing act of judgment. It is known as an actuality that itself consists in a synthesis, a synthesis that joins matter, form, and accidents into a single existent and thereby determines and individuates. It should not allow indistinctness.[25] On the other hand, what is actuated by existence may be considered in indefinite fashion, extending to everything that may possibly exist. In this way, every aspect of being may be included under the notion "he who is," when all quidditative determinations have been separated from it in "the way of removal." The content of the notion may be expressed metaphorically as an indeterminate ocean of being, including as it does drop after drop of water in indefinite sequence, each spatially apart from the others but without any definite limits appearing between them.

Why is this concept unable to signify the divine nature, the nature of being? Quidditative knowledge, in the noetic already at work in Aquinas at the time of writing the Commentary on the Sentences, is knowledge through conceptualization, knowledge through the first operation of the intellect. Through this type of knowledge the being of the thing is not grasped. Yet, in the notion of "he who is" as an indeterminate ocean of being, the representation is that of something conceived as existing in indefinite fashion. It is basically the notion of an existent nature, even though all quidditative limitations have been separated from it by deliberative thought. In Heideggerian terminology it would still be regarded as an ontic conception. It is the notion of something that has being, a common notion that is now applied to a single subject by the removal of all quidditative limits. It does not represent properly the subsistent existence reached when the existence of perceptible things is traced to the primary efficient cause.

Why does this anomaly arise? Being, in the noetic of Aquinas, is no-

25. Where being is a nature, namely in God, it determines and distinguishes just by itself. Cf.: "Ita etiam divinum esse est determinatum in se et ab omnibus aliis divisum, per hoc quod sibi nulla additio fieri potest"—In I Sent., d. 8, q. 4, a. 1, ad 1m; I, 219. "Deus enim per essentiam suam est aliquid in se indivisum, et ab omnibus quae non sunt Deus, distinctum"—De Pot., VIII, 3, c. On sensible being as a synthesis of matter, form, and accident, see text supra, n. 12.

where immediately attained by the human intellect as a nature. It is a facet that remains outside the natures of things. It is not known as a quiddity or nature, but as another actuality that synthesizes all the components of a thing. In the designation "he who is," this actuality is still regarded as present in what is designated, but it is not the nature that is thereby represented. It has the status of an actuality outside the nature envisaged, on account of the way in which it was originally known by the intellect. The nature thereby designated is not the nature of being, but rather the common nature of anything that can be, taken now without limitation. It is a melding of all possible natures, that is, all natures other than the nature of being, into a something that is regarded as existing. The one nature that is not included is the nature of being. But that is the nature it would have to express if it were to designate the nature of God. There need be little wonder, then, that "he who is" may be characterized as signifying not what God is, but rather an indeterminate ocean of substance. The nature represented is still other than the nature of being and does not include being in any quidditative way. It is the notion of an existent substance that has no quidditative limitations, containing in indistinctive fashion every possible quidditative perfection.

The situation is the same as in the case of the Anselmian argument, already discussed by Aquinas in a preceding article in the Commentary on the *Sentences*.[26] The concept of a being greater than which nothing can be thought does not tell whether or not it exists. It can be thought not to exist. The meaning is that quidditative perfection, even though extended indefinitely, does not include existence. Existence has to be known through judgment. The sum total of all conceivable perfections does not result in the nature of existence, in the nature of God. Just as there is no necessary sequence from the greatest conceivable perfection to the existence of God, so the indeterminate ocean of substance does not express what God is or what the nature of being is.

Although the object "he who is" is now found to be in a confused state, it is not said to be in darkness. It is still luminous. All concepts of definite natures have been removed from it, but the concept of "nature" or "something" in general remains. It is luminous in the way of a universal notion. It is represented as actuated by being, the actuality known through judgment. "He who is" is conceived as something that exists. The notion of "something" is an ordinary notion accessible to conceptualization, and the notion "is" continues to be that of the

26. ". . . potest enim cogitare nihil hujusmodi esse quo majus cogitari non possit; et ideo ratio sua procedit ex hac suppositione, quod supponatur aliquid esse quo majus cogitari non potest"—*In I Sent.*, d. 3, q. 1, a. 2, ad 4m; I, 95.

actuality expressed ordinarily in the synthesis of a proposition. Both elements in the notion "he who is" are still accessible at this stage to ordinary human cognition and in that way remain luminous, even though through metaphysical separation the ordinary quidditative determinations have been removed from the notion. The notion contains the whole of being (*Totum . . . esse*—Burgundio trans.) in the confused way in which a universal contains all that comes under it. "Sicut in quadam confusione" describes well enough the knowledge thereby given.

The luminosity in the notion "he who is" does not, accordingly, yield knowledge about the nature of being. It makes manifest only the synthesizing being that is found in creatures, being that is not present as a nature. Aquinas has no hesitation in making the statement: "And similarly this name 'he who is' names God through the being found in creatures."[27] If the distinction between the two original ways of knowing, namely conceptualization and judgment, is not kept in mind, the cognition of being may be looked upon as an intuition of its nature, and accordingly, the Parmenidean consequences may be drawn. Being is then regarded as entirely luminous in the way it was viewed by the Eleatic. But in the noetic of Aquinas, the being that is known in the act of judgment does not manifest the nature of being. The being of creatures is, of course, derived from subsistent being not only by way of efficient causality but also by way of exemplar causality. Yet, it reflects its exemplar too imperfectly to represent it in the way in which any nature is known. The light that "he who is" provides is that of a synthesis, not that of a nature.[28]

The knowledge reached at this stage is no longer that of the ordinary instructed Christian, but rather that of the metaphysician. The ordinary Christian does not remove from his notion of God the intelligible attributes as found in creatures, such as wisdom and goodness. He thinks of God as being good and wise quite as he sees these attributes in creatures, although on an infinite scale. He does not attempt to regard them as rendered indistinct in the one concept of being. He does not push his thought that far. This second stage is one for a metaphysician. There need be no surprise at finding it neglected by mystical writers. The mystic does, of course, reject intellectual as well as perceptual demarcations in God. But unless he is a metaphysician he has not understood the other perfections as subsumed in a confused way under

27. "Et similiter hoc nomen 'qui est' nominat Deum per esse inventum in creaturis, quod exemplariter deductum est ab ipso"—*In I Sent.*, d. 8, q. 1, a. 1, ad 2m; I, 196.

28. Text, *supra*, n. 9.

the one notion "being," and accordingly he has no call to pass through the confused state on his way to the dark cloud.

III

In the third and final step, even the synthesizing type of being is removed from the notion "he who is." Immediately, the object is in darkness. The light thrown by the being that is known through judgment, even though it is but a very imperfect reflection, was sufficient to represent the totality of being in indistinct fashion. But when it disappears in the process of removal, it takes with it all that it actuates. There is nothing luminous left in the object "he who is." Yet, according to the text, it is in this situation that cognitional union with God best takes place.

Dionysius, there seems no doubt, was referring to mystical union.[29] With the symbolism of perceptual cognition removed and the limiting force of concepts out of the way, the obstacles to mystical knowledge would be set aside. There is nothing in the text to indicate that Aquinas was not understanding Dionysius in this way. Yet, the text occurs in a theological school treatise, in which communicable knowledge is being passed from master to students. The immediately preceding stage was one of metaphysical reasoning. Does the present one remain open also to interpretation on the metaphysical level? Does it proceed in metaphysical sequence from what has already been established? No matter how well Aquinas appreciates the setting in which Dionysius speaks, is he here applying these considerations to a situation present also on the philosophical plane? Specifically, what will the "darkness of ignorance" mean, if it is interpreted in a metaphysical context?

First, it will inevitably mean the lack of conceptual knowledge. The subsistent being reached by "the way of causality" was not known in quidditative fashion. It was attained by the route of existence. The sensible thing's existence, grasped through judgment and not through conceptualization, was the basis for reasoning to its primary efficient cause, subsistent existence. No quidditative knowledge of the existence

29. On this topic, see Charles Journet, *The Dark Knowledge of God*, trans. James F. Anderson (London: Sheed & Ward, 1948), pp. 70–81. Dionysius uses the description "the darkness of true mystical nescience"—Dionysius, *Myst. Theol.*, I, 3, 85; *PG*, 3, 1001A (Journet, p. 78). The union (*henôsis*) that takes place with God in this darkness is regarded by Dionysius (*De Div. Nom.*, VII, 3; *PG*, 3, 872) as a knowledge (*gnôsis*) that surpasses understanding. For Aquinas, any knowledge is a union of knower and known. Accordingly, the metaphysical knowledge of God likewise achieves a union on its own level, in darkness but with richest philosophical content. On 'homo conjungitur Deo' in this sense, see Aquinas, *ST* I–II, 3, 2, ad 4m.

was present at any stage of the reasoning. Having demonstrated that existence subsists in this primary instance, one has thereby shown that it is in this instance a nature. It is *what* exists. But that nature has been reached in terms of existence and not through any elaboration of quidditative concepts. The result is that one cannot *conceive* it as a nature, even though one knows that it is a nature. The lack of any conceptual content in the object now before one's mind can surely be termed a darkness. More specifically, it is a darkness resulting from ignorance, since in the notion all quidditative content remains a blank. The notion can be developed to an incomparably rich content by showing that each of the transcendental and quidditative perfections known to the human mind is included in one way or another in subsistent existence. But there each of them is identified with subsistent existence. What they are at that level is existence itself.[30] What the existence is remains unknown. Accordingly, one can demonstrate that each perfection is present in subsistent existence, without knowing *what* the perfection is when it is found identified with existence. The light of conceptual knowledge is utterly and completely lacking. The question is not the same as in the problem of uniting in one concept the corpuscular and the wave notions of elementary particles and light, when both aspects have been proven to be there. Rather, it is the impossibility of any concept at all in regard to the nature of being.

Second, the intuition of existence in sensible things, as had through the act of judgment, cannot focus upon subsistent existence. It cannot give knowledge of any quiddity. Here the object is a quiddity as well as existence. It therefore cannot come under the human intuition of existence, the intuition of a synthesizing actuality. True, one can show that what is uppermost in that sensible existence is actuality and not the synthesizing facet.[31] That is enough to allow reasoning to subsistent existence. But it does not permit one to see what existential actuality is in the status of a nature instead of a non-quidditative synthesizing of something other than the existence itself. A blind person guides himself by touch and hearing; a pilot makes an instrument landing just by

30. ". . . quidquid est in simplici, est ipsum suum esse"—*In I Sent.*, d. 8, exp. lae partis textus; I, 208. *Cf.* "Quidquid autem est in Deo, hoc est suum proprium esse"—*De Ver.*, II, 11, c. Nevertheless, the formal meaning of the different attributes remains intact in this identity with subsistent existence, both because their meaning in creatures is derived from the divine model, and because that meaning would be there even though no creatures ever existed, as already explained at *In I Sent.*, d. 2, q. 1, a. 2; I, 63. On God as "utterly unknown" and "entirely unknown" in the tradition back of Aquinas, *see* Anton Pegis, "Penitus Manet Ignotum," *Mediaval Studies*, 27 (1965), pp. 212–26.

31. *See In I Periherm.*, lect. 5, Leonine no. 22.

panel readings. Neither can see where he is going, but each has the respective kind of knowledge that suffices to get him there. So a metaphysician demonstrates that the primary efficient cause is subsistent existence and that it contains all perfections in the highest degree. But he cannot conceive either its nature or any of its perfections, and he cannot intuit its existence. The ordinary light in which nature and existence are apparent to him has disappeared. Surely this merits the appellation "a darkness of ignorance." Yet, in this darkness the whole positive metaphysics about subsistent existence, in all its richness, is best developed.

IV

The passage in Aquinas about the "darkness of ignorance" in which God is best known is open, accordingly, to thoroughgoing metaphysical interpretation. It means that subsistent existence, although concluded to by demonstration from sensible things, cannot be conceptualized, and it cannot be represented through the model of the existence immediately known by the human mind. On both these counts the notion of subsistent existence remains dark. Yet, in the realization of this darkness metaphysical knowledge reaches its highest point, for then the infinitely rich attributes it predicates of subsistent being are not tarnished or diminished by the built-in deficiencies of the human cognitive processes. The "darkness" provides the way of rising above these otherwise unavoidable limitations. It blots out what is imperfect and deceptive.

At the same time, the passage illustrates how genuine metaphysics is operative in the theological reasoning of Aquinas. The setting of the passage is theological, occurring as it does in the course of a commentary on a theological text. God's name has been revealed as being, yet according to the same revelation, he is best known in a dense darkness. The theological introduction of the notion "being" prompts the metaphysical inquiry of how God, elsewhere represented as light, has to be known in darkness. Does being furnish the answer? Somewhat as the calculations of Adams and Leverrier led to the turning of a telescope on Neptune, so these theological considerations focus attention on the anomaly in the object "being." The closer metaphysical scrutiny then reveals that being was attained as a synthesis in judgment, and was not known originally by way of conceptualization. The result shows that what is intuited as "being" cannot be used in Parmenidean fashion as a nature from which the conclusions of unicity and unchangeableness may be deduced. The nature of being is in no way intuited. It is *concluded* to and only in darkness. It is not immediately the being that is known in the light of intuition.

In this manner being is located as a nature in a unique and unchangeable primary instance, while the being that is intuited by the human mind remains multiple and varying. Even with the consequent tenet that God or subsistent being is the being of all else,[32] the relation of subsistent being to all the other instances of being is that of exemplar and efficient, not formal, cause. The being that is luminous to human cognition remains accordingly multiple and variable, while the nature of being in its unicity and unchangeableness is eminently respected. But the condition is a "darkness of ignorance" in which the nature of being is attained only by way of a conclusion to something beyond the human intellect's power to intuit or conceive. The privation of both intuitional and conceptual light requires that the most refined notion of the primary efficient cause be enshrouded in this darkness in order to permit, on the metaphysical level, the successive predication of its infinite richness without the hindrance of finite restrictions.

32. *See supra,* n. 2.

CHAPTER 5.

Virtue and Law in Aquinas: Some Modern Implications

ROBERT J. KREYCHE

Introduction

In this article I wish to show the strong ethical background of St. Thomas' social-political philosophy. This I shall do in the light of his doctrine on the moral virtues, especially that of prudence as practical wisdom, and as seen not only in individual life but in the life of social institutions as well—particularly as concerns the question of "the governance of rulers." A wise ruler, for example, is one who rules not only by law, but by virtue, indeed, is one who even has a *passion* for virtue. Throughout this article I shall single out—in a manner relevant to present society—such key concepts in Aquinas' social-political philosophy as the following: the subjection of the *whole order* of creation to the rule of divine providence; the authentic role of "secondary" agents, especially those that are free; the idea that the rule of civil society, to which man *naturally* belongs, should be a rule of law by which public order is established for the *good of the whole*; the further concept that it is to this good of the whole to which all human, positive laws should be directed and ordered; the notion that the wisdom of any law is measured, not only by its justice, but by its suitability to the practical order for achieving the common good in the concrete circumstances of life; and finally, how all of these notions together can provide a basis for a modern theory of politics that is not only workable but sound, and "sound" in a way that few modern theories have been in the past.

This paper is written in the conviction that (a) there is a permanent element both of theoretical and practical truth in the "perennial" philosophy, and (b) that this same perennial philosophy cannot afford to make itself esoteric if it is to make its mark on contemporary culture.[1] Jacques Maritain stresses this same point in the following introductory remark to his book, *Redeeming the Time*.

The subject matter [of this book] is one: man in his cultural life and

1. *See, for example,* Jacques Maritain, *The Range of Reason* (New York: Charles Scribner's Sons, 1952), *passim.*

in the complex patterns of his earthly destiny . . . this is not a book of separated philosophy, separated from faith, and separated from concrete life. I believe, on the contrary, that philosophy attains its aims, particularly in practical matters, only when vitally united with every source of light and experience in the human mind. . . ."[2]

It is precisely in the spirit of the above quotation that I propose to set forth the various sections of this paper, including those that touch on the metaphysical backgrounds of Aquinas' practical philosophy.

Historical Background: The World View of Aquinas

Most persons who have taken a reflective view of the matter are ill at ease about the direction that modern society has taken with respect to the conduct both of individual and social life. Each century, of course, has had its wars, dissensions, social upheavals, and periods of violence, but just at the point when philosophers like Auguste Comte and others in the nineteenth century were hoping that the dawn of the scientific age would issue forth an unprecedented era of human peace and progress, whole new catastrophes were in the making, including the catastrophes of the wars of the twentieth century. The most distinguishing mark of our most recent wars, as compared, for example, with those of the Napoleonic era, has only been that of a greater bloodshed and cruelty because of the availability of advanced technological means.

One wonders, therefore, whether the confident belief (so rampant during the period of the Enlightenment) that man would finally, in a spirit of liberation from the philosophies and theologies of the past, be at the point of a final liberation from war, hunger, disease, and so on— whether such an optimistic belief was ever justified. This is not to deny that progress has been made, and that on a mascroscopic scale, but only to show that it is not the inevitable thing it was believed to be, and that in some important respects civilization has gone in the direction of a backslide.[3]

To say the very least, certain leading and crucial insights that *have* been part of the Western heritage have been lost, and it is because of this loss—of certain key ideas that *can* lead man in the direction of truth, the truth of himself, and the truth of human society—that men

2. Jacques Maritain, *Redeeming the Time* (London: The Centenary Press, 1946), p. *v*.
3. For an excellent historical and philosophical analysis of the rise and decline of the various philosophies of progress, *see* J. E. Sullivan's, *Prophets of The West* (New York: Holt, Rinehart, and Winston, Inc., 1970), especially Chapter 2, pp. 21–37. Note especially bibliographical references at the end of this chapter.

are suffering today. Nor is it a mere question of the simple absence of truth: whenever men are lacking the truth they need to sustain them, what they suffer is a real privation, what the Scholastics have called in line with Plotinus' philosophy, a *privatio boni*, that leads to the substitution of *false* ideas for those that are true.[4]

What I submit, therefore, to my reader is the proposal that some of the ideas I shall set forth in this article go far beyond the mere purpose of an archeological exploration of the past, as though they were merely part of a "classical" tradition that was once relevant but is no longer, is the proposal that some of these ideas, particularly those of Aquinas as inherited through the Aristotelian (and Stoic) tradition are deeply relevant to the needs of today. Nor I do take it too much for granted that even the learned reader is intimately familiar with them, and for this reason I shall stress in the first part of this article not only the strong *ethical* backgrounds of Aquinas' social-political philosophy, but the basic world-view that has given it its life and meaning.

The most important aspect of any major philosophy, be it that of a Plato, an Aristotle, an Augustine, a Spinoza, a Leibnitz, or a Hegel, is the dominant world-view or vision that governs the elaboration of its details, and the social-political philosophy of Aquinas is no exception to the rule. In context, this means that the whole of Aquinas' practical philosophy, in order to be seen in its full light, must be seen against the background of his teleological conception of man and the universe. As regards man's position in the universe it is to be noted that, although man is the most important part of material creation, he is nonetheless an *integral* part of it and therefore subject, like everything else, to the rule or domain of that higher law that leads all things to their final end or goal. This law is the very order of things themselves (that is, the whole order of the universe) as conceived in the mind of the Creator as a supremely intelligent Being, and it is quite simply known in St.

4. Compare the first five *Enneads* of Plotinus according to the text established by Paul Henry and Hans-Rudolf Schevyzer, *Plotini Opera*, Vols. I and II (Paris and Brussels, 1951–59). On the question of false ideas as having a certain mythical status, see my *Betrayal of Wisdom and the Challenge to Philosophy Today* (Staten Island, New York: Alba House, 1972), Chapter 3, "The Tyranny Of False Ideas," pp. 31–48. Note especially: ". . . Modern life is plagued with all sorts of myths like the myth of the total dominance in man of unconscious motives of behavior. However, the myths themselves would be harmless were it not for the fact that modern man has given them a credence that he has given to few religious dogmas and it is his belief in them (the myths, not the dogmas) that has led to every kind of neurotic disorder. The problem, then, in achieving any kind of cure is to get beyond the myths and the half-truths to an understanding in depth of the ultimate reality of human nature." *Ibid.*, pp. 37–38.

Thomas' philosophy as "eternal law."[5] As he understands it, the eternal law is the very plan of the universe as it exists in the mind of God and as including, not only the *knowledge* of the end or purpose of all things, but the very means by which they will be led or governed to the attainment of that end. Further, this plan of things is for Aquinas not something merely speculative, but eminently practical insofar as it includes the efficacious movement on the part of the Divine Cause of all things toward their end—not, of course, as mere automata, but according to the laws of their nature.[6]

Crucial to an understanding of this universal rule of law is to see how it applies *analogically* both to those agents that Aquinas regards as being "merely natural" and those that are free: natural agents are moved to their end without knowledge and choice and they are so moved according to those natural tendencies that are inherent in their nature. Free agents, however, (and we are here concerned with the problem of man) are those that can through their intelligence and will *move themselves* to their end. Man, in other words, differs from all other agents which are "merely natural," not in the fact that he *has* a final end but *in his manner of achieving it*, which is to say, according to his intelligence and the actual exercise of his freedom.

In St. Thomas' view all men inexorably seek happiness (as their end)

5. *See* especially *Summa Theologiae* I–II, Question 93, articles 1 to 6 inclusive. Note also the insightful titles of some of the articles: "Whether the eternal law is a supreme exemplar existing in God?" (Article 1); "Whether the eternal law is known to all?" (Article 2); "Whether every law is derived from the eternal law?" (Article 3); "Whether all human affairs are subject to the eternal law?" (Article 6). Until recently the standard translation of the *Summa Theologiae* by "The Fathers of the English Dominican Province" has been the only complete translation in English. However, a new translation published by the Dominicans has been issued in a 60-volume series with the Latin text on one side, the English on the other, with very useful introductions, notes, and critical essays (New York: McGraw-Hill). The most recent translation into English of the *Summa Contra Gentiles* has been the one by Anderson, Pegis, O'Neil, and Bourke in five paperback volumes (New York, 1955–57). The translations I have used in this text of both *Summae* are those that appear in the Pegis edition of *Basic Writings of St. Thomas Aquinas* (New York: Random House, 1945), except where otherwise indicated.

6. On this point we can see a close analogy between Aquinas' conception of divine "practical" knowledge and that *human* practical knowledge which he calls "prudence." Such knowledge contains within itself the capacity to apply itself to the order of action insofar (as Aquinas repeatedly points out) as it is "conjoined to the will." Concerning the question of prudence we shall soon see that this virtue covers as its "parts" not only counsel and deliberation, but the command of practical reason whereby that which is known to be good is applied to the order of action. On the question of *divine* practical knowledge, see *Summa Theologiae* I, Question 14, *passim*; on human prudence, *Ibid.* I–II, Q. 57, especially articles 5 and 6.

and all men are at least implicitly motivated by what he calls "the natural desire for God,"[7] but neither of these factors is a *guarantee* that they will *de facto* achieve what is their *real* end. All too often they are misled (in their search for happiness) by merely *apparent* goods that pull them away from their real end—which is the vision of God himself. Therefore, what is necessary in order for man to achieve his end is for him somehow to *know* it and even in the order of the purely natural virtues (like prudence, temperance, justice, and fortitude), in contrast to those that are supernatural (like faith, hope, and charity), to utilize his will so as to make only those choices that are appropriate to this end.

The whole schema, then, of what we might call in round terms Aquinas' "philosophy of the universe" together with his "philosophy of human life" is based on the controlling idea of a divine providence which rules over the whole of creation but in a manner that is not only compatible with the use of secondary agents, but which requires their active cooperation according to the laws of their own nature. The basic contrast between those things below the level of man and man himself is this: whereas the former are blindly ruled (from the point of view of the agents involved) by a law of nature (lex naturae) which is *set* or determined for them, the latter, namely man, is ordered to his final end by the law of his nature (lex naturalis)—which is to act as a being that is both *rational* and *free*.[8] Furthermore, what is true of man as an

7. Long before Aquinas, Augustine, too, had built into his philosophy the concept of man being endowed with a *liberum arbitrium*, a capacity of free choice. Though readily subject to abuse, this capacity is the very instrument of man's nature whereby he, in contrast to anything else in material creation, can move himself (under the impulse of divine grace) to the attainment of his end. As to the question of man's final end in Aquinas (taken together with the problem of human happiness) see *Summa Contra Gentiles*, Book III, Chapters 1 to 63, inclusive. Note also "Happiness is the great human good, the end to which all others are subordinate. It would be pernicious to a degree were happiness a matter of good luck, for then all other goods would be even more fortuitous, and so any deliberate attempt to lead a good life would go by the board." *Commentary on I Ethics*, Lecture 14.

8. The following quote epitomizes what we have been describing: "Divine providence extends to all things. Yet a special rule applies where intelligent creatures are involved. For they excel all others in the perfection of their nature and the dignity of their end: they are master of their activity and act freely, while others are more acted on than acting. They reach to their destiny by their own proper activity, that is, by knowing and loving God, whereas other creatures show only some traces of this likeness. Now in any undertaking the procedure varies according to the purposes intended and the situation that has to be met, as the method of art varies according to the end proposed and the material employed. Consequently, there is one kind of order for rational creatures under divine providence and another for irrational creatures." *Summa Contra Gentiles*, Book III, Chapter 111. A variety of English translations exist of this monumental work, such as the five-volume work of the

91

individual is also true of society as a whole: the achievement of the end of society respecting, for example, the choice of a form of government, is a "work" or accomplishment of human reason and will by which men, working together for their common end or goal, determine *for themselves* which means are best and which are not. As Aquinas notes: "In choice there are two things, the intention of the end, which belongs to moral virtue, and the preferential selection of the means to the end, which belongs to prudence,"[9] and of both of those more shall be said forthwith.

The Moral Virtues and Their Role in Human Life

Our chief concern in this paper is the Thomistic doctrine of man in his social and political life, and of how by the right use of his intelligence and freedom he can direct himself toward the attainment both of such proximate ends as the procurement of his temporal needs and, within a yet larger context, of his final end which is the Vision of God himself. This concern includes of necessity Aquinas' doctrine of the virtues both as they relate to the life of individuals and to society as a whole. Although his *ex professo* treatment of the virtues focuses mainly on their application to individual life, we shall for our own purposes examine their social implications as well, especially as they affect the life of man in a political society.[10]

In his *Summa Theologiae* I–II, from Questions 49 through 61, Aquinas provides his reader with a complete and extended analysis of his doctrine of the moral virtues. This analysis includes not only a treatment of the virtues themselves but of their necessity with respect to human life. Basically, his conception of a virtue is this: it is a "good habit" of one kind or another that every man needs in order to insure a kind of behavior that is both rational (in the best sense of the word) and in conformity with the end or purpose of human life. The need for such habits arises from the fact that men, unlike animals which are largely guided by instinct, need something to perfect the operation of

---

English Dominicans (London: Burns, Oates, 1924, Benzinger, 1928–29). *See also* a more recent American translation: Pegis, Anderson, Burke, and O'Neill (Garden City, N.Y.: Doubleday, 1955–57). Both for the accuracy of translation and liveliness of its style, I have selected the above translation from T. Gilby's, *St. Thomas Aquinas: Philosophical Texts* (New York: Oxford University Press, 1960).

9. *Summa Theologiae* I–II, Q. 56, a. 4, response to the fourth objection.

10. Here I do not mean to imply that Aquinas is indifferent to what we call today a "public morality," but only that he pretty much takes it for granted. Even so, he does show *passim* throughout his works the same basic concern that Plato and Aristotle had for the establishment of a just society.

their "faculties" or powers[11] and to insure that these same powers may be depended upon to act in a reasonably uniform way.[12]

To get the full brunt of this statement we should take note of the fact that Aquinas' ethical doctrine on the virtues is rooted in his psychology and in that part of it which is founded on Aristotle's treatise *De Anima* as well as his own extended commentary on that treatise.[13] Both for Aristotle and Aquinas man is essentially a composite being whose informing, life-giving principle (in the order of "formal," not efficient, causality) is his soul taken as a real (ontological) entity that unites with matter to form a living organism that we call a human person.[14] However, the soul of man as well as man himself (taken as a psychosomatic unit) cannot act except through those proximate principles of operation that are known in Thomistic psychology as his "powers." Whereas it is the person himself (as psychosomatic unit) that is the remote source of all the operations that man performs, it is through his powers as immediate or proximate principles of operation that he performs his activities and accomplishes his ends.

Not all of these powers, however, are the "subject" of habit and the vegetative powers are a case in point. These latter are "determined" in their manner of operation to one sort of thing, as it is the function, let us say, of the nutritive power to digest food and biologically to sustain the organism. Such powers are obviously not the subject of habit because once set in motion they "naturally" (not freely) tend to their objects and, barring such obstacles as an ulcer in the digestive system, accomplish their end or purpose (which is always for them a built-in

11. Because of the bad name which the term "faculties" has acquired in early modern psychology, the term "powers" is far preferred, especially as it directly translates Aquinas' habitual reference to the Latin "potentiae."

12. A key text for a proper understanding of the necessity of forming good habits in the soul (and by extension, within the total human composite) is the following: "If we take habit in its relation to operation, it is chiefly thus that habits are found in the soul, *insofar as the soul is not determined to one operation, but is indifferent to many*. This indifference is a condition required for a habit . . . and since the soul is the principle of operation through its powers, therefore, regarded in this sense, habits are in the soul according to its powers." *Summa Theologiae* I–II, Q. 50, a. 2c. I use "c" here to refer to the "corpus" or "body" of the article in question in contrast to that part which consists of objections or answers to objections. Italics are my own.

13. *See* Aristotle's *De Anima*, in the version of William of Moerbeke and the Commentary of St. Thomas, translated by K. Foster and S. Humphries, Introduction by I. Thomas (New Haven, Connecticut: Yale University Press, 1951).

14. Note also the fact that Aquinas accepts Boethius' traditional definition of a person as "an individual substance of a rational nature." *See Summa Theologiae* I, Q. 29, a. 1.

purpose, not one that is consciously known). So much, then, for the vegetative powers, as they are not normally subject (except in an indirect way) to human volition and control.

As to whether the sensitive powers are a subject of habit, Aquinas makes this important distinction:

> The sensitive powers can be considered in two ways: first, according as they act from natural instinct; secondly, according as they act at the command of reason. According as they act from natural instinct, they are ordained to one thing, even as nature is. Therefore, just as there are no habits in the natural powers, so likewise there are none in the sensitive powers. . . . But according as they act at the command of reason, they can be ordained to various things. And thus there can be habits in them, by which they are well or ill-disposed in regard to something [e.g., having the courage to perform an act of bravery].[15]

This is to say that the sensitive powers, particularly what we call today the "emotions," *are* the subject of habit insofar as they can be directed to a wide variety of objects and are subject to the control or command of reason. In fact, as Aquinas shows in his ethics, the very need for the important moral virtues of temperance and fortitude lies precisely in the fact that those emotions known to Aquinas and the Scholastics as the *concupiscible* and *irascible appetites* need to be brought under the control of reason for the good of a truly human life. Now it is true that the sensitive appetite for pleasure *naturally* tends toward pleasurable goods, but the question at hand is whether it normally does so in a manner that is conducive to the good of human nature. If so, there would be no need of a habit, but as everyone knows from experience the "concupiscible" appetite, which includes the desire for food and sex, needs to be subjected to rational control and is therefore subject to habit, and herein lies the need for the virtue of temperance. *Pari passu* the same must be said of the "irascible" appetite or power whereby man needs to direct himself toward those goods that are difficult of attainment. Concerning these latter, man often encounters a certain resistance to action in the lower part of his nature. In order to overcome this resistance, he needs to goad the appetite toward the attainment of the longer-range good— and he does this through the dominance both of his practical reason and the power of his will.

A more direct approach to the question of the necessity of moral virtues (both in individual and social life) lies in the question as to whether those higher powers of intellect and will are also the subject of

15. *Summa Theologiae* I–II, Q. 50, a. 3c.

94

habit.[16] Are intellect and will the subject of habit as well? To answer this question we need only consider the following argument: if it is the case that even the sensitive powers are the subject of virtue insofar as they need to be brought under the control of reason, then *a fortiori* are reason and will the subject of habit formation. The reason is that they, in a far higher sense than the sensitive powers, are "open" to a wide variety of operations and objects. In fact, it is chiefly in connection with these powers that the need for good habits (i.e., the formation of "virtue") arises since both powers, in the language of Aquinas, bear a "relation to many and various things."[17] For example, even though the will is "determined" and therefore necessitated by "the good" in the sense that whatever it selects it does so under the aspect of good ("quid-quid volitum sub ratione boni"), nonetheless it can and *de facto* does make its choices from a wide variety of goods, some of them being *really* good for man in view of his total nature and others being only *apparently* so. As for the intellect, whatever it perceives it does so under the aspect of "being" (of that which is or can be), but this too under a quasi-infinite variety of concepts, judgments, and reasonings. For example, the need for the good nonmoral habit of logic (i.e., as an "intellectual" virtue) arises from the prior need of rightly conjoining certain types of judgment so as to formulate a valid conclusion. More generally, this implies the falsity of the assumption that people are naturally (as it were, by a kind of natural instinct) logical, and experience itself is adequate testimony to this fact. In a similar and parallel manner, the "good habit" or virtue of prudence (which is both an intellectual and a moral virtue) is one that arises from the necessity of making the right kind of judgments concerning ethical and political decisions—a factor that has a very important bearing on this paper.

So much, then, as to the general need for the establishment of virtue in the life of man. Let us now return to the yet more important question

16. As background to the argument that follows, note that Aquinas considers these latter powers as being unique to man in that they alone are, strictly speaking, powers of the rational soul. As such they are only extrinsically dependent on the functioning of the organism and its various parts like the brain and the central nervous system. This means that both intellect and will are *in themselves* purely spiritual faculties or powers and it means further that *in principle* there is no truth that the human mind cannot grasp or no good that the human will cannot strive after, since the object of both of these powers, in contrast to merely sensible ones, is the universal truth or, in the case of will (as rational appetite), the universal good. This is to say there is no *upper limit* either to their mode of operation or to the nature of their object, granting, however, that they are *de facto* limited by the human bodily condition.

17. *Summa Theologiae* I–II, Q. 50, a. 6 response to the first objection.

as to the specific need for each of the moral virtues, both in individual and social life. As to the need for temperance and fortitude we shall be fairly brief. As we have already seen, the sensitive powers or appetites to which these virtues relate (namely, the concupiscible and irascible appetites) are not *in themselves* competent to be the subject of habit. Nevertheless, as Aquinas notes, *insofar as they participate in reason,* they can become the subject of habit and therefore also of virtue, which is nothing else than a good habit (whether of the intelligence or will or of some other power insofar as it is under the control of the intelligence or the will). Insofar, then, as these appetites or powers can participate in reason by conforming themselves to its demands, they can become the subject, not only of a good habit, but of what Aquinas calls a "human act."[18]

More specifically, Aquinas shows the necessity of these virtues (temperance and fortitude) by way of the following general argument: suppose that the good or morally perfect performance of an operation (like eating one's food) depends upon the conjoint operation of two distinct powers (the power of reason and the appetite for food); suppose further that one of these powers (the appetite for food) depends on the other (reason) for a properly human mode of operation; then obviously that power which is so dependent (the appetite for food) is *in need of being subject* to the person who uses it as its principal cause. Now it so happens that the concupiscible and irascible appetites *are* so dependent upon reason *as instruments* for accomplishing the purposes of human life, for *if left to themselves* (i.e., *without the regulation of reason*) they could easily go off on a tangent of their own (in the pursuit of merely apparent goods, like an excess of food). This being so, the above-mentioned appetites can and should be made subject to that other power on which they depend for their *perfect* operation and are therefore the subject of virtue. The "catch" word or rider to the above argument is the word "perfect": Aquinas is not suggesting that the above appetites cannot act at all except under the control of reason. Indeed, it is all too often they do so. His only point is that they need to be subjected to rational control in order for man to act in a way that is

18. *Summa Theologiae* I–II, Q. 56, a. 4c. Crucial to an understanding of Aquinas' ethical theory is the distinction between a mere *"actus hominis"* (an act of man) and an *"actus humanus"* (a human act). The former is indeed any kind of an act that man performs but not in his distinctively rational nature *as* man, as when he digests his food. The latter, however, is the kind of act that is subject to his rational and voluntary control and therefore also one for which he is morally responsible as a man. It is an act that is both voluntary and free.

both conducive to the real purposes of human life and to man's final end.[19]

The depth of Aquinas' psychological insight as to the potential unruliness of the human emotions and passions is one that has important ethical implications, not the least of which is the necessity, as we have just seen, of the virtues of fortitude and temperance (fortitude, generally to inhibit fear, and temperance, to inhibit an excessive concern for pleasure). However, his realization of the necessity of control does not stop at this point as he is concerned with making an important further distinction. Quoting with approval from Aristotle's *Politics I, 2* (1254b4), he suggests that "the soul rules the body with a despotic rule, as the master rules the slave,"[20] meaning by this simply that the entire movement of the body is the result of the soul in-forming it as its life-giving principle. For this reason he concludes (in language that seems strange to modern ears) that the body as such is not a proper subject of habit. Now the point of this argument is to show that the sensitive powers are not "automatically" subject to the control of reason *in the way* that the body is generally subject to the movement of the soul. As he puts it, "the irascible and concupiscible powers do not obey the reason instantly," but "have their own proper movements by which at times they go against reason."[21] This much, of course, may be taken for granted, but it is in the remark that follows as to *how* reason rules the lower level powers that we may gather some insight not only into Aquinas' psychology but into his politics as well. Thus

> ... the [power of] reason rules the irascible and concupiscible powers by a *political* rule, such as that by which free men are ruled, who *in some respect have a will of their own*. And hence there must be some virtue in the irascible and concupiscible powers.[22]

From the above quotation we may see more than a faint parallel

19. The above argument in the translated text of Aquinas is as follows: "... there *are* some virtues in the irascible and concupiscible powers. [Why?] Because an act which proceeds from one power, according as it is moved by another power, cannot be perfect unless both powers be well disposed to the act; for instance, the act of a craftsman cannot be successful unless both the craftsman *and his instrument* be well disposed to act. Therefore, in the case of the irascible and concupiscible powers, according as they are moved by reason, there must needs be, not only in the reason, but also in (these) powers, some habit aiding for the work of acting well." A little later in the same text Aquinas speaks of the need of "a certain habitual conformity of these powers to reason." *Summa Theologiae* I–II, Q. 56, a. 4c.

20. *Summa Theologiae* I–II, Q. 56, a. 5, ad 3.

21. *Ibid.*

22. *Ibid.* Italics are my own.

between Plato's approach to the question of the virtues and Aquinas'. While Plato, too, is concerned with the problem of the role of the virtues in individual life, he seldom misses a chance to show their parallel role in the life of the state. Thus in Plato we find a consistent point of analogy between the rule of reason over the passions *in the individual* as compared to the rule of the governor of the state over his subjects.²³ The analogy may, from a logical point of view, be weak or strong, but it is one that has had its influence, not only on Aristotle (as Plato's disciple) but on Aquinas as well. For Aquinas the *power* of the ruler in the state, be it legislative, judicial, or executive, is never conceived in purely voluntaristic, "despotic" terms—but in terms of a "political" rule. In much the same way, then, and according to the same point of analogy the *rule of reason* within the individual himself over the lower part of his nature is likewise a "political" rule: each of these lower powers contains within itself a certain freedom of its own, a certain inner power of resistance, and it is the role of a virtue as a habit (and a good one at that) to "overcome" this resistance, although never in such a way as to repress the power itself.²⁴

We have just encountered (in a very limited context) what amounts to one of the central insights of Aquinas' ethics, politics, and his legal theory, and it may be well for a moment to pause over the depths of its meaning. The "rule of reason" can never mean for him what it does in some voluntaristic philosophies—a *mere* "practical reason" that is divorced, as it were, from reason as a genuine power of understanding. The "rule of reason" for Aquinas always implies the idea of a *measure* of human activity, but one that is guided by insightful *knowledge* and *understanding* in the full and proper sense of the term. Furthermore, *as a measure* of legal, ethical, and in the large sense, political action, human practical reason acts not on the basis of caprice and merely on the "spur of the moment," but according to certain universal norms. However, it is not the specific content of these norms that is of concern at the moment, but the fact that their function is neither exclusively a cognitional nor a volitional one—but an integrally *human* one that *controls* the acts of the lower powers without in the least *suppressing* them. As we shall presently see, prudence as practical wisdom in the

23. *Cf. Republic,* translated by F. Cornford (New York: Oxford University Press), Part II, XII (427c–434d) and XIV (441c–445b).

24. One of the more subtle implications of the above doctrine is this: the power of reason is never meant, as in the Stoic ethic, to eradicate the emotions but only to channel their responses in a manner subject to the dictates of reason. The difference, then, between Aquinas' doctrine of the virtues and that of the Stoics is the difference between a "tyrannical" and a "political" rule.

individual never "overpowers" the activities of the other powers or even "dictates" to them in the manner of a categorical imperative, but only channels them into a properly human mode of response. In the realm of political rule likewise: a true ruler is not one who (except in cases of necessity) dictates to his subjects against their own will, but rather appeals to them in terms of their own human nature by trying to persuade them to do what is right and just. In this sense all virtue—whether it resides in the individual *as* an individual or in the ruler *as* ruler is *power of a certain kind*—but never sheer power because it is a force that carries with it the dynamics of its own conviction, that is, the power of *reason as reason* conjoined with the power of will as power of execution.[25] The dynamics of this concept of "reason" are especially evidenced in Aquinas' theory of law as an "ordinance of reason" and in his theory of the state as the capacity to establish both order and freedom in society. For now, we must return to the subject of the virtues.

So far we have seen that Aquinas' teleological conception of virtues, which is to say, his conception of their built-in end or goal is rooted in the basic necessity of getting the powers to act in a manner that is dependable in regard to what is morally good. We have seen, furthermore, that the basic idea of virtue (as derived from the Latin notion of "virtus" as a certain kind of "manliness") connotes the idea of "power," but of a kind of power which for Aquinas is never sheer "power of will" or willpower all by itself, but a real capacity within an individual or a society for accomplishing a real good under the aegis of prudence considered both as an intellectual and a moral virtue. Virtue, in other words, is neither an ineffective *velleitas* (a mere wishfulness) that lacks the support of a strong will to put it to use, nor is it, at the other extreme, a blind power of will that operates independently of and without

25. Also to be noted is the fact that this "power of reason" is affected *in its turn* by the virtue of temperance *as a power of moderation* and the virtue of fortitude, especially in those cases where a "reasonable" decision calls for a certain kind of courage in order that the "command" of reason be properly fulfilled. In other words, it is not only a case of reason establishing a certain order in the lower level appetites to help them achieve *their goal,* but one also of *reason itself* being subjected to the demands of moderation and fortitude. In the political order the implications of this last remark are considerable. Thus, a good ruler is one who is in the best sense "moderate" in his judgments about the character of other men, the method of punishing them, and so on. Further, he does not use "reason" as an excuse for inaction but as a method (through the virtue of fortitude) for prescribing and *following through* with whatever course of action needs to be pursued. In Aquinas' ethics and politics the role of reason is never separated from that of those other virtues that directly pertain to some other good than the good of reason itself. Yet in a deeper sense all goods pertain to the good of reason just as the good of reason (in the practical order) pertains to all other goods.

the surveillance of reason. Rather, it is a controlled capacity (controlled by reason) for performing good acts that need to be performed at the time and under the circumstances that such action is called for.

Before we turn to Aquinas' handling of the virtue of prudence I want to show how moral virtue for him (*all* moral virtue) is not only compatible with what he calls "passion" (that is, the use of the emotions), but of how under certain conditions the play of the emotions can even intensify the moral life. In the *Summa Theologiae* I–II, Q. 59, a. 2, he raises the question "Whether there can be moral virtue with passion?" After referring to various historical opinions, he resolves the issue on this basis:

> If, as the stoics held, the passions be taken for *inordinate* affections, they cannot be in a virtuous man, so that he consent to them deliberately. But if the passions be taken for any movements of the sensitive appetite, they can be in a virtuous man, *insofar as they are subordinate to reason.* Hence Aristotle says that some describe virtue as being a kind of freedom from passion and disturbance: this is incorrect, because the assertion should be qualified; they should have said virtue is freedom from those passions that are not as they should be as to manner and time.[26]

Addressing himself to the contrary question in Article 5 of this same section of the *Summa*, Aquinas asks "whether there can be moral virtue *without* passion," and here again he reinforces a familiar point:

> ... It is not the function of virtue to deprive the powers subordinate to reason of their proper activities, but to make them execute the commands of reason by exercising their proper acts. Therefore just as virtue directs the bodily members to their appointed external acts, so does it direct the sensitive appetite to its own regulated movements.[27]

This much being clear, St. Thomas goes on to suggest that there can nonetheless be moral virtue without the passions for the simple reason that there are some virtues, like justice, that are concerned, not about the passions as such, but about operations, which is to say, about certain *deeds* that need to be done. However, his most significant comment in this connection is the following:

> Nevertheless joy results from an act of justice, at least in the will, in which case it is not a passion. And if this joy be increased through the perfection of justice, it will overflow into the sensitive appetite, inso-

26. *Summa Theologiae* I–II, Q. 59, a. 2c
27. *Ibid.*, a. 5c

far as the lower powers follow the movement of the higher. . . . Therefore by reason of this kind of overflow, *the more perfect a virtue is,
the more does it cause passion.*[28]

This last remark gives us a profound insight into the spirit, not only of
Aquinas' ethics, but of his social and political philosophy as well, for its
intent is to show that the exercise of virtue or the living of the "good
life" is not meant to be the purely rational and somber sort of thing it
is often made out to be. St. Thomas, in other words, is no ethical puritan
but one who believes that in a society where justice flourishes, where
moderation is the order of the day, where brave men respond to the
challenges that are offered them, there not only is, but should be a
certain experience of such elevated and noble emotions as hope, love,
and joy. Contrarily, in a society where the poor are deprived of such
daily necessities as bread and shelter, where social injustice prevails, it
is not only right that these evils should be condemned and corrected,
*but that a certain true and righteous indignation provide one with a
stimulus to action.* Although justice therefore resides in the will, that is,
in the will to give each man his due, there is plenty of room in Aquinas'
social and political philosophy for a "passion for justice," and it is quite
a safe inference to assume that St. Thomas would readily agree with
Hegel's opinion that the only really important things in life are
those that are done with a certain passion. We should not, therefore,
be misled into thinking that St. Thomas' repeated insistence on
"reason" as a model for virtuous conduct in any way excludes a "flesh
and blood" approach to morality. For him reason is never an anemic,
lifeless thing, but a true and effective standard for a full human life,
both within the individual and even more importantly within society
at large.

The Centrality of Prudence

A few words now on the meaning and centrality of prudence in
Aquinas' ethics, and we shall pass on to certain larger aspects of his
social and political philosophy—together with some of the implications
they should have for society today. For the sake of general perspective
we should note that the analogy of Divine Providence (in which God
is the prudential Agent *par excellence*) plays a central role in St.
Thomas' entire practical philosophy. This analogy as it vitally affects
the life of man holds true (in Aquinas' thinking) not only for the individual, but for the home, for the conduct of education, government,
social affairs, and so on. Man is at his best as man when both as rational

28. *Ibid*. Italics are my own.

creature and as image of God he acts according to the measure of practical wisdom that comes to him, whether by a kind of human or divine inspiration, or by human industry, or by a combination of all of these factors. Furthermore, he can learn through prudence, not only how to govern himself and his own affairs, but the affairs of the family or even of the state. For St. Thomas, prudence is the master virtue which controls all of the rest.

As to the meaning of prudence, Aquinas distinguishes it from "art" (*any* kind of art) in this way: whereas both prudence and art are a "right conception" ("plan," "idea") of a certain order of things, the former (prudence) is directly concerned with the performance of *actions*, whereas the latter (art) with things to be *made*. In other words, art is *recta ratio factibilium*, the right order of *things to be made* (like making a table), whereas prudence is the *recta ratio agibilium*, that is, of *things to be done* (like repaying a debt).[29] This point of contrast is brought out even more clearly if we consider that the *end* of prudence (both as a moral and intellectual virtue) is not the "making" or production of anything, but the *very rectitude of human acts themselves*. Contrarily, in the case of that intellectual virtue (or set of virtues) generically known as "art" (whether, for example, as a mechanical or as a fine art), the end of the act or series of acts leading to the artistic products is not the perfection of the agent but the good of the things themselves. Most crucial of all, however, is this difference: taken as a moral virtue that properly directs man to his final end, prudence presupposes not only a *knowledge* of the end as well as the means that lead to it, but the "rectitude of the appetite" (or will) *insofar as it is conformed to the end*. Not so, however, in the case of art, since the goodness of a work of art is judged, not by the intention of the agent but by the product itself. As St. Thomas expresses this point: "The good of things made by art is not the good of man's appetite, but the good of the artificial things themselves, and hence art does not presuppose rectitude of the appetite."[30]

In response to the above one might readily object that many persons may be prudent in one way or another, for example, as businessmen, bank clerks, lawyers, and such like, but not in relation to a moral end. To this Aquinas would readily agree, but with the understanding that

29. *Summa Theologiae* I–II, Q. 57, a. 4c
30. *Ibid.* Note also: "Art does not require of the craftsman that his act be a good act, but that his work be good . . . . Therefore the craftsman needs art, not that he may live well, but that he may produce a good work of art . . . whereas prudence is necessary to man that he may lead a good life . . . ." *Summa Theologiae* I–II, Q. 57, a. 5c.

such prudence is not moral prudence in the proper sense of the word but mere "cleverness" or "astutia." Thus it is only in a very limited and qualified sense that a man may be said to be "prudent" as the robber of a bank—"prudent" insofar as the means he uses successfully lead to the execution of a particular end. Insofar, however, as the end in question is out of alignment with the virtue of justice and therefore with one's final end—the action is imprudent from a moral point of view. Thus: ". . . Some men, insofar as they are good counsellors in matters of warfare, or seamanship, are said to be prudent officers or pilots, *but not prudent absolutely*; for only those are prudent absolutely who give [or take] good counsel about what concerns man's entire life."[31]

The implications of this last statement are profound, and what it basically means is that the clever are not necessarily the wise. A wise man (in the full moral sense) is one who conducts his decisions in the full light of the moral law as best he can know it through the light of his reason and in consultation with others who are wise. For St. Thomas, being prudent means not only knowing the universal (moral) law, but knowing also how to apply it to particular instances and in a way that fully respects the right order of means to ends. In other words, prudence requires that (a) the ends of one's actions themselves be morally right, and that (b) the means be suited (*morally* so) to those same ends. As a case in point the preservation of "national security" properly understood and interpreted *may* be regarded as a legitimate moral end, but even at that it is not the use of any and all kinds of means that can justify its pursuit. Should "national security" become a ploy for the clandestine operations of government agents whose leading concern is to cover up their own mistakes and suspicions, as was made clear in some of the Watergate scandals of 1973, no measure of rationalization can serve to justify it either on legal or moral grounds. Indeed, true politics as taken in the best classical sense and as relating to the common good of the citizens of the state must be aligned with the virtue of prudence, in the absence of which public disorder, scandals, crime, and many other evils may be the result. For this reason it is a matter of transcendent importance that this virtue (prudence) be present in the highest degree in the top officials of the state.

On the subject of prudence, another important point should be made concerning the necessity of integrating prudence in one's private and family life with one's business and professional activity. For example, a man who is integrally prudent in the sense of having complete "rectitude of appetite" as regards the end of life—such a person will behave morally in both spheres of activity. He will not, for example, lay claim

31. *Ibid.*, response to the third objection.

to a private morality while applying the "law of the jungle" to public affairs. Nor will he, for example, give himself so completely to his business activities as to neglect his family life. The Thomistic ideal of a completely moral individual is that of the person who on balance is an "all-round" prudent man.[32]

As to the "parts" of prudence (namely, those factors or conditions that are necessary for the exercise of the virtue), St. Thomas distinguishes between counsel, judgment, and command, the first two pertaining to its intellectual side, the last to a conjoined act of the will. Thus, a prudent man is one who (1) assiduously investigates alternative courses of conduct together with the means for accomplishing a moral end; (2) who, beyond the initial process of inquiry and investigation, knows how to make practical judgments as to what needs to be done, and most importantly of all, having made his judgment, (3) *commands* through his will that a given course of action be omitted or performed.[33]

All in all, prudence in the ethics of Aquinas is that virtue of man's practical intelligence that mediates between the universal moral law and the concrete situation or event. As against the ethics of Kant which stress the need for universalizability as a condition of moral action, Aquinas considers the necessity of *applying* the universal law to the particular instance and in such a way that the application of the law being the unique product of the circumstances is *not* normally capable of being universalized. On the other hand, as against situation ethics which stress the uniqueness of moral decisions, Aquinas repeatedly insists that they must (in order to be moral) be in harmony with the law. As against the extremism of either of the above positions, the Aquinas

32. Against the objection of those who think that a good natural inclination is sufficient of itself to make a prudent man, Aquinas makes this shrewd and immensely practical observation: "The natural inclination to the good of virtue is a kind of *beginning* of virtue; but it is not *perfect* virtue. For the stronger this inclination is, the more perilous it can prove to be, unless it be accompanied by right reason, which rectifies the choice of fitting means toward the due end. Thus, *if a running horse be blind, the faster it runs the more heavily will it fall, and the more grievously will it be hurt.*" *Summa Theologiae* I–II, Q. 58, a. 5, response to the third objection. Italics are my own.

33. *Ibid.* I–II, Q. 57, a. 6c. Another aspect of St. Thomas' doctrine of prudence focuses on the need for *good memory* (a prudent man is one who can draw from the storehouse of his past experience); *circumspection*, which involves close attention to the attendant circumstances of a moral decision; and *foresight*, whereby one can reasonably project into the future consequences of a given line of action. On this last point I quote from my book, *The Betrayal of Wisdom* (Staten Island, New York: Alba House, 1972): "No man knows the future, but insofar as he can surmise the future in its present causes a prudent man can reasonably discern where his actions will lead him, and to do this is to exercise foresight." *Ibid.*, pp. 97–98.

virtue of prudence plays a mediatory role between the universal law and the particular moral decision—thus giving both his ethics and his politics a deep sense of balance and common sense.[34]

Man—Social and Political

Throughout our study of St. Thomas' treatment of the virtues we have more than hinted at their intrinsically social and political implications. At this point, however, I want to highlight in a yet more explicit manner Aquinas' teaching on the intrinsically social and political nature of man. A key text that reveals his fundamental thinking along these lines appears in his *Commentary on the Nichomachean Ethics,* I, 1:

> Now, it should be understood that, since man is naturally a social animal as needing for his life many things that he cannot prepare for himself by himself, he is naturally part of some group from which he receives help in living well. And he needs help for two things. First of all, for those things that are necessary for life . . . and in this he is aided by the *domestic* group of which he is a part . . . . In another way, man is helped by a group of which he is a part *toward perfect sufficiency of life,* namely, in order that man not only live, but *live well,* having everything that suffices for living. And in this respect man is helped by the *civil* group, of which he makes up a part, not only as to corporeal things . . . but *also as to moral things,* insofar, namely, as through the public power, unruly youths are coerced by the fear of punishment whom paternal admonition does not succeed in correcting.[35]

In this text Aquinas sets the stage of his entire social-political philosophy with the following as his basic assumptions: (1) Man is by *nature,* and not merely *accidentally,* social and political. (2) He is born into a domestic society (into a home) which supplies him with his basic biological and some of his educational needs. (3) The domestic society, basic as it is, is nonetheless imperfect in that it cannot supply all that is

34. Need we say that such a balance is lacking in much of society today insofar as many persons, reacting against the rigid formalism of an earlier ethics, feel the necessity of acting on impulse alone and as a result get carried off into contradictory currents of activity and commitment.

35. *Ut supra.* Italics are my own. Thus also: "Man is intended by nature to form a society. The group life is necessary, for if left to himself in an isolated state, the individual would be deprived of the material, the intellectual guidance, and moral support necessary for the attainment of happiness." Maurice De Wulf, *Medieval Philosophy* (Cambridge: Harvard University Press, 1926), p. 117.

necessary either for life itself or for the good (or perfect) life. (4) Man needs the life of civil society in order not only to live, but to live well—that is, as a full human being, both physically and morally.

Relative to the last of the above-mentioned points it is crucial to an understanding of Aquinas' theory of civil society and the state that the preservation of order and morality is one of its essential functions. Although man might be able for a while to survive physically in a society which operates according to the "law of the jungle," it is impossible for him to do so indefinitely as a man—unless there be a true public order which is one of law and morality. Indeed, the whole idea of law (in any sense) is that it is an ordinance of reason ordained for the common good and promulgated by the proper authority.[36] Any one of these fundamental notions (be it that of law, the common good, the inherently social and political nature of man and so on) is, of course, such that it could be developed indefinitely—although it is to be understood that they are all closely intertwined with each other.

Take, for example, Aquinas' notion of the common good. Too often today we think of the common good (the *bonum commune*) only in material terms as a kind of collection of the material resources of the state. Yet, such a notion is quite inadequate from a Thomistic point of view and no modern interpreter of the thought of Aquinas has more pointedly expressed the real meaning of Aquinas' conception than does Jacques Maritain. After indicating that the end of society is the good of the community as such, Maritain goes on to show that the common good is neither a mere collection of private goods nor is it in any sense reducible to the good of some whole or unit which sacrifices the parts to itself. In other words, no theory of the "common good" which sacrifices the rights of individuals to that of the state could ever be interpreted as being a rightful one—for the simple reason that the common good includes among other things the rights of individuals themselves:

36. *See* Aquinas' entire treatment of the subject of law, especially in his *Summa Theologiae* I–II, Questions 90 through 97. Note, for example: "Law is a kind of direction or measure for human activity through which a person is led to do something or held back." ("... Regula est et mensura actuum, secundum quam inducitur aliquis ad agendu mvel ab agendo retrahitur." *Ibid.*, Q. 90, a. 1c.) Again: "Law is nothing but a dictate of practical reason (dictamen practicae rationis) issued by a sovereign who governs a complete community." *Ibid.*, Q. 91, a. 1c. On the subject of natural law, *see* Question 91, article 2: "... This sharing in the eternal law by intelligent creatures is what we call 'natural law'." Also: "Even nonrational creatures share in the eternal reason in their own way. The way, however, for rational creatures is intelligent and reasonable; that is why their sharing is called law properly speaking, since law ... belongs to mind." *Ibid.*, response to the third objection. *See also* Question 94 in its entirety.

Thus that which constitutes the common good of political society is not only: the collection of public commodities and services—the roads, ports, schools, etc., which the organization of common life presupposes; a sound fiscal condition of the state and its military power; the body of just laws, good customs and wise institutions, which provide the nation with its structure; the heritage of its great historical remembrances, its symbols and its glories, its living traditions and cultural treasures. The common good includes all of these and something much more besides—something more profound, more concrete and more human . . . . It includes the sum . . . of all the civil conscience, political virtues and sense of right and liberty, of all the activity, material prosperity and spiritual riches, of unconsciously operative hereditary wisdom, of moral rectitude, justice, friendship, happiness, virtue and heroism in the individual lives of its members. For these things all are, in a certain measure, *communicable* and so revert to each member helping him to perfect his life and liberty of person. They all constitute the good human life of the multitude.[37]

Although there is some need to apologize for the length of this quote it is a notable expression in modern terms of what Aquinas considers to be the *finality*, the basic teleological orientation, of civil society which is or should be at least equally dedicated to the support of moral, cultural, and intellectual values as well to the material prosperity of its citizens. As Maritain further expresses the point, the common good is "not only a system of advantages and utilities but also a rectitude of life, an end, a good in itself . . . or a *bonum honestum* . . . [it] is something ethically good."[38]

This being so, a particular need exists to show the mistakenness within the peculiarly modern notion of the state of conceiving everything in terms of utility alone. The *bonum honestum* is that which is good in and of itself, an ideal worthy of attainment, regardless of any utilitarian motive that may predominate in its pursuit, and such a good is placed in contrast to that which is merely a *bonum utile*. Thus nothing within a Thomistic theory of the state or of civil society could be more mistaken than to regard such fundamental realities as law, virtue, the common good, public order, leisure, culture, and so on as having no more than a pragmatic, utilitarian value that would mistakenly place all human goods within the category of the *bonum utile*.

Much in line with this same idea of the common good as having an

37. J. Maritain, *The Person and the Common Good*, translated by J. Fitzgerald (Notre Dame, Indiana: University of Notre Dame Press, 1966), pp. 52–53.
38. *Ibid.*

essentially qualitative dimension is Aquinas' conception of the *kind* of whole or unit that the state actually is. On the one hand, it is true that the good of the state (as representing one major aspect of civil society taken as a whole) supersedes that of the individual—*but never to the point of sacrificing for the good of the state those very natural rights of the individual which it is the state's duty to defend and protect*. In other words, the individual person never literally "belongs" to the state as though he were the property of the state, if only for the reason that he exists *sui juris*—in his own right and as having a dignity, a certain inviolability with which nothing may interfere either morally or legally. On the other hand, the state too is a certain kind of whole, but as St. Thomas painstakingly points out, "this whole, which is the civic multitude . . . has solely a *unity of order*, according to which it is not something absolutely one. Therefore a part of this whole may have an operation that is not the operation of the whole, as a soldier in an army has an activity that is not of the whole army."[39]

This capital text not only indicates *that* the individual has a certain autonomy that cannot be ascribed to the state, but the *reason why*: civil society, taken as a whole, and as culminating in the authority of the state, has only a *relative* principle of unity that gives rise to its constitution or makeup—a unity of order, and *not*, as is the case with the individual person, a unity of *substance* or *being*. Whereas each individual person is by his very essence or nature a substance, the state—as a product of human "art" and reason—is through and through an "artifact"—which is to say, a man-made product.[40]

As De Wulf rightly points out in explaining Aquinas' conception of the individual in relation to the state:

> The collectivity . . . is not a substance as such . . . but rather an external unity . . . each member of the group retains his value as a person, but his activities are united or rather coordinated with that of the others. This is especially true of the state "which compromises

39. *Commentary on Nichomachean Ethics*, I, 1.
40. This last statement in no way conflicts with the earlier statement which asserts that man is essentially a political being. Although man by his nature or essence needs to organize himself into a political society, it does not follow that the peculiar form of society that he invents through his reason is itself a natural being, a substance or a quasi-organism. This being so, it is inherently dangerous to regard the state as a kind of organism—since whatever element of unity it has is such that it derives from man as its inventor. One other point: the very possibility of a variety of forms of government within civil society indicates the fact that no one of them is literally a "natural" form of government—in spite of the fact that some of them are more harmoniously ordered to the good of man's nature as such, particularly those that respect human intelligence and freedom.

108

many persons, whose varied activities combine to produce its well being." (*Summa Theologiae* I–II, Q. 9;, a. 1).[41]

Thus, although Aquinas' conception of political society was hardly that of a democratic society as we know it today, it was one which nonetheless guaranteed, in terms of a theory of natural law and natural rights,[42] the relative autonomy of the individual as person *vis à vis* the rights of the state. Accordingly, the idea of a modern totalitarian state that controls the lives of its citizens to the point of absorbing those rights within its all-encompassing eugenic, economic, and social designs, would have been for Aquinas an ethical monstrosity in direct violation both of the eternal and of the natural law.[43]

41. M. De Wulf, *Medieval Philosophy* (Cambridge: Harvard University Press, 1926), p. 118. The last point of the above quote from St. Thomas highlights the necessity of each member and of the various organizations within the state to contribute to the common good. Just as it is incumbent, therefore, for the state to insure the rights of individuals for the sake of the common good, *so too the individuals themselves and the various "parts" of the body politic need to do their part to promote the common good of the whole.* Neither a philosophy of extreme or "rugged" individualism nor one of a bland collectivism (that denies the rights of individuals) can lead to a condition of justice within the state. A truly just society is one in which both the rights of individuals and the common good of the whole are kept in a delicate state of balance with each other. This being so, it is unfair to interpret Aquinas' political theory as giving the palm either to a *laissez faire* notion of government and economics which leans to the right or that of a Marxist collectivism which is that of the radical left.

42. On the subject of natural right, *see* Leo Strauss' superbly scholarly and compact treatment of the subject in his *Natural Right and History* (Chicago: University of Chicago Press, 1968). This book is a compendium of lectures sponsored by the Charles R. Walgreen Foundation, given at the University of Chicago, October, 1949.

43. For the concept of natural law, I again refer the reader to Question 94 of the *Summa Theologiae* I–II, as well as to a variety of excellent modern commentaries and discussions on the subject. *See, for example,* G. B. Phelan, "Law and Morality" in *Progress In Philosophy* (Milwaukee: Bruce Publishing Co., 1955), pp. 177–97; E. T. Gelinas, "Right and Law in St. Thomas," *Proceedings of The American Catholic Philosophical Association,* Vol. XLV (1971), pp. 130–38. The main thesis of this author (with which I agree) is the following: ". . . Man's rational awareness of what must be done to acquire true happiness is the very essence of the thomistic notion of natural law. Instinct, whether in man or brute, is infrarational and as such is not part of the natural law." *Ibid.,* p. 131. Again: "Only to the extent that . . . inclinations are ruled by reason are they said to belong to natural law. In other words, the use of (biological) 'laws' under the rule of reason would alone lift them from the amoral area . . . to the realm of the moral. Of themselves, they do not belong to the natural law. What is biologically 'right' . . . is not the norm for the moral rectitude of an action . . . the same inclination in man is right (i.e., morally right) only insofar as sensuality is subject to reason." *Ibid.,* p. 134. For a critical examination of St. Thomas' natural law theory, *see* D. J. O'Connor, *Aquinas and Natural Law* (New York: St. Martin's Press, 1968).

On the Government of Rulers

In his excellent book, *Political Thought in the Middle Ages*, J. B. Morall makes some very sage and accurate comments concerning Aquinas' political philosophy:

> To treat St. Thomas' political theory as a separate field of study is almost as artificial as it is to treat St. Augustine's as such. Thomas wrote no complete treatise on politics, apart from a commentary on Aristotle's *Politics*, and his remarks on the social and political order have to be extracted from the main structure of his philosophical and theological works. . . . [His] political comments are contained primarily in his great *Summa Theologiae* and to a secondary degree in his *De Regimine Principum*, a manual on the art of government for the King of Cyprus . . . . Nowhere is St. Thomas, for all his aristotelianism, *ex professo* a political thinker.[44]

Be this as it may, St. Thomas does provide the modern reader with some salutary and fairly comprehensive thoughts on the subject of politics and the "government of rulers."[45] He is concerned, for example, with such large and crucially important topics as the origin of authority in the state, the need to administer justice according to the demands of natural law and right reason, the necessity of making positive laws that accord with the nature of man and the end of political authority, the abuse of authority, and so on. Yet, whatever the topic under consideration, the central concern of St. Thomas is to show that the whole of the political order, as including both rulers and ruled is one

44. J. B. Morrall, *Political Thought In Medieval Times* (New York: Harper Torchbacks, 1962), pp. 70–71.

45. For two excellent books of selections on the political thought of Aquinas, note the following: Dino Bigongiari, *The Political Ideas of St. Thomas Aquinas* (New York: Hafner Publishing Co., 1965). This book contains a fine Introduction by the editor which covers such topics as "The State as a Natural Order," "Public Power," and "Plenitudo Potestatis" ("The Fullness of Power"); *see* pp. vii to xxxvii. Selections include various texts from *Summa Theologiae* (translation of the English Dominican Province) and from the *De Regimine Principum* (the Phelan-Eschmann translation published under the title *On Kingship, To the King of Cyprus* by the Pontifical Institute of Medieval Studies, Toronto, Canada). A second superb book of selections is A. P. D'Entreves' *Aquinas' Selected Political Writings*, translated by J. Dawson (Oxford: Basil Blackwell, 1948). The latter book of selections contains a yet wider range of the political writings of St. Thomas as including, for example, selections from the *Commentary on the Sentences of Peter Lombard, On the Nichomachean Ethics*, and *On the Politics of Aristotle*. Note also in the editor's introduction remarks concerning the authenticity of *De Regimine Principum*, as well as those pertaining to the relative value and importance from a political point of view of the other works.

110

that is subject in different ways to the providence of God and the demands of the eternal law as we have explained it in the first part of this paper. In fact, natural law—which is to say, law as knowable by the light of human reason—is itself a participation in the eternal law and the objective mainspring for establishing a system of justice within the state. Accordingly, nothing is more important—for purposes of making natural law something more than a philosopher's dream—than that the positive laws of the state be both justly drawn and justly administered by the ruler.[46] No ruler of the state exists in his high office for the sake of his own personal aggrandizement *but only for the sake of the common good whose purpose it is to secure both the rights and needs—of whatever sort—of the citizens of the state.* The key, in other words, to St. Thomas' concept of the "governance of rulers" is his understanding of the end or purpose of authority within the state: authority should never be divorced from its basic teleological concept which is that of its service to the common good.

Also, for St. Thomas, all power within the state is such that *ultimately it has a divine origin* (even as it ultimately has a divine *goal*), but *this does not mean that the state as existing in any particular form is itself divine.* For St. Thomas all political societies are products of human "art" in the sense that it is man himself who through his power of reason fashions them according to his needs.[47] Thus:

46. Note also St. Thomas' insistence on the need of human laws being ultimately conformed to the eternal law: "A human law has the force of law to the extent that it falls in with right reason; as such it derives from the eternal law. To the extent that it falls away from right reason it is called a wicked law: as such it has the quality of an abuse of law, rather than of law." *Summa Theologiae* I–II, Q. 93, a. 3, response to the second objection. Note also: ". . . As St. Augustine says in the *De Libero Arbitrio* (I, 5): 'A law which is not just cannot be called a law. Such laws do not in consequence oblige in conscience except on occasion to avoid scandal and disorder." *Ibid.*, Q. 96, a. 5c. As to the contemporary relevance of these quotes, consider, for example, whether draft laws are morally valid in the case of an unjust war.

47. Being also a political "realist" in the best sense of the term, St. Thomas recognizes that these "needs" are not always either as "natural" or "ideal" as they might be, as many of them are often contrived and even immoral. Thus: "Political ideals will vary according to men's views on human destiny. Those who are persuaded that the purpose of life is pleasure, or power, or honor, will reckon that state to be best arranged in which they can live comfortably, or acquire great wealth, or achieve great power and lord it over man. *Others who think that the crowning good of virtue is the purpose of our present life will want an arrangement under which men can live virtuously and peaceably together.* In short, political judgment will be settled by the sort of life a man expects and proposes to lead by living in community." *Commentary, II Politics,* lecture 1. Italics are my own, and they are used to indicate Aquinas' view as to the right order of things.

The human reason has at its disposal, not merely the means [i.e., physical and biological means like food, and so on], but *how lives should be lived when ruled by reason* [i.e., the means of securing an ethical, cultural, and political life]. Consequently the scientific genetic method applies alike when reason would construct a ship from timbers or a house from stone and *when it would organize a single community from many individuals.*[48]

That St. Thomas leaves no doubt of his own high regard for civil society (not just *any* civil society, but one that is based on justice and natural law) as the supreme product and accomplishment of human practical reason is evidenced through the following words of his *Commentary on Aristotle's Politics:*

[Though] there are different arrangements in community groups, . . . the final and most perfect is the political fellowship which provides all that is needful for civilized life. *As men are more important than the means they use, so also is the political group superior to any other grouping the human reason can know about or constitute.*[49]

This last statement should not be taken as a doctrine of state absolutism but only as one that emphasizes the more basic importance of the state over any other artificial group within the state.[50] Accordingly also, although St. Thomas has the highest regard for ethics as political science, he nonetheless considers this science as being of less than absolute importance: "Always remember that political science is supreme, not unconditionally, but *in relation to the other practical sciences* which deal with human matters and whose purposes are social."[51]

48. *Commentary, I Politics,* lecture 1 taken from Gilby's translation in *Philosophical Texts, ut supra.* Italics are my own.

49. *Ibid.* Italics are my own. Coming from a theologian, this last statement might offhand appear rather surprising as it gives the impression that the state is superior even to the Church. However it is not the author's intent to make such a comparison, since he is explicitly talking about the state *as a product of human practical reason*—whereas, generally speaking, he regards the Church as having been directly founded by Christ himself and therefore as having a divine origin that cannot be attributed in the same way to the state. *Pari passu* Aquinas is opposed to any view of civil authority such as the divine right of kings' theory on the grounds that, although *all* authority at least remotely proceeds from a divine source, nonetheless the authority of any temporal ruler is such that it comes to him either directly through the consent of the governed or indirectly through some group of men who are vicariously responsible to the needs of the community as its "vice-regents."

50. Note the word "artificial"—so as to allow for the yet more basic importance of the family as the fundamental *natural* unit of society.

51. *Commentary, I Ethics,* lecture 2 as translated in Gilby's *Philosophical Texts, ut supra.* Italics are my own.

On the more practical side of St. Thomas' politics, there is no doubt as to his general preference for one-man or monarchical rule, *provided that the ruler be just and wise*. However, this is for him only a matter of preference, and St. Thomas allows that there is no one form of government that is best in any absolute sense. That form of government is best which under given conditions of time, place, and cultural conditions best serves the needs of the people in terms of the common good. Thus, for example, he agrees with Augustine who in Chapter I, 6 of his *De Libero Arbitrio* (P.L. 32, 1229) expresses the view that in a civil society which is basically pervaded by a sense of responsibility and moderation the people should be allowed to choose their own magistrates. Otherwise, that is, in a situation where a society is basically corrupt and degenerate, the choice should be reserved to a few men who are both good and wise.[52]

Much in agreement with Plato, Aquinas insists that although monarchy is generally the best form of government, the corruption of the best is the worst kind of corruption (*corruptio optimi pessima*)—as when monarchy degenerates into tyranny. Thus,

> If an unjust government is carried on by one man alone who seeks his own benefit from his rule and not the good of the multitude subject to him, such a ruler is called a "tyrant"—a word derived from "strength"—because he oppresses by might instead of ruling by justice.[53]

Although St. Thomas is generally moderate in the tone of his philosophical and theological writings, in Chapter XI of his *De Regimine Principum* he spares no words either as to the evil that results from the rule of the tyrant or as to the kind of punishment that should be meted out to him:

> If a man who robs or enslaves or kills another merits the maximum penalty, . . . how much more reason have we for saying that a tyrant deserves the most terrible penalties; when he has despoiled everyone, and everywhere trampled on the liberties of all, and taken life at a mere whim? To this we must add that men of this sort rarely repent: puffed up with pride, . . . hardened by adulation, it is seldom indeed that they are capable of due reparation . . . . We must further consider, besides their impenitence, the fact that they begin to think legitimate all that they have been able to do with impunity and without en-

52. *Summa Theologiae* I–II, Q. 97, a. 1c.
53. *De Regimine Principum*, Chapter 1, translated by Phelan-Eshmann, as in Bigongiari's selections in *The Political Ideas of St. Thomas Aquinas, ut supra*.

countering resistance, so that far from seeking to repair the evil they have done, they make a evil a habit and an example which leads their successors to even more flagrant wrongdoing. . . .[54]

Among the other evils of the rule of the tyrant St. Thomas mentions their greed, their manner of threatening not only the life and limb of their subordinates but even their spiritual growth, the decline of virtue within the state, the destruction of human liberty, and so on. Needless to say, whatever the form of government, the only sound one for Aquinas is that which promotes the common good, and no essentially unjust form of government like that of a tyrannical rule is either capable or desirous of accomplishing this supremely important task.

On the more positive side we may note the strength of St. Thomas' position which would combine in one form of government (that is, a "mixed" government) the elements of monarchical, aristocratic, and democratic rule:

> Two points should be observed concerning the healthy constitu-
> tion of a state or nation. One is that *all should play a responsible role
> in the governing*: this ensures peace, and the arrangement is liked
> and maintained by all. The other concerns the type of government;
> on this head the best arrangement for a state or government is for
> one [person] to be placed in command, presiding by authority over
> all, while under him are others with administrative powers, *yet for
> the rulers to belong to all because they are elected by all from all*.
> This is the best form of policy, being partly kingdom, since there is
> one [person] at the head of all; partly aristocracy, insofar as a number
> of persons are set in authority; partly democracy, *that is, government
> by the people, insofar as the rulers can be chosen from the people, and
> the people have the right to choose their rulers*.[55]

Appreciative as St. Thomas is of the principle of self-rule which lies at the basis of a democratic state, he is equally wise in assessing the dangers of an excessive freedom which fails to consider the basic limitations of democratic rights. Thus,

54. *Ibid.*, Chapter 11.
55. *Summa Theologiae* I–II, Q. 105, a. 1c. In this superb text, St. Thomas, in spite of his preference for one-man rule, does provide a democratic basis of government. Too, we should note his reservations concerning the very form of government for which he habitually expresses his preference *as a kind of ideal*: "A monarchy is the best form of government for a people, *provided it does not become corrupt*. But because of the wide powers conferred upon a king, it is easy for a monarchy to degenerate into a tyranny, unless there is perfect virtue in the one into whose hands such power is given . . . but perfect virtue is found in few persons." *Ibid.*, response to the second objection.

Even in a democratic state, where the whole people exercise power, rights are not absolute but *relative* though from the equal liberty of all subjects under the law the state may be described as predominantly egalitarian. The statutes passed by a democracy may be just, not because they reach pure and perfect justice, but because they fit the purpose of the regime.[56]

Conclusion

At whichever point we conclude this paper it is of necessity a somewhat arbitrary one since each of its leading topics is capable of indefinite expansion and application. However, we have seen enough of the fabric of St. Thomas' ethical-political philosophy to discern that it is all of one piece in the sense that St. Thomas wisely refuses, even as did Plato and Aristotle before him, to separate ethics and politics. We have seen further that the whole of his ethics and politics is governed by his world view of the universal law of providence in which man fully shares by the use of his reason and by conducting himself in conformity with natural law. Natural law, however, is not for St. Thomas a kind of *deus ex machina* or an automatic device that solves all the riddles of human existence. In fact, human intelligence is challenged to the highest degree in learning how to apply the precepts of natural law to the contingencies of human existence—a task that is accomplished by the cultivation on all levels (individual, domestic, political) of the virtue of prudence. Through prudence, the man of practical wisdom directs human actions to their overall end or purpose, and it is this virtue above all the rest that is of particular importance in the life of the ruler. However, prudence by itself is insufficient as it is necessary *through the use of prudence* to formulate just laws within the state and to *administer* them in a manner that is both fair and just, for only in this way will the citizens of the state enjoy true liberty and thus be set on the path of achieving their final goal which is ultimately happiness in God. Although it is not the purpose of the state to lead man directly to this goal (since that is the proper function of the spiritual authority of the Church), it should nonetheless promote those conditions of peace, virtue, and prosperity that will help man to lead a full human life and thus to prepare the way.

Such, then, is the general perspective of Aquinas' ethical-social-political philosophy whose applications to modern life are legion. Throughout this paper I have hinted in various contexts as to what

56. *Commentary, V Ethics*, lecture 2 in Gilby's *Philosophical Texts, ut supra.* Italics are my own.

these applications might be, leaving the reader, however, to draw his own implications. Needless to say, the general ideal of society as Aquinas envisions it is one that stands in stark contrast to the dominant pragmatism of Western society as we know it today.

One might, of course, speculate as to the reason or reasons why modern society represents such a vast departure from this "medieval" ideal, and no doubt there are a variety of reasons. However, I should like to submit as one that is dominant the fact that the very concepts of "natural law" and "common good" have been lost sight of. The modern state—be it one that exists to the right or the left—is not too far from the prototype of that of Thrasymachus as portrayed in the *Republic*, where the ideal of might as right is defended. The intellectualism of Aquinas has been replaced by a voluntaristic conception of authority and the notion of natural law has been replaced by the positivist notion of law as the expression (and nothing more than that) of the will of the lawmaker. Little wonder (in the absence of such basic conceptions as mark the "classical" view of Aquinas) that modern democracy, great as its ideal might be, has degenerated, if not into the tyranny of one-man rule, into the tyranny of a huge bureaucratic system that essentially frustrates the will of the people.

Especially in light of the Watergate experiences of recent times, has it begun to dawn on the people of one of the world's greatest democracies that not even that government which is regarded as the modern cradle of democracy is immune to the incursions of the kind of tyrannical rule that Aquinas so eloquently speaks of in both of his *Summas*, in his commentaries on Aristotle's *Ethics* and *Politics*, and in his *De Regimine Principum*. Indeed, if the reading of this article has served no other purpose than to take the reader back to the sources (ancient, medieval, and classical modern) that deal with the problem of man in society, and if he becomes convinced as a result that the older wisdom of the West is no mere archeological expedition, then the purpose of this article will have been amply fulfilled. While the date of this article corresponds to the 700th anniversary of the death of St. Thomas, it is more than reasonable to assume that given some measure of reflection on human experience and history, 1974 will serve only as a starting point for a return to a political wisdom (whatever its date) which is "ever ancient, ever new."

CHAPTER 6.

The Continuing Significance of St. Bonaventure and St. Thomas

RALPH M. McINERNY

They were both born in Italy; each joined a new mendicant order; they were elected to professorial chairs at the University of Paris on the same day; both died in 1274. Bonaventure and Thomas Aquinas, Franciscan and Dominican, respectively; both canonized by the Church—saints. One could go on enumerating the similarities between these two men; indeed, one is inclined to do so when he thinks of them across that gap of seven hundred years. Whatever their differences, they can seem all but indistinguishable to the twentieth-century eye. Whether read in translation or in the original Latin (and to the classically trained, medieval Latin itself will seem an odd patois), their works may seem only historical curiosities, contents of a time capsule, alien. The assumption of this paper is that Bonaventure and Aquinas can be read as Plato and Aristotle and Kant are read, namely, as contributors to on-going philosophizing, as voices to be taken into account. I shall concentrate on what my two medievals had to say about knowing and believing.

The topic is chosen not simply because it provides a good sample of their thought but also because it bears directly on what has seemed to many the basic impediment to learning anything philosophical from the medievals. Plato and Aristotle are distant from us in time, but their works are recognizably philosophical (as if our criteria for applying the adjective did not derive in large part from these two); Descartes and Kant may have been Christians, but that fact does not seem to animate their philosophy. The medievals, on the other hand, got things all mixed up. After all, were not Bonaventure and Aquinas Masters of Theology? Would we go to Barth for philosophy? Histories of philosophy have been written which ignore the Middle Ages, the historian assuring us that no genuine philosophy was being done during those centuries: was not being done because it could not be done, and the impossibility is one of principle. Medieval thought is permeated by faith and fervor; one who shares the religious beliefs of such authors may be interested in them, but the benefits he gains are not philosophical ones. Proscribing, censorship, ecclesiastical authority, the preeminence of theology—these features of the times indicate that prejudices against medieval thought are not unfounded. What is perhaps not sufficiently known is that the oppositions and distinctions which medievals are said not to have grasped or honored are among the most discussed topics in their writings. Any run-of-the-mill medieval author will provide you with a complex and subtle discussion of the differences between knowing and believing, philosophy and theology. Indeed, speaking historically, our way of making such distinctions is part of an unacknowledged medieval inheritance.

So much for protreptic and mild polemic. My main hope is to remove impediments to following a discussion of some medieval ways of distinguishing knowing and believing as well as such corollaries of the distinction as the differentiation of philosophy from theology. My emphasis is on Thomas Aquinas, but Bonaventure makes an important and essential contribution to what I have to say.

On several occasions St. Thomas makes use of the phrase *praeambula fidei*, preambles to faith, in speaking of those truths about God which are accessible to unaided human reason. It is well known that Thomas thought that pagan philosophers, notably Aristotle, had succeeded in proving that God exists and had come to knowledge of some of His attributes. These are the matters that "preambles of faith" is meant to cover, and it can be seen that a discussion of it can hope to cast some light on the notion of Natural or Philosophical Theology, the culminating concern of metaphysics in its traditional form.[1]

An attempt to make sense of Thomas on preambles of faith is as good a way as any to exhibit the complex and profound infrastructure which sustains a clear surface meaning. I am suggesting, again, that we have here a good sample of how Thomas works. The further significance, for our purposes, is clear. Thomas Aquinas, Christian and priest, had believed from his mother's knee in the truth of the proposition, "There is a God." The proposition is an object of faith. Yet he is saying that, for philosophers, it was an object of knowledge. More, he himself fashioned what he considered to be valid and cogent proofs of God's existence.

---

1. The central difficulty addressed in this paper is expressed in the first objection in article two of Question One of the *Summa theologiae, Pars prima*. In being asked whether it is demonstrable that God exists, the objector points out that it is of faith that God exists, what is believed cannot be known or demonstrated, ergo. In his reply, Thomas distinguishes articles of faith from matters which are preambles to those articles and counts among the latter that God exists. The phrase is already present in such an early work as Thomas' Exposition of the *De trinitate* of Boethius (q. 2, a. 3, resp., ed. Decker, p. 94).

That must mean that the proposition, "There is a God," is at once an object of knowing and believing. Nonetheless, Thomas insists that one cannot simultaneously know and believe the same truth. Bonaventure seems to be of another mind on the matter. The view of Aquinas suggests some strange overlap of knowledge and religious belief and of philosophy and theology. Is he caught in an inconsistency? He thinks not. The preambles of faith are the locus of clarification.

In order to go on, indeed, in order to grasp the incompatibility mentioned above, we must be clear on the difference between knowing and believing, a difference Thomas establishes with reference to yet other mental acts and/or states.[2] One knows or believes that something or other is true, so we can express the object of these mental acts by the usual variable for a proposition, p. Thus, what we want to know from Aquinas is the difference between "knowing that p" and "believing that p." In discussing it, as I have suggested, Aquinas will add to the mix such mental acts as "thinking (opining) that p" and "doubting that p."

(1) When I know that p, p is true and $-p$ is false.

Values for p are such that they are either true or false. Knowledge is had when there is a determination of the truth of p. St. Thomas' way of discussing the matter derives from the following elementary consideration. If p is either true or false, then if p is true, $-p$ is false, and if $-p$ is true, p is false. Thus, Thomas will say that, in knowing, the mind assents determinately to one side of a contradiction. To know that p is to know that p is true and that $-p$ is false.

St. Thomas finds it useful to make a subdistinction between knowing as *intelligere* (*intellectus*) and knowing as *scire* (*scientia*). In a narrow and proper sense of knowing, our determination of the truth of p is inferred from the truth of other propositions; to know something in this strong sense is mediated cognition. For Thomas, *scire* and *scientia* are tied to syllogism, so much so that the object of science or knowledge is the conclusion of a demonstrative syllogism which is known to be true because it follows validly from true premises. Not every proposition to which the mind gives determinate assent is mediate, however. St. Thomas also allows for immediate or self-evident truths, that is, propositions such that the connection between predicate and subject is not

2. I develop the distinctions between knowing, opining, doubting, and believing with particular reference to *Quaestio disputata de veritate*, q. 14, aa. 1 & 2. This seems to me the most concise and in several ways most precise expression given of matters which are put forth again and again in various works of Thomas. Of course, the treatise on faith in the *Summa theologiae*, Pars secunda secundae, is an obvious parallel text, but there Thomas permits himself a more spacious although no less orderly discussion.

grasped through a middle term but is grasped as soon as one knows the meaning of the constitutive terms. Needless to say, for Thomas, knowing what the terms mean is not simply a matter of knowing how we use words. When I know that the whole is greater than its part, this is not as such to know a truth about "whole" and "part," but about wholes and parts. But that is a long story.

(2) When I think (opine) that *p*, -*p* may be true.

Opinion embraces a proposition whose contradictory might turn out to be true. Needless to say, there are certain values of *p*, such that *p* and -*p* are simultaneously true. Some men have beards and some men do not have beards. In such a case, *p* and -*p* are not contradictories. We have contradictory propositions only when, if *p* is true -*p* is false and if -*p* is true *p* is false. When we think or opine that *p*, we do not with confidence reject -*p* as false. In the case of knowledge, whether it bears on self-evident truths or, in the proper sense of the term, on mediated or inferred truths, the contradictory is determinately excluded. The object of opinion may also be arrived at as a conclusion from premises but the premises do not express evidence which is conclusive for the truth of *p*. No doubt there are degrees of opinion. Perhaps that is why doubt can be associated with opinion.

(3) When I doubt that *p*, I think that -*p*.

To think that -*p* is not to be completely sure of -*p* and thus to fear that *p* may be true. But this is not to say that in thinking that -*p*, I equally think that *p*. If the evidence indicates the truth of -*p*, I will doubt that *p*. To hold that *p* v. -*p* is not to have an opinion. A jury that reported that the accused is either innocent or guilty as charged has not delivered a verdict.

Perhaps this can suffice as a first sketch of "knowing that *p*," "thinking that *p*," and "doubting that *p*." For our purposes, knowing and opining are the important mental acts or states, since it is with reference to them that Aquinas will express what he means by "believing that *p*." It may be well to say here once and for all that Aquinas, like ourselves, often uses "thinking" or "opining" to express what is here defined as "knowing." So, too, he will often use "knowing" and "believing" interchangeably, and the same can be said of "believing" and "thinking." What we have just witnessed is his assigning definite meanings to these terms for a specific purpose. In doing this, he appeals to the way we talk, and he is guided by ordinary Latin as we should be by ordinary English, but he is not engaged in an effort to say what these terms ordinarily or always mean for all purposes. The fact that "think" and "know" and "believe" can be interchangeable in some contexts is, while true, not helpful when our purpose is to assign meanings to the terms which will distinguish *different* mental acts. It is the mental acts which differ even though we may sometimes speak of them in one way and sometimes in another. Once the difference between the mental acts is clarified, "know," "think," and "believe" can be given more or less technical meanings which will cause the remarks in which they occur to diverge slightly from ordinary talk.

Given his quasi-technical accounts of "knowing that p" and "thinking that p," St. Thomas adds his account of "believing that p."

(4) We believe that p is true and that $-p$ is false on the basis of authority.

Given his definitions, Aquinas will argue for the following theses:

(5) It is impossible for a person simultaneously to know that p and to believe that p.

(6) It is impossible for a person simultaneously to think that p and to believe that p.

If "believing that p" differs from both "knowing that p" and "thinking that p," belief nonetheless bears similarities to both knowledge and opinion. In common with "knowing that p," "believing that p" totally excludes the possibility that $-p$ might be true. To believe that p is true is to have no doubt that $-p$ is false. In common with "thinking that p," "believing that p" is not grounded on conclusive evidence of the truth of p. For purposes of completeness, we can add that "believing that p" is unlike the "knowing that p" which occurs when the value of p is a self-evident truth.

If like "knowing that p," "believing that p" entails the falsity of $-p$, this is not because the believed p follows validly from true premises, nor is it because, as with "thinking that p," the preponderance of the evidence indicates the truth of p. I may think that Notre Dame will defeat Alabama; I may think that bald-headed males are more amorous than their hirsute confreres and in both cases marshal evidence to support my claim, even as I agree that one who maintains the contradictory is not willfully opaque, ignorant, obtuse, and so on. In the case of belief in the Trinity or Incarnation, it makes little sense to say that the evidence seems to indicate their truth. One's assent to the truth of p and rejection of $-p$ as false is explained, in the case of belief, not by conclusive evidence, but by reliance on authority.

It will be seen that, in this discussion, St. Thomas is concerned to clarify the nature of religious belief. Nonetheless, we can get some help toward understanding the contrasts he is drawing by appealing to instances of belief which involve one man's trusting another. Let us say that, in conversation with you, I assert that *p* and you ask me why I say that. I answer that my Uncle Seymour told me that *p*. My assertion that *p* resides on the fact that I trust my Uncle Seymour. I did not mention him when I asserted that *p*, in the scenario I have in mind, but, if pressed, I would admit to the avuncular source of my confidence. Let us assign a value to *p*. Let us imagine that what I said was, "People who lay their ungloved hands on hot stoves get burned." When you ask why I say this, I bring in Uncle Seymour. Now I could be the empirical type and arrange for a hot stove and lay my ungloved hand on it. More cautiously, I could secrete myself in a broom closet and observe the reactions of others when they lay their ungloved hands on the hot stove. Then, when you ask me why I say that *p*, I need no longer bring in Uncle Seymour as explanation of my assertion. This situation can be generalized. The student of science, the specialist in a given area of science, may assert that *p* where the value of *p* is some scientific result and yet reply, when pressed, that he asserts that *p* because Professor Seymour said so or because he has just read an article in the *"Alaskan Journal of Tropical Studies."* In such cases, believing that *p* is in principle replaceable by knowing that *p*. Trust or faith here, acceptance of *p* as true on the basis of authority, need not be a terminal mental act but only a stage on the way to knowledge. *Oportet addiscentem credere*, Aristotle said; the student must trust or believe, but not because that is his goal. His goal is knowledge.[3]

In the case of religious belief, believing that *p* is the acceptance of the truth of *p* (and the falsity of -*p*) on the authority of another and is, moreover, a mental state or attitude toward *p* that cannot, at least in this life, be replaced by knowing that *p*. When the believer asserts that there is a Trinity of Persons in the Godhead or that Christ is both God and man, the basis of his conviction is the authority of God. As St. Thomas put it, the formality under which assent is given to one side of a contradiction in the act of faith is *Deus revelans*: God revealing.[4]

The distinction between knowledge and opinion on the one hand, and faith on the other, seems to come down to a distinction between evidence and motive. When I assert a self-evident truth, the evidence is intrinsic to the judgment made. When I assert a mediated truth, as I do in both knowledge and opinion, the grounds or evidence for what I

3. The Aristotelian maxim is from *On Sophistical Refutations* (161b3) and is often quoted by Thomas. For a citation of it in connection with our concerns here, *see ST*, IIaIIae, q. 2, a. 3, c.

4. *Cf. ST*, Ia, q. 1, a. 3, c.

assert is found elsewhere than in the proposition I assert. The elsewhere, of course, is the premises from which the proposition is derived as a conclusion. If the evidence, whether conclusive or probable, of the conclusion are said to be extrinsic to it, it is not extrinsic in the same way or to the same degree as is the motive for assent to a believed truth. My knowledge that the internal angles of a scalene triangle add up to 180° may be necessarily derived from other truths, and my opinion that life exists only on earth may be grounded on a great deal of information, but in both cases there is a connection between the proposition known or opined and the propositions which express the evidence from which it is concluded. One need only think of the relation between the terms of a syllogism. In the case of belief, the motivation for assent, namely the trustworthiness of the authority, is quite extrinsic to the content of the proposition believed.

As has already been seen, we can distinguish two sorts of belief, the ordinary kind in which we take another's word that something is the case and the extraordinary kind where our authority is God revealing. Let us use subscripts to distinguish them.

(4a) When I believe$_1$ that p, I accept p as true on someone's say-so, but I can in principle establish the truth or probability of p and thus dispense with the appeal to someone's say-so.

(4b) When I believe$_2$ that p, I accept p as true on God's authority, and I cannot, in this life, replace my dependence on his authority with knowing that p.

Values of p as the object of believing$_2$ would be such truths as "There are three persons in one divine nature," and "Christ has both a human and a divine nature." In believing$_1$, so long as my mental state is one of belief, I have a motive for assenting to or accepting a proposition as true, but I have no evidence for it. The same is true of believing$_2$ with the addendum that my condition is not even in principle corrigible or alterable in this life.

In the case of believing$_1$, when attention is shifted from the content of the proposition believed to be true to our motive for thinking so, we can of course inquire into our justification for thinking that so-and-so is trustworthy. It might be said that in trusting Uncle Seymour on the truth of p, we are believing both p and Uncle Seymour. St. Thomas will say that we believe someone and something. This does not preclude our having reasons for trusting our source. In the case of believing$_1$, that justification may be found in the fact that on many occasions in the past Uncle Seymour has told me things which I took on his say-so and subsequently found to be true on the basis of evidence. Thus, the scientist might give as justification for his taking as true what he reads in a learned journal the fact that often in the past he has established to his own satisfaction the truth of its reports. In believing$_1$, taking another's word can thus be seen to be an expedient, a *pis aller*, a corrigible condition, since in any given instance of it p can in principle be known. Of course, it would be practically impossible to prove out every claim accepted on the word of others in the scientific community, say, but this is a practical and not a theoretical constraint.[5]

The veracity or trustworthiness of the authority on whom we rely for our conviction of the truth of p when we believe$_2$ that p is a different matter. It would not do to suggest that, since divine revelation has proved its veracity in the case of the Trinity, I am justified in relying on it in the case of the Incarnation, or vice versa. All instances of believing$_2$ are on the same footing. We may wish to circumvent the problem in one fell swoop by saying that God is truth or God is veracious, and that therefore it makes no sense to doubt what God says. While any human witness is fallible and may mislead, God, being what and who He is, cannot deceive. The assertion that God can neither deceive nor be deceived enters into the Catechism's Act of Faith, and this suggests that the veracity of God is an object of faith, is itself within the circle of faith, and thus could not be external to it as a truth which might prop up or support the truths constitutive of faith. We cannot show that faith is reasonable by invoking what is itself an object of faith.[6]

These distinctions and clarifications of what St. Thomas means by knowing, opining, doubting, believing$_1$ and believing$_2$ are a necessary

5. It is a simplification for present purposes to regard believing$_1$ as bearing on claims like scientific ones which are amenable to a proving procedure. Of course, it is anything but clear that all or most or indeed many of the humanly most significant examples of taking another's word fall under this rubric. I have addressed myself elsewhere to this issue. See my presidential address to the American Catholic Philosophical Association, Proceedings, 1972, "Philosophizing in Faith."

6. Signs, wonders, and miracles will occur to us as possible antecedents to the assent of faith; one who produces signs and wonders, who works miracles, gains our attention to what he says and his miracles may serve as motives for accepting as true the claims that he makes about himself. I am proceeding on the assumption that while a miracle or sign is observable by both the believer$_2$ and the unbeliever, the two interpret differently what they see. The believer interprets them as works of God, the unbeliever does not. My reasons are complex but can be suggested by the following: crowds saw and heard and witnessed Christ, yet not everyone believed. Of those who saw and heard and did not believe, we cannot say that witnessing works they recognized as divine they did not recognize them as divine. The reader is reminded of what Joannes Climacus says in *Philosophical Fragments*. For Thomas on this, *cf.* IIaIIae, q. 6, a. 1.

preliminary to understanding his conception of *praeambula fidei*. That phrase, we have seen, is taken to cover those truths about God which can be known by men independently of revelation. In other words, the truths covered by the phrase "preambles of faith" are possible objects of knowledge. The truths of faith are not, of course, possible objects of knowledge in this life.

Let us recall the thesis set down earlier that is taken to follow from the clarifications we have been examining.

(5) It is impossible for a person simultaneously to know that p and to believe that p.

Given the distinction that we have made between kinds or sorts of believing, this thesis can be construed in a number of ways. While the thesis as expressed in (5) is true of both believing$_1$ and believing$_2$, it can be restated with the types of believing in mind.

(5a) It is impossible for the same person simultaneously to know that p and to believe$_1$ that p.

The point of this restatement is to bring out the fact that objects of believing$_1$ can also be objects of knowledge. The teacher may know an astronomical truth and the pupil believe$_1$ the same truth on the teacher's say-so, the two mental acts bearing on the same truth at the same time. And, of course, the same person can believe$_1$ that p at t_1 and know that p at t_2. The thesis expressed in (5) can be restated for believing$_2$ as follows:

(5b) It is impossible for any man in this life to know that p if p is an object of believing$_2$.

This is the strongest form of the thesis. With it before us, let us select the following as examples of preambles of faith: there is a God, there is only one God. It is not our concern to give, if it could be given, a complete inventory of the preambles of faith. The ones we have mentioned are more than enough for our purposes.

We have already suggested the way to distinguish preambles of faith from truths of faith. The former are those truths about God which men can *know* in reliance on their natural powers alone; the latter are those truths God has revealed about himself, which could not otherwise be assented to, and which are accepted as true because He has revealed them, never because we know them to be true.[7] Relying on *Romans* I,

7. Of course, we can know what is to be or is believed in the sense of being able to identify the claims, propositions, and so on. Not to know what one believes in this weak sense of know is a possible human condition, and it is easy to imagine situations describable in that way. Nonetheless, this recognition-knowledge is not

19–20, St. Thomas, like many others before and after him, held that men can, from the visible things of this world, come to knowledge of the invisible things of God. At the very least, this means that the world provides evidence of the existence of God. Indeed, St. Thomas took Aristotle's proof from motion to be valid and conclusive. Thus, "God exists" can be a value for p in the schema: I know that p. But is not "God exists" an obvious value for p in the schema: I believe$_2$ that p? There would be no difficulty here if we were faced only with the thesis as expressed in (5), since that could be construed as in (5a). But is it not (5b) that comes into play, thus rendering St. Thomas' position incoherent?

To see how St. Thomas avoids contradicting himself, we must allow that the faith of the religious believer comprises both believing$_1$ and believing$_2$. That is, it seems to be a common state of affairs for the religious believer to accept on the authority of divine revelation both truths about God which are in principle knowable and truths about God which are not knowable in this life. One brought up in the faith would believe that there is a God, that there is only one God, that He is intelligent, etc., where the *et cetera* is meant to embrace any or all preambles of faith. But preambles of faith are by definition knowable in principle. Nor would the believer normally distinguish these from such other believed truths as the Trinity and Incarnation. But, if God's existence can be known, and if a believer comes to know it, he can no longer be said to believe this truth. If he knows that there is only one God, he can no longer believe it. The doctrine of preambles of faith comes down to this: among the things which the religious person believes there are some truths which are really objects of believing$_1$, although the bulk of the objects of his faith are objects of believing$_2$. Only the latter are *de fide*, of faith in the strict sense; the former are preambles of faith since they need not be believed, being in principle knowable. When this is recognized, there is no inconsistency in saying that one who first believed that there is a God comes to know that there is a God. (5a) applies to this situation; (5b) applies only to what is *de fide*.[8]

There are, of course, other ways of handling the difficulty. It might be said that the proposition "God exists" does not have the same valence when it is the conclusion of a demonstration, and thus a philosophical achievement, that it has when it is an object of faith. Pascal distin-

what is being denied when it is said that the believer does not know (understand) the propositions to which he gives his assent.

8. *See* note 1 above.

guished the God of the philosophers from the God of Abraham and Isaac, suggesting that the God who is known is not the God who is believed.[9] The position may perhaps be developed in this way. It is clear from St. Thomas' presentation of the Five Ways that he does not think that "God exists" would ever as such appear as the conclusion of a proof. After each proof, he observes that what has been shown to exist is what we mean by God.[10] What functions as the subject of the conclusions of the proofs is a given description of God, e.g., first unmoved mover, first efficient cause, and so on. It is this variety of descriptions which makes a plurality of proofs of God's existence possible. We can now put the Pascalian point in this way: God is known to exist or is proved to exist under descriptions which differ from those self-descriptions God provides in revelation. Of particular interest for our purposes, one is reminded of Bonaventure's contention that one can simultaneously know and believe the same truth, for example, that God is one, a contention which seems to conflict with (5), (5a), and (5b). His subsequent exposition nonetheless makes clear that the object of simultaneous knowledge and belief is not really the identical object. If one can know and believe at the same time that God is one, Bonaventure interprets this to mean that one knows that there is not a plurality of gods and believes that the one God is a Trinity of Persons. Since "one" is taken in several senses, "there is one God" is not the same proposition as known and as believed.

We have interpreted Pascal's point about the God of the philosophers and the God of Abraham to mean that God is known under some descriptions and believed under quite different descriptions. We then suggest that Bonaventure's point about the simultaneity of knowledge and belief is a version of this, since the divine unity turns out to be two different descriptions insofar as it is an object of knowledge and an object of faith. While there is nothing wrong with this position as stated, it is questionable whether some of its assumptions are true. If we should say, for example, that the philosopher can come to know God as first cause (and Thomists who think Thomas granted Aristotle too much in interpreting the Stagyrite as proving this, themselves go on to say that Thomas himself fashioned such a philosophical proof), it is difficult to see how knowing God in this way differs from what believers have believed of Him since their mother's knee. True, there are those who suggest that creation is a theological concept, apparently meaning by that, that apart from faith one could not grasp the total

9. See Romano Guardini, *Pascal For Our Time* (New York: 1966), pp. 113 ff. and J. H. Broome, *Pascal* (New York: 1966), pp. 75 ff.

10. *Cf. ST*, Ia, q. 2, a. 3, c.

dependence of other things on God suggested by the phrase *creatio ex nihilo*.[11] While this contention, if true, would preserve the radical difference between knowledge and faith, the difference seems bought at too high a price. Indeed, it seems headed in the direction of saying that whatever philosophers claim to know about God is false.

Bonaventure's position is actually compatible with our own earlier suggestion to the effect that religious faith incorporates both believing$_1$ and believing$_2$ and that it is therefore possible that some believers who believed$_1$ that God is one, later came to know that God is one and it is the same truth which was once believed and later known.[12] That God is one in the sense that there cannot be a plurality of gods is a truth which could first be believed$_1$ and later known. There is, as it happens, an analogous situation in the moral order. Many truths of practice have been revealed which in principle need not have been because they are naturally knowable by men. One need only utter the phrase "Natural Law" to make the point, adding St. Thomas' view that precepts of the decalogue are natural law precepts.[13] God told men that murder is wrong, although this is something men can see apart from revelation. Moreover, it must be the same truth which is believed$_1$, accepted on the authority of God, and later known and thus no longer believed. While it is often misunderstood, the Catholic position on Natural Law is quite clear. Precepts which have been revealed and thus can be accepted on the authority of God revealing are, so far as their content goes, such that the divine authority is not necessary to grasp their truth. God told men that murder is wrong but it is not wrong because He said so and thus in insisting on the precept one is not demanding religious faith of everyone. Now, the same sort of thing would seem to be true of descriptions of God. We would make a shambles of the concept of precepts of faith if we should say that the objects of believing$_1$ differ from what men can in principle know. For this reason, the Pascalian point, unless it is restricted to believing$_2$, is unacceptable. With respect to some descriptions of God, the God of the philosophers and the God of believers (as believing$_1$) is the same. Of course none of this in any

11. Thomas himself seems to hold, as in *De aeternitate mundi contra murmurantes*, that it is creation in time and not creation *ex nihilo* which distinguishes the believer's understanding of the way in which the divine causality is exercised.

12. I have attempted a discussion of Bonaventure on this point, along with the major texts, which are found in his Commentary on the *Sentences* of Peter Lombard, in *Philosophy From St. Augustine to Ockham, A History of Western Philosophy*, Vol. 2, (Notre Dame: 1970), pp. 259–67.

13. The point I am making here relies on putting together a number of texts from *ST*, IaIIae, namely, q. 90, q. 94 and q. 100, aa. 1–3.

way contests the truth that the vast majority of the objects of religious faith are objects of believing$_2$.

The animus against the concept of preambles of faith, particularly as it is associated with the traditional natural theology, arises from the apparent connotations of the term "preamble." St. Thomas chose this term because he felt it expressed well the general maxim that grace presupposes nature, builds on it, and does not destroy it. He does not, of course, mean to suggest that the community of believers consists by and large of people who, having first acquired knowledge of God, that He is, is one, and so on, come to believe$_2$ truths that He has revealed of Himself. The fact is that revelation includes things knowable in principle as well as things that can never be known in this life and that ordinary religious believers do not as a rule distinguish the one kind of truth from the other. But if the concept of preambles of faith does not entail that natural theology is chronologically prior to faith in the strong sense, it does mean that some of the truths to which we have given our religious assent are knowable *in via* and thus can be seen to be objects of believing$_1$. Our condition relative to them is not unlike the belief of the scientist that certain claims he himself has not verified are nonetheless true. As for St. Thomas, it is abundantly clear that his contention that the objects of believing$_1$ can be replaced by knowledge in no way commits him to the thesis that, in this life, the objects of believing$_2$ can be known to be true.

Now we approach the most delicate matter of all. If some of the truths to which we have given the assent of faith can be known, what is the importance of this knowledge, when had, for those truths which are and remain *de fide*? It will be appreciated how easily the claim that men can come to know truths about God which they previously believed can be misunderstood if we have not distinguished believing$_1$ from believing$_2$. And yet, do we not want to say that believing$_2$ is affected in some way by the success of the program suggested by the phrase *praeambula fidei*? No doubt, but let us be clear as to how it is not affected. The fact that we can come to know a truth that we previously believed$_1$, for example, that there is a God, that He is one, in no way diminishes the necessity that the believer, be he wise or simple, accept as true, solely on the authority of God, the Trinity, the Incarnation, the Resurrection, the Forgiveness of Sins, and so forth. The most accomplished metaphysician is in exactly the same condition as the most unsophisticated sacristan with respect to what is *de fide*. What is more, and this is of crucial importance, knowing that there is a God, knowing that He is one, knowing any of the preambles of faith, does not entail any of the *de fide* truths. That accomplished metaphysician we mentioned may very well be a nonbeliever; his knowledge that there is a God does not compel him to believe₂ what God has revealed of Himself. It was Kierkegaard's unfounded fear that natural theology commits one to this absurdity. The mental state of believing₂ remains anomolous; in it the intellect is rendered captive in that its assent is gained, not because of the clarity and intelligibility, for us, of what is proposed, but by the promise of an eternal happiness if we will but restrain that hubris which demands that whatever is intelligible be seen to be so by us.[14] By definition, the believer does not know, does not understand, the truths to which he gives his assent. Is religious faith thereby irrational?

A negative answer to the question reposes on such considerations as the following. First, the believer believes that the truths to which he gives his assent are intelligible and make sense even though he does not see that they do. It is a false description of religious faith to say that it is the teleological acceptance of manifest nonsense. Second, the notion of preambles of faith gives indirect support to this conviction. If some of the things God has revealed can be known to be true, this suggests that the rest is intelligible, although it is not the case that what is and remains *de fide* can in any way be deduced or known from what is understood. And, of course, it is basic to faith that the believer hold that eventually, *in patria*, faith will give way to seeing. Again, no proponent of the absurdity or irrationality of faith has, to my knowledge, maintained that one truth of faith contradicts another truth of faith. Thus, internally to the body of believed truths, the basic demand of rationality, the principle of contradiction, is honored. St. Thomas held further that nothing we know to be true can be in conflict with what we believe₂ to be true. If this is itself a truth of faith, it is also a program for the theological task, or at least a part of it. Indeed, we can find here one of the motives for the interest the community of believers has always taken in the task of natural theology. It is not that a proof of God's existence is direct support for truths of faith in the strong sense. But if God is known to exist, one impediment to accepting that He has revealed truths about Himself is removed. Nor could the community of believers ignore claims that it is nonsense to assert that there is a God. Believed₂ truths cannot be derived from truths known about God but, negatively, if it were known that there is not a God, believed₂ truths

14. In the paper cited in note 5, I have argued for the compatibility of the views of Thomas and the Kierkegaard of the *Philosophical Fragments*. Knowing the truth of the proposition that there is a God in no way commits one to the acceptance of truths about God which cannot be known, but if we knew the falsity of the proposition that there is a God, this would be devastating for all truths of faith.

would *eo ipso* be destroyed. A God known not to exist cannot reveal truths about Himself.

As for attacks on faith proper, St. Thomas maintained that the theologian could either refute the attack or, if that be impossible in the strong sense of refutation, he can at least show that the attack is not compelling, necessary, cogent. This seems to allow for cases where evidence would tell against a truth of faith, although the evidence would not be conclusive.[15] I think it is clear that none of these activities would make any sense if religious faith were indifferent to rationality, if it were indeed a leap into the manifestly absurd entailing a general devaluation of reason and logic. Nevertheless, there is much truth in the Kierkegaardian description of faith as a crucifixion of the understanding. Faith is humbling for one who honors the demands of reason as themselves deriving from God and yet assents to truths which he does not understand but holds to be in themselves understandable.

Our discussion has suggested the all but identical views of Aquinas and Bonaventure and, so far as the matters discussed go, in the way we have discussed them, this is accurate enough. Nonetheless, it would be misleading in the extreme to leave the impression that Thomas and Bonaventure were of one mind on the relation between faith and philosophy. It has been said that the Bonaventure of the Commentary on the *Sentences* of Peter Lombard, an early work which reflects the saint's brief university career, must not be identified with the man who, shortly after receiving his chair of theology at Paris, was elected Master General of the Franciscans and eventually became a cardinal.[16] The writings of Bonaventure which reflect his pastoral concerns see Aristotle not as the apotheosis of natural reason but as an antagonist, an enemy of the faith. Were we to take three positions which were either held by Aristotle or thought to be held by him, namely, the eternity of the world, the unicity of the agent intellect with its consequences for personal immortality and, finally, the description of the divine knowledge as thought thinking itself with the implication that God knows only Himself with obvious consequences for the notion of Providence, we could exhibit the differences between Thomas and Bonaventure in a

15. On these various tasks of the theologian, *see,* for example, the exposition of Boethius' *de trinitate*, q. 2, a. 3.

16. For the many and diverse differences between Thomas and Bonaventure, *see* Fernand Van Steenberghen, *La philosophie au XIIIe siecle,* (Louvain: 1966); Joseph Ratzinger, *The Theology of History in St Bonaventure,* (Chicago: 1971), pp. 119 ff. Here, as in so many other instances, the work of Gilson has been seminal. A recent expression of his interpretation can be found in *History of Christian Philosophy in the Middle Ages* (New York: 1955). My own modest contribution may be found in the work cited in note 12.

striking way. Thomas, confronted with such difficulties, is first of all concerned to see what exactly, behind the filigree of the Islamic commentaries, Aristotle meant and, given that, whether it is indeed inimical to the faith. On all three points, he ends with an interpretation of Aristotle which makes the great pagan philosopher compatible with Christian belief. I myself reject the view that he was either consciously or actually reading Aristotle wrong when he did this. Others, alas, hold that Aristotle did not say what Thomas takes him to say on these matters and that Thomas either knew this but interpreted him "genially" or did not know it and was simply wrong. A surprising number of Thomas' defenders portray him as wrenching texts to his own fleeting advantage. My reading of the *De unitate intellectus* and the *De aeternitate mundi* prevents me from finding this devious explicator.

Bonaventure, confronted with the three difficulties mentioned, is quite willing to assume that Aristotle said what he is said to have said and that what he said is incompatible with the faith. From this enormous difference in antecedent attitude toward the most impressive representative of philosophy known to the two men flow a great many other differences. But that is another and lengthy discussion.

CHAPTER 7.

Bonaventure and Aquinas on the Divine Being as Infinite

LEO SWEENEY, S.J.

Rather recently Patterson Brown suggested that one aspect of Bonaventure's conception of infinity anticipates Georg Cantor's definition.[1] When disproving the world to be eternal, the medieval author "pointed out that, if the world were infinitely old, then there would have been an infinite number of annual revolutions of the sun around the ecliptic. But during each such period there occur (roughly) twelve revolutions of the moon, i.e., lunar months or lunations. Thus there would be one infinity which was twelve times another"—and this, he concludes, is impossible. What this disproof amounts to in modern terms is, if one views a revolution of the sun as the period between successive vernal equinoxes, this *reductio ad absurdum*: "If there could be an infinite set of past lunations, then clearly it could be put in a one-to-one correspondence with a proper sub-set of itself—viz., with the set of past lunar months during which vernal equinoxes occurred. But this consequence is preposterous; no set could be so correlated with its own sub-set. Therefore the set of past lunar months cannot be infinite, and the world must have had a beginning." (*Ibid.*)

Other than this brief note, as well as an occasional other paper,[2] Bonaventure's theory of infinity has not received much attention since the

1. "A Medieval Analysis of Infinity," *Journal of History of Philosophy* [hereafter: *JHP*], 3 (1965), pp. 242–43. Bonaventure's text is *In II Sent.*, d. 1, p. 1, a. 1, qu. 2 (Quaracchi ed. minor, II, 13).

2. See E. Magrini, "Dio perfezione infinita in S. Bonaventura," *Incontri Bonaventuriani*, 5 (1969), pp. 55–79. There is no lack of recent studies on topics other than infinity in Bonaventure, as one can realize by checking the apposite volumes of *Bulletin de théologie ancienne et médiévale, Bulletin Signalétique* (Section 519), *Bibliographie de philosophie* and the like. Also see L.-J. Bataillon, "Bulletin d'histoire des doctrines médiévales," *Revue de sciences philosophiques et théologiques* [hereafter: *RSPT*], 56 (1972), pp. 511–20; F. Van Steenberghen, *La philosophie au XIIIe siècle* (Louvain: Publications Universitaires, 1966), pp. 190–271. On this last, see G. H. M. Therán, "Van Steenberghen y su reajuste de la filosofia del s. XIII," *Sapientia* 23 (1968), pp. 59–66; M.-B. Petene, "La philosophie de S. Bonaventure," *Études Franciscaines*, 20 (1970), pp. 335–42.

mid-sixties. Nor did it in previous years, as Jean Prather made clear in 1964. "Papers have been contributed in regard to Bonaventure's doctrine in psychology, epistemology, mystical theology, metaphysics, aesthetics, Trinitarian theology, causality, and some of the divine attributes. Some writings compare Bonaventure with other theologians and another series takes up his life and writings." But "no previous work has been devoted solely to his notion of divine infinity."[3]

Hence, this topic seems apt for discussion during the septicentenary anniversary of his death in 1274, especially if we also study it in Thomas Aquinas, who died the same year.[4] This discussion will consist of four parts, in the first two of which we shall briefly reconstruct the intellectual climate within which they wrote by noting what some of their immediate predecessors thought on the subject. Then we shall turn to Bonaventure's and next to Aquinas' first major treatises: their commentaries on the *Sentences* of Peter Lombard.[5]

In authors just prior to those two we can detect at least three attitudes on the question of whether the divine being is itself infinite. Someone

3. "Divine Infinity in Selected Texts from Saint Bonaventure's Commentary on the *Sentences*," (St. Louis University: M.A. Thesis, 1964), p. 20. See the helpful bibliography, pp. 150–65.

4. Among the rather rare papers on infinity in Aquinas, one may note these: J. Owens, "Aquinas on Infinite Regress," *Mind*, 71 (1962), pp. 244–46; O. Argerami, "El infinito actual en Santo Tomás," *Sapientia*, 26 (1971), pp. 217–32. As with Bonaventure, so with Thomas: abundant studies have recently appeared on other topics, as will be seen by checking the bibliographic volumes listed above, note 2, to which should be added: *Bulletin Thomiste*, 12 (1968), pp. 209–435; L.-J. Bataillon, *RSPT*, 57 (1973), pp. 143–55.

5. Controversies exist on when the two wrote their commentaries. For a survey of opinions on Bonaventure, *see* J. F. Quinn, "Chronology of St. Bonaventure (1217–1257)," *FS*, 32 (1972), pp. 168–86, who argues that Bonaventure was reading the *Sentences* as a *baccalaurius sententiarius* during 1251–53 and was officially recognized as a doctor of theology in 1254 (his formal recognition, however, was delayed until Oct. 23, 1257). In this chronology he would presumably have been composing his Commentary on the *Sentences* between 1251 and 1254. Others date its composition between 1250 and 1252—*see* I. C. Brady, "Bonaventure," *New Catholic Encyclopedia* [hereafter: NCE], 2 (1967), p. 658; A. Wolter, "Bonaventure," *Encyclopedia of Philosophy* [hereafter: EP], 1 (1967), p. 340. J. Guy Bougerol, *Introduction to the Works of Bonaventure* (Patterson, N.J.: St. Anthony Guild Press, 1964), p. 101, thinks (with L. Lemmens and J.-Fr. Bonnefoy) that "in writing these *Commentaries*, Bonaventure did not follow the numerical order of the Books themselves. . . . [It is] more than probable that Bonaventure began with the fourth *Book of Sentences* and ended with the third."

A problem in determining the date of composition of Thomas' commentary is the possibility that parts of it may have existed also in a revised version. At the end of a long paper, "Textes inédits de S. Thomas. Les premières rédactions du *Scriptum Super Tertium Sententiarum*," *RSPT*, 45 (1961), pp. 201–28; 46 (1962), pp. 445–

like Hugh of St. Cher, who taught theology at the University of Paris from 1231 to 1235, seems totally unaware of the doctrine. As Richard McCaslin has established from studying nine sections of his Commentary on Lombard's *Sentences* (written *ca.* 1231),[6] the Dominican theologian infrequently and only briefly mentions infinity. Twice he makes it equivalent to incomprehensibility, once to eternity, once to divine supremacy. Nowhere does he apply it to God's essence.[7] One can only conclude that "Hugh simply did not see infinity [of the divine being] as a problem; and, not seeing the question, he never formulated an answer."[8]

---

62 and 609–28, P.-M. Gils concluded that "nous ignorons quand cette oeuvre a été publiée." For each passage we must ask whether it is "la première redaction ou de la revision" (*ibid.*, p. 627; for a history of the controversy, *see* G. F. Rossi, "S. Tommaso ha fatto due edizioni del 'Commento alle Sentenze'?" *Divus Thomas*, 65 [1962], pp. 412–15). But it seems best to agree with W. A. Wallace and J. A. Weisheipl ("Thomas Aquinas," NCE, 14 [1967], pp. 103–104 and 111) that Thomas became a *baccalaurius sententiarius* in the Fall of 1252 and a doctor of theology in 1256 (with formal recognition, together with Bonaventure, on Oct. 23, 1257), and that he elaborated his Commentary on the *Sentences* between 1252 and 1256 while lecturing at Paris. Also see G. E. Ponferrada, "Tomás de Aquino en la Universidad de Paris," *Sapientia*, 26 (1971), pp. 233–62.

At any rate, Bonaventure's Commentary preceded Aquinas' by at least two years, whatever their respective dates may be. *Cf. also* J. Weisheipl, *Friar Thomas d'Aquino: His Life, Thought and Works* (New York: Doubleday, 1974), pp. 67–80, 94–95.

6. "Divine Infinity in Some Texts of Hugh of Saint Cher," *The Modern Schoolman* [hereafter: *TMS*], 42 (1964), pp. 47–69. The sections studied are Book I, distinctions 2, 8, 9, 19, 31, 34 and 43; Book III, distinctions 13 and 14. Peter Lombard composed his *Libri Sententiarum* sometime between 1155 and 1158—*see Magistri Petri Lombardi Sententiae in IV Libris Distinctae* (3rd ed.; Grottaferrata: Editiones Collegii S. Bonaventurae, 1971), I, i, pp. 117*–29*).

7. McCaslin, *art. cit.*, p. 68. The absence of such an application is what one might expect in the light of the fact that a similar absence occurs in Lombard's own texts. The latter uses "infinity" solely to express God's omnipotence, eternity, omniscience, incomprehensibility, and the identity in nature of the three divine persons. *See* L. Sweeney, S.J., "Divine Infinity: 1150–1250," *TMS*, 35 (1957), pp. 41–47; *idem*, "Lombard, Augustine and Infinity," *Manuscripta*, 2 (1958), pp. 24–40. Lombard himself was in good company, since Augustine, his main mentor, restricts infinity to God's incomprehensibiilty, power, and freedom from place, as well as to the absence of distinction between the three persons. *See ibid.*, pp. 26–31.

8. *Ibid.*, *art. cit.*, p. 69. The same conclusion seems valid for Robert Grosseteste in his *Commentarius in VIII Libros Physicorum Aristotelis*, written *ca.* 1228–32. God "est infinitum quia ipsum est et potencie et sapiencie et bonitatis infinite et secundum quod Plato et Augustinus loquuntur de numero: numerus et sapiencia idem sunt et sapiencia Dei numerus est infinitus et infinite sunt ydee sive raciones rerum in

135

Infinity for a second group of authors was definitely a problem, encountered when they discussed the beatific vision of God by the saints in heaven. In the course of this discussion they felt obliged to deny that God's being was infinite.[9] For instance, Guerric of Saint-Quentin, who taught at the University of Paris from 1233 to 1242, was asked in a *quaestio quodlibetalis*, presumably held there and rather recently transcribed by B.-G. Guyot,[10] whether the divine essence will be seen by the blessed in heaven (I, 1: "Quaerebatur primo si videbitur divina essentia"). Yes, he replied, although it will be seen not as essence but as power, which alone is directly related to knowledge (I, 83–85:

sapiencia divina" (R. C. Dales' edition [Boulder: University of Colorado Press, 1963], p. 54; also see *ibid.*, p. 69).

9. One can understand their quandary better if he recalls that in 1241 the Bishop of Paris (William of Auvergne; d. 1249) condemned the proposition that in heaven neither men nor angels see the divine essence itself: "Primus [error], quod divina essentia in se nec ab homine nec ab angelo videbitur. Hunc errorem reprobamus . . . . Firmiter autem credimus et asserimus, quod Deus in sua essentia vel substantia videbitur ab angelis et omnibus sanctis et videtur ab animabus glorificatis" (H. Denifle and E. Chatelain, *Chartularium Universitatis Parisiensis* [Paris, 1889–97], I, 170). That condemnation says nothing of infinity but it was influential on the doctrine nonetheless. At least one reason which renders the blessed in heaven incapable of seeing the divine being itself was (so some maintained) its infinity, which prevents its being comprehended and seen. But, if according to the condemnation of 1241, "God in his essence or substance" is seen by the angels and the blessed, then one perhaps should infer that God's essence is finite—the position we are now considering.

On that condemnation see the following informative studies, each of which lists other helpful references: M.-D. Chenu, "Le dernier avatar de la théologie orientale en Occident au XIIIe siècle," *Mélanges A. Pelzer* (Louvain: Éditions de l'Institut Supérieur de Philosophie, 1947), pp. 159 sqq.; H.-F. Dondaine, "L'objet et le 'medium' de la vision béatifique chez les théologiens du XIIIe siècle," *Recherches de théologie ancienne et médiévale* [hereafter: RTAM], 19 (1952), pp. 60–99; P.-M. de Contenson, "Avicennisme latin et vision de Dieu au début XIIIe siècle," *Archives d'histoire doctrinale et Littéraire du moyen âge* [hereafter: AHDL], 26 (1959), pp. 29–97; idem, "S. Thomas et l'avicennisme latin," *RSPT*, 43 (1959), pp. 3–31; idem, "La théologie de la vision de Dieu au début du XIIIe siècle," *RSPT*, 46 (1962), pp. 409–44; J. M. Alonso, "Estudios teologicos sobre la vision beata. La sintesis pretomista y postomista," *La Ciudad de Dios*, 178 (1965), pp. 5–32. On Hugh of St. Cher's position *re* the beatific vision, *see* H.-F. Dondaine, "Hughes de S. Cher et la condamnation de 1241," *RSPT*, 33 (1949), pp. 170–74: Hugh was among those who prior to 1241 denied the divine essence *as essence* was seen.

10. B.G. Guyot and H.-Fr. Dondaine, "Guerric de Saint-Quentin et la condamnation de 1241," *RSPT*, 44 (1960), pp. 225–42, where Guyot has edited three *quaestiones*, the first running pp. 230–33, the second pp. 233–38, the third pp. 238–41. The editions are preceded by Dondaine's remarks on the doctrines of the *quaestiones* (pp. 227–29). Our references will be to *quaestio* and line, thus: I, 85 = Quaestio prima, line 85.

"Essentia videbitur . . . . Sed non videbitur ut essentia quia essentia non erit ratio intelligendi, sed potentia"). Only the Trinity sees the essence as essence and thus they alone have full vision of it. A human intellect will see the divine essence as power and hence will lack that fullness (I, 99, 104–108: "Videbitur essentia, sed non plene . . . . Non videbitur ut essentia, sed ut virtus. Si videretur ut essentia, quia essentia simplicissima est, videretur plene; unde a quibus videretur ut essentia, videretur plene sicut a Patre et Filio et Spiritu Sancto. Sed dico quod ab humano intellectu videtur ut virtus").[11] But what of the argumentation against even that partial vision based on Damascene's saying that God is infinite in whatever pertains to him? The argument runs thus: what is infinite is incomprehensible; but God is infinite in whatever pertains to him; therefore, he is incomprehensible in whatever pertains to him and, thus, he is not comprehended either fully or partially (I, 64–65: "Item. Damascenus: Deus secundum quodlibet sui est infinitus. Infinitum, incomprehensibile; igitur Deus secundum quodlibet sui est incomprehensibilis, ergo nec plene nec semiplene est comprehensibilis"). Damascene's words on infinity pertain, Guerric responds, to God's power and not to his essence [which accordingly is not infinite].[12] But if his power is infinite, why can it be known? Because when considered as identified with God, who is supremely good and powerful, it is finite and thus intelligible. But if considered with reference to the particular existents [it causes, which are endless], then it too is infinite and thus cannot be known (I, 122–26: "Ad illud 'quodlibet Dei est infinitum est,' solutio: Illa nominant ut virtutem, non ut essentiam. Sed essentia ut virtus potest dupliciter considerari: in ratione universali, sic est finita et sic est intelligibilis; rationes universales sunt quod summe bonus, quod summe potens, etc. Si vero consideretur in ratione particularium, sic sciri non potest").

In the light of Guerric's own rather elliptical words, then, God's essence is not infinite, nor is his power except when described with reference to his innumerable effects.[13] When in the "responsio" of a

11. Not even the soul of Christ sees the divine essence as essence but only as power—see II, 73–81, especially lines 75–76: "Anima Christi . . . videt sive cognoscit essentiam, sed non ut essentiam, quod facit Trinitas."

12. Here and later brackets indicate explications, which the text demands or at least allows.

13. Such a description is through "extrinsic denomination": infinity does not pertain to the power itself but to its effects, which are infinite in number, variety, etc. Such an interpretation is applicable also to texts in Lombard and Augustine (see articles cited above, n. 7), as well as in Aristotle, Plotinus and John Damascene. See L. Sweeney, S.J., "L'infini quantitaif chez Aristote," Revue philosophique de Louvain, 58 (1960), pp. 505–28; idem, "Infinity in Plotinus," Gregorianum, 38

later *quaestio quodlibetalis* he retracted his previous position on the beatific vision,[14] he felt no need to distinguish between essence and power but affirmed simply that "the divine essence is seen in itself . . . . God is beheld in himself, directly in his very substance" (III, 79, 82–83: "Ipsa essentia in se ipsa videbitur . . . . [Deus] videbitur in se ipso, in sua substantia nuda"). He made the distinction, though, in his rejoinder to those objecting that God cannot himself be seen because of his simplicity and infinity (see III, 41 sqq.). Indeed God is, Guerric granted, both simple and infinite. But infinity and simplicity arise from different sources. Simplicity has to do with essence, and thus infinity does not prevent the divine essence as essence from being seen in its entirety. A saint does, then, comprehend the entire essence as essence, but not as power [which is, properly understood, infinite] (III, 165–72: ". . . bene verum est quod Deus simplex est et infinitus, et non ex eadem ratione est infinitas et simplicitas. . . . Unde cum simplicitas sit ex parte essentiae, ex parte illa non erit infinitas; et ideo infinitas non impedit quin essentia in ratione essentiae tota videatur. . . . [Hence, a saint comprehends] totam essentiam in ratione essentiae, non tamen in ratione virtutis").[15]

After this clear indication by Guerric that the divine essence is simple *and finite*,[16] we move to a final and almost opposite position—

(1957), pp. 713–32; *idem*, "John Damascene and Divine Infinity," *New Scholasticism*, 35 (1961), pp. 76–106. On Alexander of Hales and Albert the Great, see below, n. 16.

14. For data on his retraction, *see* Guyot and Dondaine, *art. cit.*, pp. 227–29.

15. *See also* III, 57–60 (italics added): "Infinitas est secundum potentiam et virtutem quia *non potest in tot quin possit in plura*; unde infinitas determinatur in Deo *secundum fluxum ad creaturas*. Essentia de se non dicit fluxum, ergo infinitas ibi non est ex parte essentiae." Divine power is infinite through extrinsic denomination because of its reference to endless creatures; God's essence has no such reference directly and, hence, is not infinite. In Guerric's *quaestio* contained in Codex Vat. Lat. 4245, folio 68rb, infinity occurs only once and concerns divine power: "Quaeritur quomodo ex finitis actibus intelligitur infinita Dei potentia . . . . Dicendum quod homo videns omnia mutabilia non potest sistere donec recurrat ad aliquod immutabile, et videns finitos actus recurrat ad infinitatem, et ad hoc ducitur per imperfectionem creaturarum" (*see* L. Sweeney, "Human Knowledge According to Guerric," *Arts Libéraux et philosophie au moyen âge* [Paris: Vrin, 1969], p. 1129, n. 2).

16. Alexander of Hales in his *Glossa* on the *Sentences* (written ca. 1225) is similar to Guerric in that for him the beatific vision is not of the divine essence *per se* but *per speciem* and infinity merely locates God with reference to creatures, none of which can contain or circumscribe him (*see* Sweeney, "Some Mediaeval Opponents of Divine Infinity," *Mediaeval Studies* [hereafter: *MS*], 19 (1957), pp. 241–42, n. 31; de Contenson, *RSPT*, 46 [1962], pp. 427–29). Albert the Great is even more akin to Guerric in his *Commentary* on the *Sentences* (ca. 1243): although he allows

that of Richard Fishacre, who taught at Oxford from *ca.* 1236 to 1248. True, Richard's view has similarities with Guerric's: he elaborates it while studying the beatific vision; he aligns infinity with simplicity;[17] he centers his discussion on divine power.[18] But doctrinal similarity vanishes when he grounds the compatibility of infinity with simplicity on the freedom of an agent from matter and potency. Let us distinguish, he begins, what is infinite quantitatively from what is infinite virtually (lines 286–87). Let us further distinguish between what is virtually infinite through addition and what is so through separation or elongation from matter, which if present makes an agent's *virtus* be less in act and more in potency (lines 292–300, especially 299–300: "[virtus] elongata ab impedimente et faciente eam in potentia et minus in actu; et hoc est a materia"). Only the last sort is compatible with simplicity, as this consideration discloses. Light, for example, is less powerful when embodied than when not embodied, not because in the latter state any addition is made to light but rather because light is "elongated" from the factor which makes it less powerful. Again, the rational faculty is more powerful than the sensitive, not because it is more composite but because it is less flesh-bound; and the more it withdraws itself from flesh, the more powerful it is with respect to its operation (lines 300–

God to be called infinite with reference to creatures (hence, through extrinsic denomination), he affirms that in one sense he is "the most finite of all his power and in whatever else he is" ("finitione qua finis dicitur finitus, finitissimus omnium Deus et potentia sua et quidquid ipse est"). *See* Sweeney, *MS*, pp. 244–45, nn. 37–40; F. J. Catania, "Divine Infinity in Albert the Great's Commentary on the 'Sentences' of Peter Lombard," *MS* 22 (1960), pp. 27–42; *idem*, "Albert the Great, Boethius, and Divine Infinity," *RTAM*, 28 (1961), pp. 97–114; de Contenson, *RSPT*, 46 (1962), pp. 435–39. On Jean Pagus (whose *In Sententiarum* is dated *ca.* 1243–45), *see* de Contenson, *ibid.*, p. 436, n. 103; *idem*, *AHDL*, p. 81, n. 190; P. Glorieux, "Les annees 1242–1247 a la Faculte de Theologie de Paris," *RTAM*, 29 (1962), 240 sq.

17. See his listing of questions to be discussed in his *Commentary* (written shortly before 1245) on the *Sentences*, I, d. 2, as edited by C. J. Ermatinger, *TMS*, 24 (1958), p. 216, lines 2–6: "Hic de Dei visione in patris quaeratur. Gratia cuius primo quaeritur an Deus sit infinitus; . . . tertio, quomodo se compatiantur infinitas vel numerositas et simplicitas summa"). References will be to lines in this edition, which runs pp. 213–35.

18. *See* L. Sweeney, S. J., and C. J. Ermatinger, "Divine Infinity According to Richard Fishacre," *TMS*, 35 (1958), p. 199 (although God is infinite in power, wisdom, and goodness, the last two presuppose the first), pp. 199–205 (the "infinite distance" argument proves power to be infinite), pp. 206–10 (the blessed soul can see the infinite God because of the soul's own innate power and because of the divine power elevating the soul and actuating its power). The "infinite distance" notion shows up at least once in Guerric too—*see* Guyot and Dondaine, *RSPT*, p. 237 (Qu. II, lines 161–63).

309). This argumentation again is not based on any addition to power (which would mean an increase in composition) but rather on an "elongation" from impediments. The conclusion to be drawn, therefore, is that an increase of power understood in terms of *elongatio ab impedimentis* does not involve greater composition but rather greater simplicity (lines 310–21).

When, then, is an agent's power *infinite* according to the latter sort of increase? Manifestly, when he is absolutely and infinitely removed from impediments and from matter (*propter infinitam elongationem ab impedimentis et a materia*). And such removal and infinity are eminently consonant with simplicity (lines 322–26). God is such an agent. A substance which is completely separated from all else, a being who is simple in himself and who enters into composition with nothing outside, he is virtually infinite in his infinite separation from impediments and matter (lines 327–31: "Quia ergo Deus in se simplex est et carens compositione cum alio, ut sit pars compositi, patet quod est infinitus virtualiter, non propter additiones virtutis factas in infinitum, sed potius quia in infinitum elongatus est ab impedimentis et materia, cum sit substantia omnino separata").[19]

According to that excerpt, Fishacre is aware not merely that the divine power is infinite but that *God Himself* is infinite ("Deus in se ... est infinitus virtualiter"). *He* is infinitely removed from matter because *he* is a completely subsistent substance ("in infinitum elongatus est ... cum sit substantia omnino separata"). True enough, he does not explicitly state that the divine essence or being is infinite, but that statement seems only a step away. It is a step Bonaventure and then Aquinas will both take, as we are about to see. But were they the first? Between the time Fishacre wrote his Commentary on the *Sentences* in the mid-forties and Bonaventure and Aquinas wrote theirs in the fifties, had anyone else explicated the infinity of God's essence?

"Summa Fratris Alexandri"

What of the compilers of the *Summa Theologica* attributed to Alexander of Hales (d. 1245)? Although this did not achieve its final form as published in the Quaracchi edition until *ca.* 1260, it existed in an initial

---

19. The previous two paragraphs are taken from Sweeney and Ermatinger, *TMS*, pp. 203–205. D. E. Dubrule considers Fishacre to have influenced Gerard of Abbeville on infinity in *Quaestio Quodlibetalis*, XIII, (written ca. 1265)—*see* "Gerard of Abbeville ... ," *MS*, 32 (1970), pp. 128–37. For a recent dissertation, *see* R. J. Long, "Problem of Soul in Richard Fishacre's *Commentary* on the *Sentences*," (University of Toronto: Doctoral Dissertation, 1968).

version by 1245.[20] It explicitly asks whether or not the divine essence is infinite and answers affirmatively.[21] But that response can be misleading. The divine essence is infinite but solely with reference to creatures and, thus, through extrinsic denomination. This seems clear if we run through several *sed contra* arguments which the authors of the *Summa* set down and the *solutio* itself.[22]

God's essence is infinite because it is one with His power (*Sed contra* #a, p. 55a), which is infinite because no matter how many created essences it may be present in, it still can be in more (*Sed contra* #b, p. 55a: "[Respectus sunt in essentia] prout intelligitur secundum extensionem, secundum quod dicimus quod se extendit divina essentia in omni esse rerum, sicut sua potentia in omni posse; sed hoc modo essentia est infinita.—Probatio quia potentia eius est infinita: quia non est in tot nec potest esse in tot quin adhuc posset esse in plura; ergo, si similiter non est dicere de divina essentia quod ita sit in essentiis rerum nec possit esse in pluribus, constat quod ipsa est infinita").[23] Again, just as goodness or power is said to be infinite inasmuch as it is the source of all goodness or power and none greater can be conceived, so too that being will be described as infinite which is the source of all being and none greater can be conceived—such is the divine being, which accordingly is infinite (*Sed contra* #c, p. 55b: "Ergo et illud esse dicetur infinitum a quo est omne esse et quo maius excogitari non potest; sed tale est esse divinum; ergo illud est infinitum"). Even if God's essence were not identified with but extended beyond his power, it would still be infinite since God is everywhere and thus can be beyond any place one may think of. Just as a body might be called infinite if it filled and went beyond the entire world, even if these were infinite, so the divine es-

20. That initial version consisted of all of Book I (except perhaps q. 74), besides most of Bk. II and fragments of Bk. III. *See* A. Emmen, "Alexander of Hales," *NCE*, 1 (1967), pp. 296-97; V. Doucet, *Alexandri de Hales Summa Theologica*, Tomus IV: *Prolegomena* (Quaracchi: Collegii S. Bonaventurae, 1948), *passim*; I. Brady, "Alexander of Hales," *EP*, 1 (1967), pp. 73-75. The "authors" of the *Summa* include Alexander himself, John of Rochelle (who is almost certainly responsible for Book I) and others. On an anonymous Commentary on the *Sentences* found in three manuscripts, which is an important source of the *Summa* and which is likely to have been written by John of Rochelle, *see* B. Carra de Vaux Saint-Cyr, "Une source inconnue de la *Summa fratis Alexandri*," *RSPT*, 47 (1963), pp. 571-605.

21. *S.T.*, I, tr. 2, q. 1, c. 1 (Quaracchi ed., p. 54): "Utrum divina essentia sit finita vel infinita." Subsequent references will be to the Quaracchi edition (1924).

22. That they agree with the considerations under "Sed contra" *see ibid.*, ad 3 (p. 57b): "sicut etiam probatum est in rationibus quae sunt ad veram partem."

23. Infinity is in fact defined in *sed contra* #a (p. 55a) as extension beyond what is finite: "Cum infinitum dicat extensionem ultra finitum . . . ."

sence should be called infinite (*Sed contra* #d, p. 55b: "Deus est ubique, nec tantum potest cogitari ubi sit quin adhuc possit dici quod ultra sit. Sicut ergo corpus diceretur infinitum quod totum mundum repleret et ultra, si essent mundi infiniti, ita divina essentia debet dici infinita").[24] Moreover, since God is the goal or final cause of all else, [every created essence is finite as "finalized" by something other than itself but] His essence is infinite [because non-"finalized" by anything outside Himself] (*Sed contra*, #f, p. 55c).[25]

In the *solutio* the same approach is continued. The divine essence is infinite since nowhere in sacred Scripture does one find mention of its finitude. (p. 56a) Consequently, God is infinite in substance (unless one takes "finite" as synonymous with perfection),[26] in accord with John Damascene's view that the best name for God is "He Who is" since "His being is like an infinite and indeterminate sea of substance because it embraces all reality within itself" (*ibid.*).[27] But can one explain that infinity more exactly? Yes, the divine essence is infinite because it is "finalized" by nothing else and yet it "finalizes" all else (see above, note 25). Second, the infinity of the divine essence is completely opposed to finitude: what is finite pertains only to so many and no more, whereas the divine essence is in all else, even if these were infinite (*solutio*, p. 56b–c: "Adhuc [essentia] est infinita, quia habet disparatam dispositionem respectu finitatis: dicimus enim aliquid finitum, cum in tot est quod non potest esse in plura. In Deo autem est dispositio disparata respectu huius, quae est quod divina essentia est in omnibus et extra omnia, et adhuc, si essent infinita, impleret illa").

Essence infinite because it is identified with power; essence infinite

24. Also see *sed contra* #e (p. 55c); *ibid.*, inq. 2, tr. un., q. 5, *resp.*, p. 488c.

25. *Finis* as goal receives much prominence—*see* ad 1 and ad 2 (pp. 56–57). The author of this portion of the *Summa* seems attracted to the idea that while God can be called "infinite" with respect to any extrinsic goal, he is himself "finite" because he is his own *finis*. *See solutio*, p. 56a: "Proprie ergo est dicendum ipsum esse infinitum secundum substantiam et non finitum, nisi dicatur finitum "completum'." One must eliminate, though, from "finitum" any connotations of passivity to prevent God being thought of as perfected—*see ibid.*, ad 2, p. 57a.

26. *See above*, note 25.

27. The quotation is from Damascene's *De Fide Orthodoxa*, I, c. 9 (PG, 94, 835): "... totum enim in se ipso comprehendens habet esse velut quoddam pelagus substantiae infinitum et indeterminatum." What the compiler of the *Summa* appears to intend here is this: God contains an infinite number of creatures (no matter how many created existents there are, there can be still more) and, thus, can himself be termed "infinite" with respect to them. The texts from Damascene, *ibid.*, c. 8, quoted in the *solutio* also and in *sed contra* #h (p. 55d), admit a similar interpretation. Besides my article on Damascene cited above, note 13, also see "John Damascene's 'Infinite Sea of Essence'," *Studia Patristica*, 6 (1962), pp. 294–309.

inasmuch as it is present in an endless number of creatures as their source; essence infinite because not finalized by anything other than itself; substance infinite since it contains innumerable created beings— such is the position found in the *Summa Theologica*. Infinity is predicated of God's essence with reference not to itself so much as to creatures and, hence, through extrinsic denomination (see above, note 13). Nowhere—and this seems especially significant—is an attempt made to ground that infinity in the divine essence's freedom from matter, as had occurred with Fishacre.[28]

If our interpretation is accurate, what may have happened is this. Rejecting Guerric's view which depicted the divine essence as finite,[29] the compilers of the *Summa* affirmed it to be infinite. But unaware of or unimpressed by the metaphysical basis which allowed Fishacre to say God is Himself infinite, they aligned essence with power and computed its infinity in terms of the creatures it causes, contains, and is present in and not in terms of its separation from matter and potency.[30] This last computation Bonaventure and Aquinas will make in approaching the problem.

Bonaventure

In at least two texts Bonaventure analyzes infinity within a context of matter and form.[31] In the first, he is discussing whether the trinity of divine persons might entail the presence in God of a material principle. He notes the attempt of some to prove its presence by arguing that finiteness in creatures comes from form but infiniteness from matter; but everything in God is infinite; therefore, a material principle is present in God.[32] That argument is invalid, he replies, since there are

28. The *Summa* mentions prime matter in ad 5 (p. 57c) but only as that which leads one to acknowledge God's power as its infinite efficient and exemplar cause: "Unde prima materia, quae est infinita in potentia passiva, ducit in potentiam Dei infinitam, . . . in ratione qua ordinatur ad ipsum ut ad efficiens et exemplar." Also *ibid.*, I, p. 1, inq. 1, tr. 1, q. 3, [objectio] 1, p. 53a.

29. On Alexander's own earlier view in his *Glossa* of divine infinity as somewhat similar to Guerric's, *see above*, note 16.

30. For my criticism of a different interpretation of the *Summa, see International Philosophical Quarterly*, 6 (1966), pp. 139–43.

31. J. Prather, *op. cit.*, pp. 22–27, lists 71 texts on the *Sentences* in which Bonaventure mentions or discusses infinity.

32. *In I Sent.*, d. 19, p. 2, a. un., q. 3, *videtur quod* 4, p. 288b: "In rebus creatis finitas a forma venit, sed infinitas a materia; sed omne quod est in Deo, est infinitum; ergo cum Deo maxime conveniat passio consequens principium materiale, maxime competit et ipsum." An attempt to identify matter and God had previously been made by David of Dinant, who together with others was condemned in 1210. *See* P.-M. de Contenson, *AHDL*, pp. 49–51 (with references to other studies); M.

two sorts of infiniteness: that arising from lack of perfection belongs to matter but not to God, whereas that which issues from the absence of limitation pertains to God and pure form but not to matter (*ibid.*, ad 4, p. 289c: "Ad illud quod obicitur de infinitate, dicendum quod est infinitas ex defectu perfectionis, et haec competit materiae sed non Deo; et est infinitas ex privatione limitationis, et haec Deo et formae liberrimae, non materiae competit").

That short reply appears to suggest these points. Since matter without form is imperfect *and infinite*, the function of form must be both to perfect and *to determine* matter. Second, since form without matter is perfect (because without limitation) *and infinite*, the function of matter is both to render form less perfect and *to determine* it.

The second passage occurs when Bonaventure asks whether the divine power is infinite (*ibid.*, d. 43, a. un., q. 1: "Utrum potentia Dei secundum quod huiusmodi sit infinita"). Some answer negatively, he notes, because in created powers infiniteness is from matter but finiteness is from form; but divine power is solely form having no possibility whatever; hence, it is simply finite and in no way infinite.[33] In his rebuttal Bonaventure observes that something can be infinite in two ways: through lack of completeness or perfection and through absence of limitation. The first sort is a passive or recipient potency and is exemplified best in matter. The second is act and, hence, truly and properly characterizes him who is solely act—pure and most perfect act (*ibid.*, ad 3, pp. 607–608: "Ad illud quod obicitur quod infinitum est passio potentiae materialis, dicendum quod hoc verum est de infinito per privationem completionis sive completi esse; sed non est verum de infinito per privationem limitationis. Primum enim est infinitum potentia passiva sive receptiva, et ita primo inest materiae; secundum est infinitum actu, et ideo in illo solo vere est et proprie, qui est tantum actus et actus purus et perfectissimus").

That brief text intimates, in a way somewhat similar to the first, that whatever is infinite is so through an absence either of perfection or of limit, each of which would be a determinant if present; that limit is matter or potency, perfection is act or form; that matter or potency

---

Kurdzialek, "David von Dinant und die Anfaenge der Aristotelischen Naturphilosophie," *La filosofia della natura nel medioevo* (Milano: Vita e Pensiero, 1966), pp. 407–16. Bonaventure reports an argument which seems inspired by David in *In I Sent.*, d. 19, p. 2, a. un., q. 3, *videtur quod* 6, p. 288b.

33. *Ibid.*, *sed contra* 3, p. 606b: "Videmus in potentiis creatis, quod infinitas est a materia, sed finitas est a forma; ergo cum potentia Dei sit omnino forma sive formalis, nihil omnino habens possibilitatis, ergo simpliciter est finita et nullo modo infinita."

would be *infinite* if lacking form or act; that act or form is an *infinite* perfection when free from potency or matter; that God is pure act and thus is genuinely infinite.

In the light of those two passages Bonaventure would seem aware of the fact that infinity of the divine essence had been (at least could be) conceived through God's freedom from matter and potency.[34] Elsewhere, he frequently calls God "pure act" and (often enough) "infinite" for that very reason.[35] But other factors in his position raise the question of how deeply and personally he was committed to that conception of infinity. He tends to think of matter not as Aristotle's pure potency in bodies but as Augustine's "almost nothing" ("prope nihil")[36] or as Boethius' "that by which something is" ("quo est").[37] He finds it even within angels.[38] Moreover, limitation or restriction ("arctatio") of a form or act, although grounded on occasion in the matter or potency receiving it,[39] appears more frequently to result in a more extrinsic manner. For example, a creature's being is limited by the fact it is composed of genus and species (*In I Sent.*, d. 8, p. 2, q. 2 *respondeo*, p. 134b: "Creaturae autem compositae sunt . . . quia habent esse limitatum et ita in genere et specie per additionem contractum"). Again: if God were not pure act but had some limitation and restric-

34. Was Bonaventure aware of Fishacre's conception? Almost certainly. He is said, in fact, to have had a manuscript copy of his Commentary. *See* W. A. Hinnebusch, *Early English Friars Preachers* (Romae: Ad S. Sabinae, 1951), pp. 364–69. But he does not here use Richard's language ("elongatio a materia et impedimentis").

35. For instance, *see In I Sent.*, d. 8, p. 1, a. 2, q. 1, *videtur quod* #c, p. 121d; *ibid., respondeo*, p. 122c; *ibid.*, d. 19, p. 2, a. un., q. 3, ad 2, p. 289b; *ibid.*, d. 34, a. un., q. 1, *videtur quod* 2, p. 467b; *ibid.*, d. 37, p. 1, a. 1, q. 1, *respondeo*, p. 507a; *ibid.*, d. 43, a. un., q. 3, *respondeo*, p. 612d; *In II Sent.*, d. 13 ,a. 2, q. 1, ad 4, p. 321d.

36. *See In I Sent.*, d. 19, p. 2, a. un., q. 3, *sed contra* #b, p. 288c; *In II Sent.*, d. 3, p. 1, a. 1, q. 2, *sed contra* 1, p. 83d; *ibid.*, ad 1, p. 87a.

37. *Ibid.*, d. 8, p. 2, a. 2, *videtur quod* #a, pp. 132–33; *ibid.*, d. 19, p. 2, a. un., q. 3, *videtur quod* 5, p. 288b.

38. *See In II Sent.*, d. 3, p. 1, a. 1 ("De simplicitate essentiae in angelis"), which consists of these three questions: "Utrum angeli sint compositi ex materia et forma; Utrum materia, ex qua compositi sunt angeli, sit eadem cum materia corporalium; Utrum materia corporalium et incorporalium sit una numero" (pp. 79–92). For Avicebron's (*seu* Solomon ibn Gabirol) theory of "spiritual matter," which is influencing Bonaventure here, *see* Et. Gilson, *History of Christian Philosophy in the Middle Ages* (New York: Random House, 1955), pp. 226–29.

39. *See In II Sent.*, d. 3, p. 1, a. 1, q. 1, *videtur quod* #c, p. 80a: "Cum hypostasis angeli sit finita et arctata et limitata, . . . necessario oportet quod ultra formam addat aliquid arctans substantiale sibi; hoc autem non potest esse nisi materia"; *In I Sent.*, d. 9, p. 2, a. un., q. 3, ad 3, pp. 289–90; G. P. Klubertanz, "*Esse* and *Existere* in St. Bonaventure," *MS*, 8 (1946), pp. 184–88.

tion, he would be finite; accordingly, a creature cannot be pure act or be infinite [but is limited and restricted in being] by the very fact it is a creature: it has received its being from what is outside and other than itself and is from nothing. In short: every creature is limited because it is from nothing and entails composition.[40]

But what makes the Franciscan's personal acceptance of the alignment of infinity of essence with separation from matter and potency ever more suspect is that he is almost completely silent on it in his *ex professo* handling of the topic. "Is the divine essence infinite?" he inquires in *In I Sent.*, d. 43, a. unicus, q. 2 (p. 608b) and answers affirmatively for several reasons. It is infinite because it is one with God's power which is infinite;[41] because such infinity is more harmonious with our Creed, according to which God is immense;[42] because it harmonizes better with [the divine immensity which Alexander of Hales and other] contemporary teachers ascribe to God;[43] because it agrees more with

40. *Ibid.*, d. 8, a. un., q. 3, *respondeo*, pp. 612d and 613a: "Infinitum enim in actu est actus purus, alioquin, si aliquid haberet de limitatione et arctatione, esset finitum; sed quod est actus purus, est suum esse per essentiam, et nihil tale accipit esse ab alia essentia nec ex nihilo. Si igitur creatura, eo ipso quod creatura, aliunde est et ex nihilo, nullo modo potest esse actus purus, nullo modo potent esse infinita. . . . Necesse est omnem creaturam esse limitatam, eo quod ex nihilo, et eo ipso quod composita est"; *ibid.*, d. 37, p. 1, a. 1, q. 1, *respondeo*, p. 507a–b.

41. *Ibid.*, *videtur quod* #a–#c, p. 508c. Even the statement of the question is significant: "Utrum *essentia* sit infinita *sive divina potentia* sit infinita *quantum ad esse*" (italics added). "Essence" is equivalent to "power of being." In *ibid.*, *videtur quod* #d–f, the divine essence is considered on its own—a consideration which concentrates on its goodness and magnitude (#c), its being most perfect and best (#e), its nobility and goodness (#f) rather than on its independence of matter and potency.

42. *Ibid.*, *respondeo*, p. 610a: "Et hoc [quod essentia omnino infinita sit actu] concedendum est et tenendum est tamquam verum, et quod magis est consonum fidei, quae dicit Deum immensum." Bonaventure would be referring to "Symbolum 'Quicunque' ": ". . . immensus Pater, immensus Filius, immensus (et) Spiritus Sanctus . . . nec tres immensi . . . sed unus immensus" (H. Denzinger and A. Schönmetzer, *Enchiridion Symbolorum* [32nd ed.; Friburgi, Brisg.: Herder, 1963], #75) or to "De Fide Catholica" of the Fourth Lateran Council held in 1215: "Firmiter credimus et simpliciter confitemur quod unus solus est verus Deus, . . . immensus" (*ibid.*, #800).

Immediately after referring to the Creed on God as "immensus," Bonaventure states that his view on the divine essence as infinite agrees also with the authoritative position of the Fathers of the Church—for example, John Damascene says that God is "quoddam pelagus substantiae infinitum" (*loc. cit.*, *respondeo*, p. 610a). In light of the context Bonaventure must think Damascene's text has to do with immensity. For interpretation of that quotation, see articles cited above, n. 27.

43. *Ibid.*, *respondeo*, p. 610a: ". . . magis etiam consonum magistrorum." That the then current "magistri" would include Hales and other compilers of the so-called

reason itself, as this consideration discloses. Infinity in God is the absence from him of anything which would terminate his perfections—an absence which is due to his supreme immensity (*loc. cit., respondeo*, p. 610b: "Alio modo [abnegatio finis qui est terminus potest intelligi] negative, quod non habet terminum nec est natum habere; et hoc modo ponitur in Deo propter summam immensitatem").

And why is God supremely immense? Because his essence extends to the same infinite extent as his power: he cannot make so many creatures but what his substance is present in them.[44] Again, there is no end to what his power can do (which is entirely in act and thus is truly infinite), and his essence can be proved to involve the same situation: [there is no end to where it can be].[45] Infinity is negative only in etymology and not in fact. What actually corresponds to it is full possession of perfections: nothing can be immense unless it has supreme and most perfect actuality with nothing restricting or determining it[46] to producing or to being present in merely a definite number or kind of

Summa Fratris Alexandri is an inference from the contents of that *Summa*. The second tractate of its Book I, is entitled "De immensitate divinae essentiae," which then considers in its first question this topic: "De immensitate Dei quantum ad se seu de infinitate eius." The first *caput* of this question asks "Utrum divina essentia sit finita vel infinita" (see above, for analysis), and part of its answer is a description of the immensity of God's presence in creatures (*see Summa*, I, tr. 2, q. 1, c. 1, *sed contra* #b, p. 55a; *ibid., sed contra* #d, p. 55b; *ibid., solutio*, p. 56b-c; for exegesis, *see above*).

44. *In I Sent., videtur quod* #c, p. 608c: "Nunquam Deus potest facere tot, quin eius substantia possit esse in tot." Also *see ibid., respondeo*, p. 609d: "Ad quidquid se extendit potentia sua ratione potentiae, et essentia." This is a refutation of "quidam," who solved the problem of how the blessed could see the divine essence itself by making it finite as essence but infinite as power (see above re Guerric; Bonaventure's explanation of that position is very good—*see ibid.*). Also *see ibid.*, ad 2 *ad finem*, p. 610c.

45. *Ibid., respondeo*, p. 609d: "Ipsa [potentia] non habet statum in possendo, et iterum est omnino actu, et ideo ponitur vere infinita; sic etiam probari de essentia." Here Bonaventure is refuting "aliqui," who solved the problem of the beatific vision mentioned in the previous note by postulating the divine essence and power to be finite in themselves and infinite only *re* creatures (on that position, *see above*, esp. note 16). Interestingly enough, Bonaventure himself does not hesitate to call God "finite" in the sense that the divine reality does not exceed the grasp of divine intellect. *Ibid., sed contra* 3, p. 609a: "Divina essentia est veritati divinae cognitionis finita quia Deus ipsam comprehendit et novit perfecte." *Ibid.*, ad 3, p. 610d: "Secundo modo [i.e., essentia non excedit comprehensionem ipsius Dei] Deus est finitus quia se non excedit cum sit infinitus."

46. *Ibid.*, ad 6, p. 611a: "Respondet ei [i.e., infinito divino] summa positio. Nihil enim dicitur immensum nisi quod habet summam et perfectissimum actualitatem et nihil coarctans et determinans."

effects with limited duration.[47] God's presence in all things is, in fact, necessitated by his very perfection. Since he is supreme simplicity itself, he is supremely immense and infinitely powerful: he is within all creatures, which can *be* only through his presence conferring being upon them.[48]

In his *ex professo* treatise on the infinity of God's essence, then, Bonaventure makes it equivalent to immensity, which in turn is equivalent to omni- or infini-presence: his causative being *is in* however many creatures there may be and is itself termed infinite only with respect to their potentially infinite number and kind. Infinity, accordingly, describes the divine essence with reference to creatures rather than directly in itself, as it would have done had Bonaventure continued the approach he made in the two earlier texts analyzed above. But instead of locating infinity in the divine being's freedom from matter and potentiality, Bonaventure appears to have preferred to identify it with divine immensity and omnipresence, as his Franciscan confreres had done earlier in the *Summa Fratris Alexandri*.[49]

Thomas Aquinas

Aquinas' *ex professo* treatise on infinity occurs, as does Bonaventure's, in connection with Book One, d. 43, of Lombard's *Sentences*. But unlike the Franciscan, who discusses four questions,[50] the Dominican asks only two: "Utrum potentia Dei sit infinita" and "Utrum omnipotentia sua, quae convenit sibi secundum infinitatem potentiae, sit creaturae communicabilis" (*In I Sent.*, d. 43, q. 1, [*introductio*];

47. *See ibid.*, q. 1, *respondeo*, p. 606b: "Et ideo [divina potentia] est habens in se plenam et perfectam actualitatem respectu infinitorum."

48. *Ibid.*, d. 37, p. 1, a. 1, q. 1, *respondeo*, pp. 506–507: "Necessitas autem existendi Deum in omnibus sumitur . . . a parte ipsius propter summam immensitatem et summam potestatem; et utriusque ratio est summa simplicitas. Quia enim summe simplex est, ad nihil arctatum, ideo in omnibus invenitur tamquam immensum; quia summe simplex, ideo in infinitum virtuosissimum, et ideo virtus idem est quod substantia, et ideo necesse est quod sit in omnibus. Ex parte creaturae est necessitas . . . [quia] non potest esse nisi per praesentiam eius qui dedit ei esse." Also *see ibid.*, q. 2, *respondeo*, p. 509a.

49. Our interpretation of Bonaventure differs, then, from J. Prather's (*op. cit.*, pp. 119, 135–36), who thinks he makes that location in most if not all relevant texts. No one seems yet to have studied infinity in his writings subsequent to the commentary on the *Sentences*.

50. *See* Quaracchi ed. minor, p. 605a: "Primo quaeritur utrum potentia Dei sit infinita. Secondo, dato quod sic, quaeritur utrum ipsa essentia divina sit infinita, sicut potentia. Tertio quaeritur utrum Deus possit producere opus infinitum. Quarto, utrum ratio operandi sit infinita."

Mandonnet ed., p. 1001). Although "essentia divina" does not appear in the formulation itself of either question, it is at the center of each *solutio* since the status of power as infinite or finite is decided by whether the essence whence power issues is infinite or finite, and the infiniteness or finiteness of essence is computed explicitly in terms of the absence or presence in it of matter and potency. Thus, in the first *solutio* God's power is infinite since it is consequent upon an essence which is infinite because the divine *esse* is "absolutum et nullo modo receptum in aliquo" (*ibid.*, a. 1, *solutio*, p. 1003).[51] In the second, the power of no creature can be infinite because power there follows upon an essence which is not infinite since *esse* in a created existent is not subsistent but is received and limited by that very essence (*ibid.*, a. 2, *solutio*, p. 1005: "Unde impossibile est ut essentiae finitae sit virtus infinita. Impossibile est autem aliquam essentiam creatam esse infinitam, eo quod esse suum non est absolutum et subsistens sed receptum in aliquo"). And the key to what makes something be finite (or infinite) in its very nature is disclosed with admirable clarity: every item becomes finite through that which determines and confines its essence (*ibid.*, a. 1, *solutio*, p. 1003: "Sic dicitur unumquodque finiri per illud quod determinat vel contrahit essentiam suam"). By implication: an item is infinite if it is without that which would determine and restrict its essence.

Let us study that first *solutio* more in detail. Despite its clear disclosure of the principle guiding Aquinas' approach to infinity and finiteness, it is awkward and a bit misleading in other ways because Thomas makes two divisions of infinity which overlap. The first is in line with whether what is absent from something (thereby called "infinite") ought to be present. If it ought to be present, the absence is a privation or deficiency; if it ought not be present, the absence is merely a negation.[52] The second division concerns what is and what is not quantitative. A quantitative item (e.g., a line) is finite or infinite when considered with or without that which terminates it (its final

51. This rooting of the infinity of power in that of essence will be constant throughout Thomas' later texts on divine power. See *Summa Contra Gentiles*, I, c. 43; *Compendium Theologiae*, I, c. 19; *De Potentia*, q. 1, a. 2 resp.; *S. T.*, I, q. 25, a. 2. For an exegesis *see* L. Sweeney S.J., "Divine Infinity in the Writings of Saint Thomas Aquinas," (Ph.D. dissertation, School of Graduate Studies, University of Toronto, 1954); *idem, TMS*, 48 (1970), pp. 88–89.

52. *Ibid., solutio*, p. 1002: "Respondeo dicendum quod infinitum potest dupliciter sumi: privative . . . vel negative." Also see *ibid.*, ad 1, p. 1004: ". . . de infinito quod privative dicitur, quod scilicet natum est habere formam et non habet"; *ibid.*, d. 3, q. 1, a. 1, ad 4, p. 92.

point).[53] Something which is itself without quantity is finite or infinite inasmuch as its essence is with or without what determines and confines it (*ibid.*: "Dicitur alio modo finis quantum ad essentiam rei. . . . Et sic dicitur unumquodque finiri per illud quod determinat vel contrahit essentiam suam"). Thus, a generic essence, e.g., "animal," is finite when determined by a specific difference ("rational"), but infinite when thought of without that determination (*ibid.*). Or prime matter is finite as determined in a composite by a substantial form, e.g., human soul, but infinite because it itself is indifferent to all forms: it can receive any form (*ibid.*: "Et materia prima, quae de se est indifferens ad omnes formas, unde et infinita dicitur, finitur per formam"). Likewise, form is made finite by the matter receiving it, although it is also infinite insofar as it transcends any one matter (*ibid.*: "Et similiter forma, quae quantum in se est potest perficere diversas partes materiae, finitur per materiam in qua recipitur").[54]

Granted that here Aquinas has unmistakably explicated two important points: an item's finitude or infinitude resides in its possessing or not possessing a determinant and, second, such determination is twofold: form (or, more generally, act) determines matter (or potency) by perfecting it, whereas matter (or potency) determines form (or act) by limiting it. But that explication is permeated with rather awkward and troublesome expressions. Logical conceptions (genus *re* specific difference), prime matter, and form are all listed under the same sort of infinity. Yet infinity for the first two is coterminous with imperfection (because it lacks specific determination, a generic nature is less perfect than a specific nature; prime matter of itself is pure potency and without any formal determination or perfection), while infinity for a subsistent form connotes perfection. Infinity for the first two is a privation, for the last a negation.

This trouble arose from Thomas' dividing items according to whether they are or are not directly quantitative. Lines and other mathematical conceptions are in obvious contrast with logical notions, with prime matter and with form, in none of which is quantity itself a constituent. But otherwise the last three are so different that any attempt to bind

53. *Ibid.*: "Finis vel terminus multipliciter dicitur. Uno modo terminus quantitatis, sicut punctus lineae; et hoc modo dicitur a positione et a privatione talis finis finitum et infinitum, secundum quod est passio quantitatis." Thomas' concern with this second division arises most likely from his awareness (*see ibid.*) of "quidam," who restrict infinity entirely to quantity, thereby predicating it solely of God's *virtus* and not of his essence, which thus can be the object of the beatific vision. On "quidam," see above *re* Guerric and n. 9.

54. That is, form as a specific perfection can perfect any one of many individual members of that species.

them together under one common sort of infinity was bound to come apart, and Aquinas no longer attempted it in his latest treatises.[55] But even here it does not interfere with his description of God's infinity itself, which grows out of his conception of form and act,[56] as the rest of the *solutio* shows.

The divine essence is, he concludes there, infinite through negation of whatever would determine and restrict it [namely, potency and matter], for form as form is infinite (*loc. cit.*: "Et a negatione talis finis essentia divina infinita dicitur. Omnis enim forma in propria ratione, si abstracte consideretur, infinitatem habet").[57] Consequently, that whose *esse* is absolute and in no way received in something else—in fact he *is* his *esse*—is strictly infinite. Hence, his essence is infinite, his goodness is infinite, all his other attributes are infinite: none of them is limited since limitation arises when a perfection is received in something, which thereby limits it to its own capacity (*ibid.*: "Et ideo illud quod habet esse absolutum et nullo modo receptum in aliquo, immo ipsemet est suum esse, illud est infinitum simpliciter; et ideo essentia eius infinita est, et bonitas eius, et quidquid aliud de eo dicitur; quia nihil eorum limi-

55. *See S. T.*, I, q. 7, a. 1, *resp.*, where the division of finite/infinite is according to matter and form; also *ibid.*, q. 86, 2, ad 1; *ibid.*, III, q. 10, a. 3 ad 1; *Quaestio Quodl.*, III, q. 2, a. 1 resp. Between *In I Sent.*, d. 43, q. 1, a. 1, and these texts there is a series of texts in which Thomas tries to reformulate his approach through quantity: *In III Sent.*, d. 13, q. 1, a. 2, *sol.* 2; *De Veritate*, q. 2, a. 2 ad 5; *ibid.*, q. 20, a. 4 ad 1; *ibid.*, q. 29, a. 3 resp.; *S.C.G.*, I, c. 28 and c. 43. But he completely abandoned that reformulation in the late texts listed above. In view of the awkward complexities in his expressing his position on infinity in *In I Sent.*, d. 43, I would judge it to be a first rather than a revised version—if such a distinction be valid (*see above*, note 5, second prgr.).

56. For similar descriptions in earlier texts *see ibid.*, d. 8, q. 1, a. 1, ad 1, p. 196; *ibid.*, a 2, *contra* #b, p. 197; *ibid.*, q. 2, a. 1, *solutio*, p. 202; *ibid.*, a. 2, *solutio*, p. 205; *ibid.*, q. 4, a. 1 ad 1 and ad 2, pp. 219–20; *ibid.*, a. 2, *contra* #b, pp. 221–22; *ibid.*, q. 5, a. 1, *contra* #b, p. 226; *ibid.*, d. 35, q. 1, a. 1, *solutio*, p. 809; *ibid.*, d. 42, q. 1, a. 1, *solutio*, p. 893.

57. As the Latin quotation shows, Thomas actually says "form as form, *if abstractly considered*." He explains the italicized words by the example of whiteness. "In whiteness as abstractly taken, the nature of whiteness is not limited on the level of whiteness, although in it the intelligible natures of color and of being become determined and drawn within a definite species." That is, whiteness considered precisely as whiteness possesses all the perfection of whiteness and, thus, can be said to be infinite within the domain of whiteness. It is, however, not absolutely infinite, for whiteness is only one species of color and thereby is finite when considered precisely as color; similarly, whiteness is only one of the four species of quality, which in turn is only one of the nine general modes of accidental predication; accordingly, it is also finite when viewed qua being. Thomas continues to use whiteness as an example of partially infinite forms even in his late works; *see S. T.*, I, 50, 2 ad 4.

tatur ad aliquid, sicut quod recipitur in aliquo limitatur ad capacitatem eius").[58]

But what of the question Thomas originally raised on God's power? Is it infinite? His answer consists of the single sentence he next adds: "And from the fact that the divine essence is infinite, it follows that the divine power is infinite also" (*ibid.*: "Et ex hoc quod essentia est infinita, sequitur quod potentia eius infinita sit").

Manifestly, Aquinas' theory of the infinity of divine being differs deeply from Bonaventure's. The former concentrates on essence, whence he moves to power; the latter concentrates on power and thence moves to essence. The former grounds the infinity of God's essence in its freedom from potency and matter: it is subsistent, God *is* existence. The latter (with the exception of two brief texts) identifies the infinity of the divine essence with its immensity: it is present in all creatures, however many and varied they may be.

Aquinas' theory on divine infinity is another proof that his is a universe of *being*, which is analogously common to God and to creatures.[59] In it form and actuation cause determination wherever found and, accordingly, matter can be considered as infinite because of itself it is without any form or act. But matter and potency are genuinely real as actually existing components in material things and, thereby, also are determinants by limiting the forms and acts which they receive and which are themselves determinants by conferring perfection on their recipients.[60] Now each creature is a being and God is Being. But each creature is a *finite* being because a composite of acts received and determined by potency, whereas God is *infinite* Being because an entirely subsistent Act and so without any recipient potency. Perfect *Being* because He is subsistent Actuality, God is *infinite* Being as free from the limiting determination of matter and all potency. Here infinity, al-

58. On the meaning of *esse* as existence and its relation to essence, *see* L. Sweeney, S.J., "Existence/Essence in Thomas Aquinas' Early Writings," *Proceedings of American Catholic Philosophical Association*, 37 (1963), pp. 97–131; *idem, A Metaphysics of Authentic Existentialism* (Englewood Cliffs, N.J.: Prentice-Hall, 1965), pp. 67–95, 127–30.

59. For a list of 36 texts on analogy in *In I Sent., see* G. P. Klubertanz, *St. Thomas on Analogy* (Chicago: Loyola University Press, 1960), pp. 165–76.

60. Such a view of matter and potency is basically Aristotelian—at least as Aquinas read the *Physics* and *Metaphysics*. If Bonaventure and other medieval authors do not approach divine infinity through form/matter and act/potency, it may indicate their basic metaphysics is radically un-Aristotelian. Some recent studies have challenged (unsuccessfully, I would say) the medieval interpretation of prime matter in Aristotle—for instance, *see* Robert Sokolowski, "Matter, Elements and Substance in Aristotle," *JHP*, 8 (1970), pp. 263–88 (with references to H. R. King, D. C. Williams).

though a negation and an absence, belongs properly and directly to the divine being itself because what is negated is within the very sphere of being: matter and potency belong, in their own way, to being as truly as do form and act, since matter and potency too are genuinely real in their own way. And just as their presence in an existent has actual repercussions on his very being by making it limited, so their absence in an Existent has genuine repercussions on his very being which thereby is unlimited. And this being is Thomas' God, whose infinity thus permeates his very entity.[61]

61. His description of God is in contrast with Plotinus', for whom God may be infinite in his very reality (= unity) but only because he transcends being. See L. Sweeney, S.J., "Another Interpretation of *Enneads*, VI, 7, 32," *TMS*, 38 (1961), pp. 289–303; *idem*, "Plotinus' Conception of Neoplatonism," in F. N. Magill and E. G. Weltin (ed.), *Great Events From History* (Englewood Cliffs, N. J.: Salem Press, 1972), II, pp. 823–28. For the meanings the Pre-Socratics gave to *apeiron*, *see idem*, *Infinity in the Presocratics: A Bibliographical and Philosophical Study* (The Hague: Martinus Nijhoff, 1972); for its meaning in Gregory of Nyssa, *see* E. Mühlenberg, *Die Unendlichkeit Gottes bei Gregor von Nyssa* (Göttingen: Vandenhoeck u. Ruprecht, 1966).

CHAPTER 8

The Question of the Eternity of the World in St. Bonaventure and St. Thomas—A Critical Analysis

FRANCIS J. KOVACH

It is always intriguing to observe two philosophers discussing an issue on which they disagree. Accordingly, it is extremely fascinating to study the controversy between St. Bonaventure and St. Thomas Aquinas over the question of the eternity or temporality of the world, i.e., whether the created world did or did not begin to exist, and it is greatly interesting for two reasons. First, in that the opponents involved in the debate are among the greatest of all philosophers or, at least, of all scholastic thinkers. Second, because the issue about which these two great thinkers argue is among the truly enduring questions in the history of philosophy—indeed, a question on which the earliest known opinion, the Assyro-Babylonian *Enuma elish,* dates back to c. 2000 B.C.; whereas the most recent views are being formed in the minds of contemporary philosophers, theologians, and astrophysicists.

This paper aims to both study and evaluate the cosmogonic views of Bonaventure and Thomas. Correspondingly, it is comprised of two main parts—an historical and a doctrinal.

I. *Historical Analysis*

The purpose of this historical investigation is properly and exactly to classify the positions taken by Bonaventure and Aquinas on the cosmogonic question. To achieve this end, it will be necessary to offer first a reasonably comprehensive classification of the cosmogonic views on a logical rather than a chronological basis.

A. *Classification of the Cosmogonic Views*

This classification will be carried out at two levels: the level of fact and the level of possibility. For one may ask first, Did or did not the world begin to exist?, i.e., Is the world, as a matter of fact, eternal or temporal? and, second, If either temporal or eternal, could the world be otherwise? or, more specifically, If the world is temporal, is it necessarily temporal, or could it be eternal?

1. At the factual level, all cosmogonic views fall into two categories: the radically irrationalist and the radically rationalist views. According to the former, the cosmogonic question is meaningless for either metaphysical reasons (Gorgias of Leontini)[1] or epistemological reasons; and if meaningless for the latter reasons, it may be held implicitly and generically (A. J. Ayer),[2] or explicitly and specifically (M. Scriven).[3]

According to the radically rationalist views, the cosmogonic question is meaningful and either can or cannot be answered. The agnostic views are either irreligious (not based on religious faith) or religious. The former are either immoderate or moderate. The immoderate irreligious agnostic views are either epistemologically (Maimonides as a philosopher)[4] or metaphysically (Cajetan)[5] or cosmologically (Kant)[6] founded. The moderate irreligious agnostic views are presented either implicitly, avoiding any definitive answer (Algazel),[7] or explicitly. The explicit views declare that no definite answer is known to anyone (Galen, R. Tolman, T. Davies, E. J. Öpik)[8] or to the holder of the view (G. Lemaitre)[9], and either do (Aristotle, Robert Schlegel)[10] or do not prefer one of the two alternatives (Galen, Tolman, Öpik).[11]

Religious agnosticism holds the temporality of the world as certain by faith but unknown by reason (Duns Scotus, Hervaeus Natalis, J. Gredt),[12] or as certain by faith and probable by reason, maintaining this

1. For Gorgias, see Sextus Empiricus, *Adv. Mathem.* VII (= *Adv. Log.* I), nn. 65–76 (Loeb-ed. II. 34–40).

2. Ayer, *Language, Truth and Logic*, chap. 1 (New York: Dover, 1952), p. 36.

3. Scriven, "The Age of the Universe," *British Journal for the Philosophy of Science*, (henceforth *BJPS*) V/ 19 (Nov., 1954), p. 182.

4. Maimonides, *The Guide of the Perplexed*, II, p. 17. S. Pines, tr. (Chicago: University Press, 1963), p. 295.

5. Cajetan, *Comm. in Summ. Theol. S. Thomae A.*, p. I, q. 46, a. 1, comm. I; Leonine-ed. of *S. Thomae A. Summa Theologiae*, Vol. IV (1888), p. 480a.

6. Kant, *Critique of Pure Reason*, First Antinomy, A 426–29, B 454–57.

7. Al-Ghazali's *Tahafut al-Falasifah* (*Incoherence of the Philosophers*), problem 1. S. A. Kamali, tr. (Lahore: Pakistan Philosophical Congress, 1963), pp. 13–53.

8. Galen, quoted by Maimonides, *op. cit.*, II, 15, p. 292. Tolman, *Relativity, Thermodynamics and Cosmology* (Oxford: Clarendon, 1934), p. 488. Davies, "The Age of the Universe," *BJPS*, V / 19 (Nov. 1954), p. 191. Öpik, "The Age of the Universe," *BJPS*, V / 19 (Nov., 1954), p. 213.

9. Lemaitre, *The Primeval Atom*. B. H. and S. A. Korff, trs. (New York: D. Van Nostrand Co., 1950), pp. 79, 163. Cf. pp. 82, 86, 101 and 134.

10. *Compare* Aristotle, *Top.* I, 11, 104b 12–17 *with Phys.* VIII, 1, 251a 7–b 27 or any other classic text of eternalism in his works. R. Schlegel, "The Age of the Universe," *BJPS*, V / 19 (Nov., 1954), pp. 233, 235, 236.

11. *See* note 8 above.

12. Hervaeus Natalis, *Quodlibetum*, II, q. 1; partially reprinted in *Controversia de aeternitate mundi* (*Pontificia Universitas Gregoriana, Textus et Documenta,*

probability consistently (B. Jungmann)[13] or inconsistently (St. Albert).[14]

The realist views, which constitute the second main version of the radically rationalist views, are either eternalist or temporalist or eternalist-temporalist. In the eternalist views, the eternal world is held to be either uncaused or divinely caused, and each group of views can be further classified as either cyclic or noncyclic. The noncyclic positions on the uncaused eternal world are either postulatory (Thales, Heraclitus, H. Spencer),[15] or demonstrative by *a priori* (Chalcidius, Alexander of Aphrodisias, Themistius, Avicenna, Averroes)[16] or *a posteriori* arguments (Theophrastus, Critolaus, S. Arrhenius, F. Hoyle, H. Bondi).[17] Similarly, the cyclic positions on the uncaused eternal world are postulatory (Anaximander, Anaximenes, Diogenes of Apollonia, Leucippus, Democritus, Nietzsche)[18] or else argumentative either in an *a*

Series Philosophica 6), nn. 48–50. M. Gierens, ed. (Romae: apud aedes Pontif. Univ. Gregorianae, 1933), pp. 74, 77. J. Gredt, *Philosophia Naturalis* (*Elementa Philosophicae Aristotelico-Thomisticae*, I), nn. 369–71. Editio octava (Barcelona: Herder, 1946), pp. 286–88. For Duns Scotus, *see* note 37 below.

13. Bernard Jungmann, *Institutiones Theologiae Dogmaticae Specialis, Tractatus de Deo Creatore*, nn. 6, 15–16 (Ratisbonae, Romae et Neo Eboraci: F. Pustet, 1900), pp. 5, 11, 12.

14. *Compare* "nihil probabilius" in *In II. Sent.* d. 1 B, a. 10, sol. (Borgnet-ed. II, 29a) *with* "Et hoc est concedendum" in *Summa theol.* II, tr. 1 q. 4 m. 2 a. 5 p. 1, in contr. 4 and sol. (XXXII, 96b).

15. For Thales, *see* Aristotle, *Met.* I, 3, 983b 6–21. Heraclitus, Fr. 30, Diels, 12 B 66 (Clement, *Strom.* V, 104, 1). H. Spencer, *First Principles*, part II, ch. 6, § 62; (New York: A. L. Burt, ND), p. 167.

16. Chalcidius, *In Tim.* cc. 305–307; in *Platonis Timaeus interprete Chalcidio cum eiusdem commentario*, J. Wrobel, ed. (Lipsiae: B. G. Teubner, 1876), pp. 333, 334, 336. Avicenna, *Metaphysices Compendium*, I, p. 3 tr. 1 cc. 2–6; N. Carame, tr. (Romae: Pont. Inst. Orientalium Studiorum, 1926), pp. 134–50. Averroes, *Destructio destructionum philosophiae Algazelis*, disp. 1–3, B. H. Zeller, ed. (Milwaukee: Marquette University Press, 1961), pp. 69–226.

17. For Theophrastus and Critolaus, *see* Philo, *De aeternitate mundi*, c. 11, n. 55–c. 13, n. 69 and c. 29, nn. 118f., c. 25, nn. 132–137, c. 23, nn. 120–123, c. 26, nn. 138–142, c. 24, nn. 130f., c. 27, nn. 145–149, respectively. Arrhenius, *The Life of the Universe*, II, chap. IX (New York: Harper, 1914), pp. 223–25. Fred Hoyle, *Frontiers of Astronomy* (London: Mercury Books, 1963), pp. 320, 321, 342; and *The Nature of the Universe* (New York: Harper and Brothers, 1950), pp. 122, 123, 128, 130. H. Bondi, *Cosmology* (Cambridge University Press, 1952), chap. 12.

18. For Anaximander, Leucippus and Democritus, *see* Simplicius, *Phys.* 1121, 5; in Kirk-Raven, *The Presocratic Philosophers*, n. 115 (Cambridge University Press), 1963), p. 124. For Anaximenes, *see* Theophrastus in Simplicius, *Phys.* 24, 26; Kirk-Raven, *op. cit.* n. 143, p. 144. Diogenes, Fragm. 2, Theophrastus in Simplicius, *Phys.* 25, 1 (DK 64 A 5). Nietzsche, *Thus Spoke Zarathustra*, ch. 46; Thomas Common, tr. in *The Philosophy of Nietzsche* (New York: The Modern Library, 1927), p. 174.

priori (Lucretius)[19] or *a posteriori* (B. Abramenko)[20] fashion. The cyclic positions on the divinely caused eternal world are held by reason alone or by both faith and reason (Origen).[21] Those held by reason alone are either postulated (Epicurus, Marcus Aurelius)[22] or demonstrated *a posteriori* (Solon's tale in Plato's *Timaeus*).[23] The noncyclic positions on the divinely caused eternal world are held by faith (Gnostics, Arians),[24] by reason, either by postulation (Plato, Apuleius, Plotinus)[25] or by *a priori* (Manicheists, Boethius)[26] or *a priori* and *a posteriori* arguments (Hermogenes),[27] or else by both faith and reason (St. Justin, Erigena).[28]

The temporalist positions are held by faith (Catholic Church, Mutakallimun, Basil, Chrysostom, Bede, Peter Lombard, Giles of Rome,

19. Lucretius, *De natura rerum*, I, pp. 483–634; *cf.* II, pp. 529f., 574.

20. B. Abramenko, "The Age of the Universe," *BJPS*, V / 19 (November, 1954), pp. 237–52.

21. Origen's theological arguments are in *Peri archon*, III, 5, 1; Migne, *Patrologia Graeca* (henceforth *PG*), 11, 326 AB; *Contra Celsum*, VI, 49 (*PG* 11, 1374C–1375A); and *Comm. in ev. Ioan.* II, 4 (*PG* 14, 115). For arguments of reason, *see Peri archon*, III, 5, 2 (*PG* 11, 327a); III, 5, 3, col. 327–328B.

22. Epicurus, Fragment 55, in *The Stoic and Epicurean Philosophers*, W. J. Oates, ed. (New York: The Modern Library, 1940), p. 50. Marcus Aurelius, *Meditations*, IV, 50; *cf.* IX, 32 and XII, 7 and 32 in the light of IV, 43; *The Stoic and Epicurean Philosophers*, pp. 558, 580, 584, 514.

23. *Tim.* 21a–23d. *Cf.* Aristotle, *Meteor.* I, 14, 351a 19 and St. Augustine, *De civ. Dei*, XII, 10; Migne, *Patrologia Latina* (henceforth *PL*), 41, 357f.

24. For the Gnostics, *see* Iraeneus, *Adv. hereses*, I, 1, 1 (*PG* 7, 446f.); I, cc. 3, 8, 11, 14, 18 (*PG* 7, 466–78, 519–38, 559–70, 593–612, 691–704). For the Arians, *see* Athanasius, *Orationes contra Arianos*, I, 29 (*PG* 26, 71A).

25. Plato, *Tim.* 52a speaks of eternal space; and *Tim.* 30a implies the preexistence of chaotic matter. The text is explicitly so interpreted by innumerable authors; e.g., Simplicius, *Phys.* 1122,3; Justine, *Cohortatio ad Graecos*, cc. 6 and 7 (*PG* 6, 254–255); Apuleius, *De Platone*, V, pp. 190f., VII, p. 194, *Opera*, III, P. Thomas, ed. (Lipsiae: B. G. Teubner, 1921), pp. 86f., 88f.; Chalcidius, *In Tim.* cc. 283, 298, 305–307, *ed. cit.* pp. 312, 327, 333f., 336; and Apuleius, *De Deo Socratis*, in *The Works of Apuleius, A New Translation* (London: G. Bell and Sons, 1899), p. 354. *Cf.* Augustine, *De civ. Dei*, XII, 10, 1 (*PL* 41, 357). Plotinus postulates the eternity of the universe (III, 2, 2) or the cosmos (II, 9, 7 and 8; II, 1, 1) and the circular motion of the heavens (III, 2, 3). The only nonpostulated element in his eternalist theory is in II, 9, 4 and 8, echoing somewhat Aristotle, *Phys. VIII*, 1, 251a 22–28.

26. Augustine, *De Gen. contra Manich.* I, 2, 3 (*PL* 34, 174). John Chrysostome, *Homiliae in Gen.* II, n. 3 (*PG* 53, 29f.). Boethius, *De consol. phil.* V, 6 (*PL* 63, 858f.).

27. Tertullian, *Adv. Hermogenem*, cc. 2–3 (*PG* 2, 222f.).

28. Justin, *Apologia I pro Christianis*, c. 10 (*PG* 6, 339f.) *Cf.* c. 59 (*PG* 6, 413, 418) and *Cohortatio ad Graecos*, cc. 6–7 (*PG* 6, 254, 254–55.). Erigena, *De divisione naturae*, II, 20–21; III, 5–9 (*PL* 122, 556–62; 635–42).

Stephen Tempier, J. Ussher),[29] by reason, postulating (Hesiod, Locke)[30] or demonstrating temporality either in an *a priori* (Anselm)[31] or *a posteriori* fashion (J. Donat, A. Eddington, G. J. Whitrow),[32] or else by both faith and reason (Philo, Irenaeus, Tertullian, Athanasius, Ambrose, Augustine, Robert Grosseteste, Alexander of Hales, S. Reinstadler, J. J. Urráburu).[33]

29. Fourth Lateran Council, c. 1, in H. Denzinger, *Enchiridion Symbolorum*, n. 428, ed. 30 (Friburgi Brisgoviae: Herder, 1955), p. 199. First Vatican Council, sessio IIII, Constitutio dogmatica de fide, c. 1; *ed. cit.* n. 1783, p. 491. For the Mutakallimun, *see* Maimonides, *op. cit.* part II, introduction, *ed. cit.* p. 241. Basilius, *Hom. in Hexaem*. I, 3 (*PG* 29, 10 B). Chrysostom, *Hom. in Gen*., II, 3 (*PG* 53, 29–30). Bede, *Hexaem*. I, princ. (*PL* 91, 13A). Peter Lombard, *Sent*. II, d. 1, nn. 1–2 (*PL* 192, 651 f.). Giles of Rome, *Errores philosophorum*, cap. 1, nn. 1–4, 6; c. 2, nn. 1–6; cc. 3, 4, and c. 5, n. 5; c. 6, nn. 2, 4, 5; c. 7, nn. 2, 5; c. 8, nn. 1, 2; c. 9, nn. 1–3; c. 12; J. Koch, ed. (Milwaukee: Marquette University Press, 1944), pp. 2–4, 10, 12, 14, 20, 26, 28, 36, 38, 44, 58. Bishop Tempier's condemnation of 219 theses include four (nos. 87, 89, 90, 99) professing the eternity of the world. *See* D. E. Sharp, *Franciscan Philosophy At Oxford In the Thirteenth Century* (Oxford University Press, London: H. Milford, 1936), p. 275, n. 2. Archbishop Ussher, *The Annals of the World Deduced from the Original Time* (London, 1658), I; cited in G. J. Whitrow, "The Age of the Universe," *BJPS*, V / 19 (November 1954), p. 219.

30. Hesiod, *Theogony*, lines 116–34. Locke may imply the temporality of the world in *Essay Concerning Human Understanding*, II, 15, 5.

31. *Monologium*, c. 24 (*PL* 158, 178A).

32. Donat, *Cosmologia (Summa Philosophiae Christianae*, IV), nn. 438–46, 449–51 (Oeniponte: F. Rauch, 1936), pp. 331–40, 342–44. Sir Eddington, *The Expanding Universe* (New York: Macmillan, 1933), pp. 121 f., 178. G. J. Whitrow, *art. cit.* (n. 29 above), pp. 218, 225.

33. Philo, *Quaestiones et solutiones in Genesim*, I, 1 (Loeb-ed. I, 2); *De opificio mundi*, IV, 16 (I, 15); *De fuga*, II, 12 (V, 16f.); *De somniis*, I, 12, 76 (V, 336f.) postulate temporal creation as a scriptural truth; but *De opificio mundi*, LXI, 171 (I, 135) offers an *a priori* proof. Iraeneus, *Adv. hereses*, II, 34, 2–3; III, 8, 3 (*PG* VII, 835f., 867f.). Tertullian's arguments of faith are in *Adv. Hermogenem*, cc. 3, 19, 20 (*PL* 2, 223–225, 238f., 239f.); his arguments of reason, *op. cit.* cc. 4–6 (*PL* 2, 225–227). Athanasius' argument of faith, *De incarnatione Verbi*, n. 3 (*PG* 26, 1096f.); his argument of reason, *Contra Arianos*, or. I, c. 29 (*PG* 26, 71). Ambrose's theological treatment of the issue is in *In Hexaem*. I, 1, 2 and 5; I, 3, 8 (*PL* 14, 134A, 135, 137); two arguments combining faith and reason, *op. cit.* I, 3, 10 and 10–11 (col. 138, 139); and his terse philosophic summation, *ibid.* I, 6, 20 (col. 143B). Augustine offers Biblical reasons in *De civ. Dei*, X, 4, 1 (*PL* 41, 310); *In Gen. ad litt.* I, 9, 15; I, 14, 28 (*PL* 34, 251f., 256f.); and philosophical reasons, in *Conf.* XI, 10–12; *De civ. Dei*, XI, 4–6; XII, 15–17. Grosseteste, *Hexaemeron*, 142^r a–b, 143^{v}b. MS Brit. Mus. Reg. 6 E. V. Fol. 140^{r}b–184^{v}b; in D. E. Sharp, *op. cit.*, (n. 29 above), pp. 43f. Alexander, *Summa theol.* contains a purely philosophical and a philosophico-theological statement on the issue: I–II, i. 1 tr. 2 q. 2 tit. 4 c. 1 a. 1, sol. (Quaracchi-ed. II, n. 67, p. 86b.) Reinstadler, *Cosmologia (Elementa Philosophiae Scholasticae*, I), editio 13a (Friburgi Brisgoviae: Herder, 1929), pp. 529 n. 4, 529–31. Urráburu, *Cosmologia (Institutiones Philosophicae*, III), n. 81 (Vallisoleti: typis viduae ac filiorum a Cuesta, 1892), pp. 265–74.

In the eternalist-temporalist view, held by both faith and reason, the created world is eternal in one respect and temporal in another (Meister Eckhart, Nicholas of Cusa).[34]

2. At the level of possibility, the cosmogonic theories are epistemologically twofold: realist and agnostic. According to the former, the possibility or impossibility of the eternity or temporality of the world is strictly demonstrable; according to the latter, it is not. The former views are themselves twofold: eternalist and temporalist.

In the eternalist view, the world is necessarily eternal or impossibly temporal (Avicenna, Averroes, Avicebron).[35] In the temporalist view, the world is necessarily temporal or impossibly eternal (Athanasius, Philoponus, Robert Grosseteste, Albert, Thomas of York, John Peckham, Richard of Middleton, Pseudo-Grosseteste, Aureolus, Stephen Langton, S. Tongiorgi).[36]

The agnostic position contends that the world is neither necessarily eternal nor necessarily temporal; or, in other words, it can be either eternal or temporal, with the necessity of neither alternative being strictly demonstrable. This generic position has two versions: one, that the whole world can be eternal; and the other, that only a part of the world can be eternal. Those who hold the possibility of the whole world being eternal maintain three specific views. In the first of these views, it is argued that the whole world *probably* can be eternal (Maimonides,

34. For an excellent comparative summary of the eternalist-temporalist theories of the two thinkers, see the chapter "Ewigkeit und Zeitlichkeit" in Herbert Wacker-zapp, *Der Einfluss Meister Eckharts auf die ersten philosophischen Schriften des Nikolaus von Kues* (1440–1450), J. Koch, ed., *Beiträge zur Geschichte der Philosophie und Theologie des Mittelalters*, (henceforth *Beiträge*) XXXIX/3 (Münster, Westf.: Aschendorff, 1962), pp. 119–30.

35. For Avicenna and Averroes, see n. 16 above. Avicebron, *Fons vitae*, V, 31. C. Baeumkehr, ed. *Beiträge*, I, 2–4 (1895), pp. 314f.

36. Athanasius, *Contra Arianos*, I, 29 (PG 26, 71). Philoponus, *De aeternitate mundi contra Proclum*, I, 3, H. Rabe, ed. (B. G. Teubner, 1899), pp. 5–13. Albert, *Summa theol.* II, tr. 1 q. 4 a. 5 p. 3, quaestio incidens, obi. 5 and 6 (XXXII, 107b, 108a). For the relevant texts in R. Grosseteste, *Hexaemeron* and *De finitate motus et temporis*, Thomas of York, *Sapientiale*; J. Peckham, *Quaest. disp.* and *Quaest. quodlibeticae*; and Richard Middleton, *Quaest. disputatae*, see D. E. Sharp, *op. cit.* (n. 29 above), pp. 44, 107f., 207, 276. For Pseudo-Grosseteste, see C. K. McKeon, *A Study of the Summa philosophiae of the Pseudo-Grosseteste* (New York: Columbia University Press, 1948), pp. 106, 107, 107n. 34. Petrus Aureolus, *In II. Sent.* q. prooem. art. 2, and d. 1 q. 1 aa. 3–4, in Capreolus, *In II. Sent.* d. 1 q. 1 a. 2, p. II: argumenta Aureoli; Paban, Pegues, eds., *Defensiones theologiae divi Thomae Aquinatis*, III (Turonibus: A. Cattier, 1902; reprint: Frankfurt/Main: Minerva, 1967), 5a–8b. Cardinal Langton, *In II. Sent.* d. 1 c. 3 n. 3, in *Beiträge*, XXXVII/1 (Münster, Westf.: Aschendorff, 1952), p. 69. Tongiorgi, *Cosmologia*, II, 2, 4, prop. IV, n. 286 (Parisiis: Soc. Gen. Libr. Cath., 1862), p. 334.

Scotus, Zigliara).[37] According to the second of these views, it is affirmed that the whole world can *certainly* be eternal (Capreolus, Cajetan, H. D. Gardeil);[38] and it can be eternal in such a way that (1) neither the eternity nor the temporality of the world is more probable (Hervaeus Natalis),[39] or that (2) the temporality of the world is definitely more probable (the early Albert).[40]

The view that only a part of the created world can be eternal is itself generic, with four specific versions. The first specific version holds that all creatures and all motion probably can be eternal and that only generation cannot (G. Vasquez). The second version holds that all permanent creatures, also the successive creatures unchanging for an infinite period of time prior to their state of changes and, possibly, continuous circular motion can be eternal; but no other change and no changing successive creature can (D. Soto).[41]

The third specific theory holds that permanent creatures and the successive creatures unchanging for an infinite period of time prior to their state of changes can be eternal, but that no kind of change and generation can (Suarez, E. Rolfes).[42] Finally, according to the fourth version, the permanent creatures can be eternal, but motion and successive creatures cannot. This last theory is itself advocated in three forms. According to the first version, permanent creatures *certainly* can be eternal, whereas motion and successive creatures *certainly* cannot (Durandus a S. Portiano).[43] According to the second version, permanent creatures *certainly* can be eternal, whereas motion and successive

37. Maimonides, *op. cit.* II, Introduction and chap. 16, pp. 241, 294. Duns Scotus, *In II. Sent.* d. 1 q. 3 (Vivès-ed. XI, 69–87); *Rep. Par.* II, d. 1 q. 4 (XXII, 538–548). F. T. M. Zigliara, *Cosmologia*, I, 3, 2, nn. IV–V (Parisiis: Delhomme et Briguet, 1902), p. 48.

38. Capreolus, *Defensiones theologiae divi Thomae Aquinatis in II. Sent.*, d. 1 q. 1 a. 1, *ed. cit.* pp. 1–3. Cajetan, *Comm. in I. Summae Theol. S. Thomae Aquinatis*, q. 46, art. 1–2, in the Leonine-ed., vol. IV (1888), pp. 480f., 482f. Gardeil, *Cosmology.* J. A. Otto, tr. (St. Louis: Herder, 1958), p. 129.

39. Hervaeus, *Quodlibetum*, III, q. 11; *ed. cit.* (n. 12 above), n. 51, pp 77–80.

40. *See* the "nihil probabilius" text in n. 14 above.

41. Vasquez, *Comm. ac di sput. in I. Summae Theologiae S. Thomae*, disp. 117, c. 5. Editio novissima (Lugduni: Jacob Cardon, 1631), p. 284. Dominic Soto, *In VIII. Phys.*, q. 2, concl. 3. Editio secunda (Salamanticae: Andrea de Portinaris, 1555), 122b–125.

42. Suarez, *Metaphysicae Disputationes*, disp. 20 sect. 5, nn. 6, 7, 13, 15, 16; in *Opera omnia*, 25 (Parisiis: L. Vivès, 1866), pp. 780–84. E. Rolfes, "Die Controverse über die Möglichkeit einer anfangslosen Schöpfung," p. IV, *Philosophisches Jahrbuch*, X (1897), pp. 19–21.

43. Durandus, *In II. Sent.* d. 1 q. 2, resp. (Venetiis: ex typographia Guerraea, 1571), I, n. 14, p. 126d.

creatures *probably* cannot (John of St. Thomas, Urráburu).[44] According to the third version, the permanent creatures *probably* can be eternal, but the successive creatures *probably* cannot (C. R. Billuart).[45]

B. *Classification of Bonaventure's and Thomas' Views*

Using the above classification of cosmogonic views at the two levels, we may attempt now to classify the theories of Bonaventure and Thomas.

1. Considering first Bonaventure's position at the level of fact, we find it, first of all, to be evidently not irrationalist, because he formally raises the question of . . . "whether the world was produced in time or eternally"; moreover, instead of rejecting it as meaningless, he proceeds to discuss the arguments for both alternatives.[46] Consequently, his position is radically rationalist. Second, Bonaventure is not agnostic on this issue. For, after discussing the eternalist and the temporalist arguments, he proceeds to give a definitive *conclusio* rather than an *ignoramus* type answer. Thus, his position is realist. Third, this realist position is not eternalist, because the author considers eternal creation totally contrary to truth;[47] he explicitly asserts that the world did, in fact, begin to exist.[48] Fourth, Bonaventure's temporalist theory is founded on both faith and reason. The theological foundation is shown by the explicit and repeated references to *Genesis*, I, 1 and 4 as the source and confirmation of his factual temporalism,[49] and also by texts employing no Biblical quotations but declaring that the temporal beginning of the world is a fundamental article of faith.[50] The rational basis of this temporalist theory is expressed by the famous remark that eternal creation is "completely against reason (*omnino est contra*

44. John of St. Thomas, *Philosophia Naturalis (Cursus Philosophicus Thomisticus*, II), pars 1, q. 24, aa. 1–2. Nova editio a B. Reisner (Torino: Marietti, 1948), pp. 477b, 478a. Urráburu, *op. cit.*, n. 84, pp. 285–291.

45. C. R. Billuart, *Summa S. Thomae . . . accommodata*, II, diss. 1, art. 6, dico 20 et 30, (Paris: V. Lecoffre, 1904), pp. 243f.

46. Bonaventure, *In II. Sent.* d. 1 p. 1 a. 1 q. 2 *Opera omnia*, 11 vols., Pp. Collegii a S. Bonaventura, ed. (Ad Claras Aquas, Quaracchi: ex typographia Collegii S. Bonaventurae, 1883–1901), vol. II, p. 19a.

47. *Ibid.*, concl. (II, 22.)

48. *Comm. in Ecclesiasten*, c. 1 p. 1 a. 1, quaestiones, resp. (VI, 14b.) Cf. *Coll. in Hexaem.* VI, 4 (V, 361a).

49. *De donis Spiritus Sancti*, coll. VIII, 16 (V, 497b); *Breviloquium*, II, 2 and 5 (V, 219b, 222b–223a); *In Hexaem.* VII, 1 (V, 365a); *Comm. in Sapientiam*, 5:1 (VI, 204a); *In ev. Ioannis*, prooem. (VI, 245b); *Sermones de tempore*, Dominica II post Epiphaniam, sermo 3 (IX, 182b).

50. *In Hexaem.* IV, 13 (V, 351); *Brevil.* II, 1 (V, 219a).

rationem)"[51] and also by the temporalist arguments (to be discussed later).

Turning to the level of possibility, Bonaventure leaves no doubt as to his position that the world is necessarily temporal and impossibly eternal. He uses six arguments for this thesis, of which one is used once in a purely philosophical form and once as a partly philosophical and partly theological argument;[52] another, the sixth listed in the main text, is the one on the basis of which Bonaventure considers eternal creation so totally contrary to truth and reason that he would not have believed even the poorest philosopher (*nullum philosophorum quantumcumque parvi intellectus*) would advocate it.[53]

In the light of this unequivocal advocacy of temporal creation at both levels, it is not surprising that the classification of Bonaventure's cosmogonic position on either level has not been a controversial issue. This, however, cannot be said of the classification of Thomas' theory.

2. At the factual level, Thomas' cosmogonic position is, first of all, not that of the radical irrationalist. For, like Bonaventure, he repeatedly raises the question of whether the world is eternal, along with several related issues, and invariably and unhesitatingly proceeds to deal with it. Second, Thomas answers the cosmogonic question in a definitive rather than an agnostic fashion, and, more specifically, in the temporalist way. In his temporalist view, God has not willed the world to exist from eternity,[54] i.e., always.[55] Instead, God willed the world to begin to exist after nonbeing,[56] i.e., after it was not.[57] Correspondingly, the world has not existed from eternity[58] (always).[59] Instead, it began

51. *In II. Sent.* d. 1 p. 1 a. 1 q. 2, concl. (II, 22).

52. This is the fifth argument in the main cosmogonic text, from the impossibility of an infinite number of souls; connected with the theology of happiness in *Coll. in Hexaem.* VI, 1 (V, 361b). Even the sixth and main argument is theologically founded: *Brevil.* II, 5 (V, 222b–223a).

53. *In II. Sent.*, d. 1 p. 1 a. 1 q. 2, concl. (II, 22.) Cf. *In I. Sent.*, d. 44 a. 1 q. 4, concl. (I, 788a); *In Hexaem.* IV, 13 (V, 351).

54. *In librum De causis*, prop. 11, n. 271. *Nota bene*: the paragraph numbering in *all* the works of St. Thomas is taken from the Marietti-edition.

55. *De pot.* 3, 17, ad 9; *In II. Sent.*, 1, 1, 5, ad 9. Cf. *Summa contra gentiles* (hereafter: *S.c.g.*), II, 36, 1123.

56. *In II. Sent.*, 1, 1, 5, ad 14. Cf., *ibid.*, ad 9; *Summa theologiae* (hereafter: *S. th.*), I, 46, 1, ad 9.

57. (Ponamus) secundum nostrae fidei sententiam, quod non ab aeterno produxerit res, sed produxerit eas postquam non fuerant. *In VIII. Phys.*, lect. 2, n. 974.

58. *S.c.g.*, II, 35, 1113.

59. *De pot.* 3, 17, ad 8; *S. th.* I, 46, 1, ad 6. Cf. *In I. De caelo*, 6, 64.

to exist[60] after it was not[61]; i.e., it did not exist before,[62] except as a possibility.[63] Moreover, God can will to have the world as a new effect[64] and to have it exactly *then when* (*tunc quando*) He wills it to begin existing.[65] Accordingly, the world was a new, yet eternally, predetermined effect of God[66]—a new effect, which came into existence exactly *when* (*quando*) God willed it to become,[67] rather than *whenever* (*quandocumque*) the divine nature or divine will is;[68] that is, at the predetermined moment of the beginning of time.[69] Moreover, God actually willed the world to have a certain quantity (measure) of time,[70] and correspondingly, the world has exactly that much time or quantity of duration as God has predetermined for it.[71] Thomas makes it quite clear that he holds this temporalist position at the level of fact, on the basis of faith alone. For not only does he quote a variety of relevant texts from the Scriptures in support of his factual temporalism,[72] but also remarks that the idea of eternal creation is contrary to the Catholic faith (incompatible with that faith), and theologically erroneous.[73] Moreover, Thomas repeats over and over again that the factuality of temporal creation is an article of faith[74] and nothing else,[75] and, consequently, *per se* indemonstrable.[76]

At the level of possibility, Thomas changes his dogmatic tone. He

60. *In VIII. Phys.* 2, 987.
61. *S.c.g.,* II, 33, 1102; 36, 1126.
62. *S. th.* I, 46, 1, ad 5; *In I. De caelo,* 29, 287.
63. *De pot.* 3, 17, ad 10; *S. th.* I, 46, 1, ad 1; *Comp. theol.* c. 99, n. 190.
64. *S.c.g.* II, 36, 1123; *In lib. De causis,* pr. 11, n. 272.
65. *De pot.* 3, 17, ad 9; *Comp. theol.* 99, n. 187; *S.c.g.* II, 35, 1113, 1114, 1116.
66. *S.c.g.* II, 35, 1112; *De pot.* 3, 17, ad 12.
67. *S.c.g.* II, 35, 1115; *De pot.* 3, 17, ad 4.
68. *De pot.* 3, 17, ad 4 and 6; *In I. De caelo,* 6, n. 66.
69. *In I. De caelo,* 6, n. 64.
70. *S. th.* I, 46, 1, ad 6; *De pot.* 3, 17c. fin.
71. *Comp. theol.* c. 98, n. 187; *In I. De caelo,* 6. n. 66.
72. *Gen.* 1:1 and *Prov.* 8:22 in *S.c.g.* II, 37, 1134; *Prov.* 8:24 in *De pot.* 3, 17, sed contra 1; *Gen.* I: 1 in *Quodlib.* III, 14, 2, sed contra and *S. th.* I, 46, 3, sed contra and corpus; *Prov.* 8:22 and *John,* 17: 5 in *S. th.* I, 46, 1, sed contra; and *Peter* II, 3:3 in *In Symb. Apost.,* a. 1, n. 880.
73. *S.c.g.* II, 38, 1150; *In VIII. Phys.* 2, 986; *In I. De caelo,* 6, n. 64; *De subst. sep.* c. 9, n. 100; *In I. De gen.* 7, n. 57. *In II, Sent.* d. 1 q. 1 a. 6, sol.; *S. th.* I, 46, 3c; *In Symb. Ap.,* a. 1, n. 880.
74. *De pot.* 3, 17c.; *De aeternitate mundi,* n. 295; *S.c.g.* II, 37, 1134; *De pot.* 3, 14c; *In VIII. Phys.* 2, nn. 974, 986; *In I. De caelo,* 6, 64; 29, 287; *Quodlib.* III, 14, 2, sed contra; XII, 6, 1; *S. th.* I, 46, 2, sed contra.
75. *S. th.* I, 46, 2c.
76. *Ibid.;* also, a. 1c.; *Quodlib.* III, 14, 2; XII, 6, 1; *In II. Sent.* d. 1 q. 1 a. 5, sol.; *In VIII. Phys.* 2, 989, fin.

holds, first of all, that the world, although actually temporal, is not necessarily temporal so as to be demonstrable either cosmologically (since the Aristotelian arguments do not take God, a universal cause, into consideration)[77] or metaphysically (since eternal creation, as a matter of fact, is not contradictory).[78] At the same time, he maintains that the world is not necessarily eternal.[79] Since, then, neither alternative is necessarily true, while each is possible; and since God is absolutely free in choosing between eternal and temporal creation as well as in determining the measure of time to allot the world, without divine revelation there is no way in which human reason could possibly learn whether the world is actually eternal or temporal.[80] This seemingly unyielding cosmogonic agnosticism is mitigated by Thomas on one point only. Thomas thinks that, while both eternal and temporal creation are equally possible, the temporality of the world is more probable than eternal creation, by reason of the end which the divine will has for creation. But Thomas hastens to add even to this reasoning that it can be considered a temporalist argument only so far as the human intellect can truthfully be said to comprehend things divine, while the secrets of divine wisdom necessarily escape its comprehension.[81]

3. At this point the question arises whether this unquestionable agnosticism on the cosmogonic issue is unqualified or qualified, i.e., whether Aquinas considers the whole world or only some parts of the world to be capable of eternal existence. In fact, one of his most faithful and greatest disciples, John of St. Thomas, asserts that his (John's) own cosmogonic thesis, viz., that *only* the permanent creatures can exist eternally, is explicitly taught (*expresse asseritur*) by St. Thomas, and lists four texts from the works of *divus Thomas* in support of this interpretation.[82] If this allegation be true, St. Thomas' cosmogonic theory is evidently a qualified one, as are most of the theories of the fourteenth- to seventeenth-century schoolmen. This issue must be investigated now.

In the first Thomistic text listed by John, Aquinas explains that prior to creation, the world was possible not in terms of some pre-existent, eternal matter as a passive potency but in virtue of God's active power.

77. *De pot.* 3, 17c.
78. *De aet. m.*, n. 306; *De pot.* 3, 14c.
79. *S.c.g.* II, 31, 1085; *S. th.* I, 46, 1c; *De pot.* 3, 17c; *In XII. Met.* 5, n. 2499; *Comp. theol.*, cc. 98–99.
80. *S. th.* I, 46, 1c, 2c; *Quodlib.* III, 14, 2; XII, 6, 1, etc.
81. *In VIII. Phys.* 2, 989.
82. John of St. Thomas, *op. cit.*, I, q. 24 a. 1, *ed. cit.* II, 478a, lists St. Thomas, *S. th.* I, 46, 1, ad 1; *De pot.* 3, 14, ad ibi. in opp.; *S.c.g.* II, 38; and *De aeternitate mundi.*

But this is entirely different from John's teaching that material or "successive" creatures cannot be eternal. In the third cited text, the sixth argument and the reply to it,[83] indeed, deal with "permanent creatures," i.e., the immortal souls of men. But what St. Thomas teaches here is merely that, according to some thinkers, an actually infinite member of immortal souls is not impossible—a thesis evidently different from John's that only permanent creatures can be eternal. In the second listed text, only the reply to the ninth temporalist argument has any connection with John's first thesis. But even in that reply Thomas does no more than call the spiritual (John's "permanent") creatures eternal, while contrasting them with the *per se* successive material creatures in terms of their respective measures of duration, *aevum* and time. From this statement alone, however, although it is the best of the four cited,[84] it does not follow that only the immaterial creatures can, in Thomas' opinion, be eternally created.

But John of St. Thomas quotes Aquinas also in support of his second thesis, *viz.*, that successive creatures cannot be eternal. If John is right in doing so, St. Thomas must be classified not in the way as, let us say, Capreolus or Gardeil must (i.e., as one holding without qualification the possibility of eternal creation), but rather as one who held the same cosmogonic view as, e.g., Durandus did. The text quoted by John is taken from St. Thomas' *De aeternitate mundi*. What is being expressed in the context in question is that a material being caused by an agent acting by way of motion (*per motum*) cannot be simultaneous with its producing cause and, consequently, cannot be eternal.[85] But in the same text, St. Thomas' point is precisely that an effect caused by an agent acting instantaneously *can* be simultaneous with its own cause—a principle from which Thomas concludes that God the Creator being an instantaneously acting cause and eternal, the creature *can* be eternal. From this, it is evident that the views of St. Thomas and John of St. Thomas on the possibility of the eternity of the successive creature are anything but identical. For St. Thomas speaks in this context of *creature* in general, while John excludes the successive creature.

This, however, is not the only text John quotes from Aquinas in support of his second thesis. Somewhat later in the discussion of the two basic reasons for what he considers to be Thomas' position, John points to a text in which Aquinas actually concedes that it *might be* held that

83. *S.c.g.* II, 38, nn. 1141, 1148.
84. The *De aeternitate mundi* text will be discussed in the next paragraph, in connection with John's second thesis.
85. *De aet. m.*, nn. 299, 297. Cf. *In VIII. Phys.* 2, 987, 989; *In II. Sent.* 1, 1, 5, ad 1 in contr.

man cannot be eternally created.[86] From this, John endeavors to prove that this patently *particular* concession to temporal creation on Aquinas' part implies, by analogy, the impossibility of all eternal generations and all eternal motions, i.e., that no successive creatures can be eternal.[87] But John overlooks here several important points. First, that the particular concession in question, made in the *Prima*, was retracted by Thomas some five years later in his *De aeternitate mundi* on the basis of the realizations that God could create the world without men in it, and that it had not been demonstrated that God could not create an actually infinite number of beings. The second point overlooked by John is that his argument is one of false analogy because, simply from the impossibility of the eternal generation of creatures with immortal souls, the impossibility of the eternal generation of creatures without immortal souls does not follow. The third and very important point is that Thomas explicitly teaches the possibility of eternal generation, including man's.[88] Finally, the fourth and most enlightening point overlooked by John is the remainder of the text in which St. Thomas makes a qualified concession to temporal creation. For in that text Thomas remarks that even if it be true that, unlike some creatures, human beings cannot be eternally created, he is concerned only with the universal or generic problem of the possibility of eternal creation, whereas the question whether the eternal generation of man is possible is a particular or specific issue.[89]

This last remark leads us to the final solution of the overall problem of the classification of Thomas' cosmogonic theory: *If* or insofar as Thomas did concede the impossibility of the eternal creation of some kind of successive creatures, Thomas' position, according to its *objective content*, is in the same *generic* group of views as the views of Durandus or John of St. Thomas; but, according to Thomas' *personal interest* in the question and his own mode of approaching the issue of eternal creation, Aquinas' theory is *generically* opposed to the group of cosmogonic views expounded by a number of fourteenth- to seventeenth-century schoolmen, such as Durandus, Suarez, Vasquez, and John of St. Thomas.[90]

86. John, *ibid., ed. cit.* II, 482b, referring to Thomas, *S. th.* I, 46, 2, ad 8.
87. *Ibid.,* p. 483a.
88. *S. th.* I, 46, 2, ad 7. *Cf.* Cajetan's commentary on this reply, *ed. cit.* IV, 483.
89. *S. th.* I, 46, 1, ad 8.
90. The change from Thomas' generic to the later schoolmen's specific interest in the cosmogonic problem may have been due to the sharp contrast between Albert's (*Summa theol.* II, tr. 1 q. 4, q. incidens II, n. 5; vol. 32, 107b) and Bonaventure's unyielding temporalist view that eternal creation is both impossible and unintelligible, and Thomas' explicit and Scotus' implied views that eternal creation is both

With this conclusion in mind, we can turn now to the doctrinal analysis of the cosmogonic theories of Bonaventure and Aquinas.

II. Doctrinal Analysis

Like the historical analysis, this analysis will consist of two parts, of which the former, the descriptive, is the means to the latter, the critical, as the end.

A. Doctrinal Comparison

1. A careful reading of the cosmogonic views of Bonaventure and Thomas leads to the recognition of the following points of agreement:

(a) *At the Level of Facts*: First, taken in the strict proper sense, as meaning an immutable, successionless and interminable duration,[91] eternity belongs to God alone.[92] Second, the world is actually temporal.[93] Third, this factual temporality of the world is a matter of faith[94] and as such, strictly indemonstrable.[95] Fourth, the eternity of the world is incompatible with or contrary to the Catholic faith.[96] Fifth, inas-

---

possible and intelligible. For such a basic disagreement between great thinkers naturally motivates subsequent philosophers to attempt a reconciliation of the radically different views, and such attempts almost inevitably result in the kind of proliferation of distinctions which we find for centuries in the works of post-Thomistic and post-Scotistic authors on the issue of the possibiilty of eternal creation. *Cf.* the "Et propterea cauti sint Thomistae in concedendo mundum potuisse esse ab aeterno" passage in Cajetan, *comm. cit. in I. Summae Theol.* q. 46, a. 2, ad 7, n. IX (IV, 483b).

91. Bonaventure: aeternitas est nunc simplicissimum in quo nulla omnino cadit diversitas. *In I. Sent.* d. 44 a. 1 q. 4, concl. (I, 788b). Cf. *In I. Sent.* d. 9 a. 1 q. 4, contra 3 (I, 186a); d. 31 p. 2 a. 1 q. 3, resp. (I, 544a). Thomas, *S. th.* I, 10, 1c; *In lib. De causis,* pr. 2, n. 48; *Quodlib.* X, 2, 1, 4a. Their common source is Boethius, *De cons. phil.* V, 6 (PL, 63, 858a). *Cf.* Proclus, *Institutio theologica,* c. 52; E. R. Dodds, ed. (Oxford: Clarendon, 1963), p. 50.

92. Bonaventure, *Comm. in Eccles.* c. 1 p. 1 a. 1, quaest. resp. (VI, 14b). Thomas, *S. th.* I, 10, 3c; *Quodlib.* X, 3, 1c; *In Dion. De div. nom.* c. 10, lect. 3, n. 869.

93. For Bonaventure, *see* n. 48; for Thomas, nn. 54–63 above.

94. For Bonaventure, *see* nn. 49–50; for Thomas, n. 95.

95. Bonaventure implies this doctrine by his replies to the eternalist arguments in *In II. Sent.* d. 1 p. 1 a. 1 q. 2, ad 1–6 (II, 23–24) and by his view that eternal creation is impossible. Thomas explicitly expresses this doctrine in *S. th.* I, 46, 1c, and implies it in *In XII. Met.* lect. 5, nn. 2497–2499, as well as in the replies to the eternalist arguments: *In II. Sent.* 1, 1, 5, ad 1–14; *S.c.g.* II, 35–37; *De pot.* 3, 17, ad 1–30.

96. Bonaventure, *De donis Spir. Sancti,* coll. VIII, 16 (V, 497b); *In Hexaem.* IV, 13 (V, 351a). For Thomas, see n. 73 above.

much as the world is actually temporal, the time prior to creation is merely imaginary.[97]

(b) *At the Level of Possibility*: First, the temporality of the world is *per se* possible.[98] Second, despite the possibility of temporal creation, the eternity of the world is also possible and conceivable from the *cosmological* point of view.[99] Third, it is possible that Aristotle himself did not consider his eternalist arguments metaphysically conclusive and universally valid.[100] Fourth, an earlier creation (but not necessarily of *this* world) is possible.[101]

2. The points of disagreement can be summed up in the following fashion.

At the level of facts, there is only one point of disagreement: Bonaventure affirms, and Thomas denies, that the temporality of creation is knowable by reason alone, independent of faith.[102]

At the level of possibility, there are several points of disagreement:

(1) Contrary to Thomas, Bonaventure affirms that creation is neces-

97. Bonaventure, *In I. Sent.* d. 44 a. 1 q. 4, concl. (I, 788b). Thomas, *S.c.g.* II, 36, 1126; *In II. Sent.* 1, 1, 5, ad 13; *In XII. Met.* 5, 2498; *Comp. theol.* 98, n. 188.

98. Bonaventure evidently implies this in his statements on both the necessity of temporal creation (*Brevil.* II, 1; vol. V, 219) and the impossibility of eternal creation: *In I. Sent.* d. 44 a. 1 q. 4, concl. (I, 788a); *In II. Sent.* d. 1 p. 1 a. 1 q. 2, concl. (II, 22); *In Hexaem.* IV, 13 (V, 351). Thomas expresses this possibility by teaching the non-necessity of temporal creation (*S.c.g.* II, 38, 1135–1148; *De pot.* 3, 17c; *In II. Sent.* 1, 1, 5, sol. fin.), on the one hand and by the theological fact of temporal creation, on the other.

99. Bonaventure, Si Aristoteles posuit mundum non incepisse secundum naturam, verum posuit . . . (*In II. Sent.* d. 1 p. 1 a. 1 q. 2, concl. 3; vol. II, 23a.) Cf. *also* the two Neoplatonic analogies inspired by Augustine, *De civ. Dei*, X, 31 (*PL* 41, 311) in Bonaventure, *ibid.*, p. 22b and *In Hexaem.* VII, 2 (V, 365b). Thomas, Sic ergo patet quod . . . *De aet. mundi*, n. 306; *In VIII. Phys.* 2, 986, 974; *In I. De caelo*, 29, n. 287; *In I. De gen.* 7, n. 57; *S. th.* I, 46, 2c.

100. Bonaventure, *In II. Sent.* d. 1 p. 1 a. 1 q. 2, concl. 3 (II, 22b–23a); *In Hexaem.* VI, 4 (V, 361a). Thomas, *In II. Sent.* 1, 1, 5, sol; *S. th.* I, 46, 1c and ad 2; *De pot.* 3, 17c and ad 15; *In XII. Met.* 5, 2497. Cf. Augustine, *De Gen. contra Man.* I, 6, 10 (*PL* 34, 178); and Maimonides, *op. cit.*, II, 15, pp. 289–93. Thomas speaks differently, however, in *In VIII. Phys.* 2, 986.

101. Bonaventure holds this view in the sense that, in his opinion, God could create *another* world before this one: *In I. Sent.* d. 44 a. 1 q. 4, resp. (I, 789b). Cf. *ibid.* arg. 1–4 and ad 1–4 (I, 787a–788b; 789b). Thomas explicitly states this view in *In II. Sent.* 1, 1, 5, ad 7, and implies the same in his statement that God is free to decide the measure of time this world should have: *De pot.* 3, 17c. fin.; *Comp. theol.* 98, n. 187; 99, n. 190; *In VIII. Phys.* 2, 988–989. Cf. Augustine, *De civ. Dei*, XI, 4, 2 (*PL* 41, 319f.).

102. Bonaventure, *In II. Sent.* d. 1 p. 1 a. 1 q. 2, concl. (II, 22). Thomas, *Quodlib.* XII, 6, 1.

sarily or demonstrably temporal, i.e., impossibly eternal.[103] Thomas holds, instead, that creation can be either temporal or eternal[104] and in such a way that the temporality of creation can be shown to be the more probable alternative. (On this point, Bonaventure is in the company of a formidable array of patristic and scholastic authorities, whereas, on the possibility of eternal creation, Thomas may have no more than one scholastic predecessor—Erigena.[105])

(2) Bonaventure maintains, while Thomas denies, that eternal creation is unintelligible.[106]

(3) According to Bonaventure, *this* world could not be older; Thomas implies that it could.[107]

(4) While Bonaventure does not object to the question, "Could this world have been made before?" Thomas suggests that, instead, one should ask, "Why did God will to appoint this amount or measure of time to the world (rather than another amount or measure)?" or, "Why did God not will the world to be eternal?"[108]

(5) According to Bonaventure, the question, "Why was the world not created before?" is not simply analogous (*non est omnino simile*) to the question, "Why was not the world created larger or in another place?" According to Thomas, however, the questions concerning the measure of time and the size of the universe are simply analogous. Bonaventure's reason is that the given moment (*illud nunc*) from

103. Bonaventure, *ibid.* and ad opp. 6 (II, 22a); *In I. Sent.* d. 44 a. 1 q. 4, concl. (I, 788a); *Brevil.* II, 3 (V, 219b.). Thomas, S. *c.g.* II, 38, 1142–1148; *Quodlib.* III, 14, 2; *S. th.* I, 46, 2; De pot. 3, 14c.

104. *In II. Sent.* 1, 1, 5, sol.; *De pot.* 3, 14, remark after ad 9; *ibid.* 3, 17, ad arg. in opp. *Compare also* S.c.g. II, 35–37, showing the weaknesses of the eternalist arguments, with *S. c. g.* II, 38, 1143–48 pointing out the weaknesses of the temporalist arguments.

105. S. *c. g.* II, 38, 1149; 35, 1117–1118; *De pot.* 3, 17, ad 8; *S. th.* I, 46, 1, ad 6 and 9; *In VIII. Phys.* 2, 989. *See* nn. 36 and 106, respectively.

106. Bonaventure expresses this view by holding eternal creation to be a contradictory or impossible idea: *In I. Sent.* d. 44 a. 1 q. 4, concl. (I, 788a); *In II. Sent.* d. 1 p. 1 a. 1 q. 2, concl. (II, 22). Thomas implies his view by maintaining that eternal creation is possible (*see* n. 98 above). In this respect, Bonaventure is in the company of Augustine (*De civ. Dei*, XII, 15, 2; *PL* 41, 364) and Albert (*Summa theol.* II, tr. 1 q. 4 a. 5 part. 3 q. incidens I, n. 5; vol. 32, 107); whereas John Scotus Erigena (*De divisione naturae*, I, 72; II, 20f.; III, 5–9; *PL* 122, 517f., 556–562, 635, ө642) may be the only medieval schoolman anticipating Thomas on this issue).

107. Bonaventure, *In I. Sent.* d. 44 a. 1 q. 4, resp. (I, 788b). Thomas, S.c.g. II, 35, 1115; *De pot.* 3, 17c. fin.; *Comp. theol.* 98, n. 187.

108. Bonaventure's formulation is, Utrum Deus potuerit facere mundum *antiquiorem* and *altiorem*: *In I. Sent.* d. 44 a. 1 q. 4, concl. (I, 788a, 789a). For Thomas, *see* S.c.g. II, 35, 1116; *In I. De caelo*, 6, n. 66. However, Thomas himself uses occasionally the phrase *before* (*antequam*), e.g., in *Comp. theol.* c. 98, n. 187.

which we measure the amount of time elapsed in the past would not be the same moment if God had created the world before He did, whereas this world would be the same even if the heaven were larger or farther from the earth.[109]

(6) Bonaventure considers the argument from the incompatibility of the terms "eternal" and "created" the strongest proof for the necessity of temporal creation, and apparently never uses the argument from divine immutability. In contrast, Thomas finds the temporalist argument from the infinite number of human souls the most difficult to refute (*inter alias fortior*); whereas, of all temporalist arguments, the one from the suitability of a temporal world to God's end for creation is, to his mind, the most efficacious (*efficacissima*), and, among the eternalist arguments, the one from the immutability of the Creator.[110]

Of all these points of doctrinal disagreement, the first is the basic or central, whereas the sixth is an indication of the fundamental difference between Bonaventure's and Thomas' metaphysical view on the eternity of the world. For this reason, the subsequent critical comparison will concentrate on these two points.

B. *Critical Comparison*

There is no need to compare Bonaventure's and Aquinas' evaluations of the eternalist arguments, because both thinkers consider those arguments inconclusive. However, what causes the fundamental metaphysical disagreement between the two philosophers on the cosmogonic issue is their respective opinions about the temporalist arguments. For this reason Thomas' treatment of Bonaventure's six temporalist arguments seems to be the most convenient and most proper point of departure in this critical comparison.

1. Beginning with the first of the six temporalist arguments, as listed in Bonaventure's principal cosmogonic text, Thomas answers the

109. Compare Bonaventure, *In I. Sent.* d. 44 a. 1 q. 4, concl. (I, 789a) *with* Thomas, *De pot.* 3, 17c. fin.; *Comp. theol.* 98, n. 187; *In II. Sent.* 1, 1, 5, ad 7; *In XII. Met.* 5, 2498; *In lib. De causis,* pr. 11, n. 272; and *S. th.* I, 46, 1, ad 8.

110. Bonaventure, *In II. Sent.* d. 1 p. 1 a. 1 q. 2, concl. (II, 22b); *In I. Sent.* d. 44 a. 1 q. 4, concl. (I, 788). Thomas, *In II. Sent.* 1, 1, 5, ad 6 in contr.; *De aet. mundi,* n. 310; and *S.c.g.* II, 38, 1148; *S.c.g.* II, 38, 1149; and Haec enim videtur esse efficacissima ratio ponentium aeternitatem mundi, quae sumitur ex immobilitate Factoris. (*In lib. De causis,* pr. 11, n. 264.) For the earliest history of this argument from the immutability of God, see Aristotle, *Phys.* VIII, 1, 251a 24–27; Philo, *De aet. mundi,* XVI, 83f. in the light of *ibid.,* XXII, 116; Origen, *Peri archon,* III, 5, 3 (PG 11, 327); Plotinus, *Enn.* II, 9, 8; Augustine, *De Gen. contra Manich.* I, 2, 3 (PL 34, 174f.); *Conf.* XI, 10, 12 (PL 32, 814); *De civ. Dei,* XI, 5; XII, 17, 1 (PL 41, 320f., 366).

premise, "The infinite cannot be increased," by pointing out that the number of celestial revolutions or days in an eternally created world is only potentially infinite and, as such, can be increased at the end where it is actually finite.[111] Bonaventure disagrees with this reply without offering a reason for his view and counters the reply with an argument that is open to the same Thomistic reply as the original.[112]

The second argument, that the numerical infinite cannot have an order whereas the celestial revolutions do, is answered by Thomas with the Aristotelian principle that these revolutions constitute an infinite series that is arranged *per accident* only.[113] Bonaventure insists, however, that if the world were eternal then it would consist also of a set of *per se* arranged efficient causes, *viz.*, the generations of animals. Thomas disputes the latter contention,[114] and altogether refutes the counter-argument by pointing out that the premise, "The world has not been without animals," is an arbitrary and untrue postulate, since God can create the world without animals.[115]

This last reply also constitutes Thomas' ultimate solution of the fifth temporalist argument in Bonaventure, *viz.*, that there cannot be simultaneously an infinite number of beings—which would be the case with human souls in a beginningless world. But before realizing that Bonaventure's Aristotelian reasoning, according to which the world is never without man because the world is for man, is a *non sequitur*,[116] Thomas repeatedly struggles with this argument. Thus, in the first and the second *Summa*, he merely lists the conceivable theories which *could* resolve the argument *if* they were true and theologically acceptable

111. *In II. Sent.* 1, 1, 5, ad 4 in contr.; *S.c.g.* II, 38, 1146 in reply to n. 1130. *Cf.* Algazel as quoted and answered in Averroes, *Destructio destr.*, disp. 1, ed. cit. pp. 78f.

112. Bonaventure, *In II. Sent.* d. 1 p. 1 a. 1 q. 2, 1a in opp. (II, 20b–21a). *Cf.* Thomas, *S.c.g.* II, 38, 1145. A modern critic of Thomas' cosmogonic theory, E. Rolfes, remarks on Aquinas' reply to this argument that it defends a contradictory notion, *viz.*, infinite time. (*Art. cit.* p. 14.) But obviously, he overlooks here Thomas' distinctions between the actually and the potentially infinite and between eternity in the essential and the accidental sense. (Thomas, *S. th.* I, 10, 4c; a. 3, ad 2; a. 4, ad 2 and 3; *De pot.* 3, 14, ad 9 in opp.) Besides, Rolfes' argument is directed not against Thomas' reply to the temporalist argument in question but against Thomas' generic view on the possibility of eternal creation—an issue to be discussed later.

113. Aristotle, *Met.* II, 2, 994a 16f. Thomas, *S. th.* I, 46, 2, ad 7; *S.c.g.* II, 38, 1147.

114. *In II. Sent.* 1, 1, 5, ad 5 in opp.; *S.c.g.* II, 38, 1147.

115. Bonaventure, *In II. Sent.* d. 1 p. 1 a. 1 q. 2, 2a ad opp. (II, 21a.) Thomas, *De aet. mundi*, n. 310.

116. Bonaventure, *ibid.* ad opp. 5 (II, 20b–21a). *Cf.* Aristotle, *Phys.* II, 2, 194a 35. Thomas, *De aet. mundi*, n. 310.

(which, he knows, they are not). In the latter *Summa* he even concedes that one may hold the impossibility of an eternally created mankind,[117] and in the Commentary on the *Sentences* and in another passage of the first *Summa*, he resorts to arguments of authority.[118] Nevertheless, the important point is that Thomas does succeed in resolving this problem in a way which not only is borne out by the findings of modern science, but also admirably fits into Thomas' principal argument for his cosmo-gonic agnosticism: that it depends entirely on God's will *when* He creates the world in general and man in particular.[119]

Ironically, Thomas seems to have found the resolution of Bona-venture's principal temporalist argument more easily than that of the above discussed fifth argument. Nevertheless, it may be more than mere coincidence that Thomas mentions this argument, which his great Franciscan opponent thought to be conclusive, more often than any other Bonaventurian argument—in fact, not less than 16 times. Bonaventure construes this argument in two versions: (1) The world is totally produced by God, i.e., out of nothing (*ex nihilo*). "Out of nothing" refers not to matter but to origin. Therefore, the world is pro-duced and exists *after* nonbeing (*habet esse post non-esse*). (2) That which is created becomes and, as such, has a beginning, whereas that which is eternal has no beginning. Therefore, the "created eternal" both has a beginning (being created) and has no beginning (being eternal), and is, as such, a contradictory notion.[120]

Thomas' principal reply to this argument is in his *De aeternitate mundi*, where he discusses the broader issue of whether "created" and "eternal" are contradictory, either on the part of God as the efficient cause of the world or on the part of the creature. In this work Thomas, in effect, rejects the principal temporalist argument of Bonaventure, arguing that it fails to distinguish between priority of duration and priority of nature—a distinction made by Avicenna.[121] Thomas was so sure of the sufficiency of this solution that, spanning the years from his Commentary on the *Sentences* to his period of maturity, he uses it no

117. *S.c.g.* II ,38, 1148; *S. th.* I, 46, 2, ad 8.

118. *In II. Sent.* 1, 1, 5, ad 6 in contr.; *S.c.g.* II, 81, 1622 in reply to n. 1616.

119. *De aet. mundi*, n. 310. It is interesting that Thomas never applied his dis-tinction between the actually and the potentially infinite, used in resolving the first Bonaventurean argument, to this argument, although this application could also lead to the rejection of the temporalist argument at hand.

120. Bonaventure, *In. II. Sent.* d. 1 p. 1 a. 1 q. 2, arg. 6 ad opp. (II, 22a); *In I. Sent.* d. 44 a. 1 q. 4, resp. (I, 788).

121. Thomas, *De aet. mundi*, nn. 302–306; Avicenna, *Met.* tr. 6, cc. 1–2. *Cf.* Augustine, *De civ. Dei*, XII, 5, 2 (PL 41, 352f.).

less than 11 times.[122] In the light of these facts, it is truly surprising to find Thomas himself formally using once this same argument in the same way as Bonaventure.[123]

At this point the fourth argument of Bonaventure may be considered briefly. Bonaventure argues that, if the world were eternal, a finite power, a spiritual creature, would know an infinite number of truths connected with the celestial revolutions. Regrettably, Thomas never includes this among his more than 60 temporalist arguments (as opposed to the more than 100 eternalist arguments, not counting the repetitions in their use)—perhaps because of its patent weakness.[124] This weakness is indicated by the numerous postulates Bonaventure explicitly lists in the argument and by others which he implies—some of them ranging from the somewhat questionable to the seriously questionable (e.g., that the pure spirits do know every celestial revolution singly rather than by one intelligible species and that every single revolution has its own diverse effects). For these reasons it is difficult to believe that anyone could be convinced of the temporality of creation solely on the basis of this argument.

Now we come to the third temporalist argument offered by Bonaventure which is based on the premise that it is impossible to traverse the infinite. Thomas uses this argument four times, and answers it in two ways. One answer is familiar to us: only the actually infinite cannot be traversed; the potentially infinite can.[125] The other type of reply runs as follows: "Transition" means moving from the first to the last mem-

122. *In II. Sent.* 1 ,1, 5, ad 2 in contr.; *De pot.* 3, 13, ad 1–5; 3, 14, ad 4, 7, 8, 10; *S. th.* I, 46, 2, ad 2. In the other five texts dealing with this argument, two replies utilize the "simultaneously acting cause" angle of *De aet. mundi,* n. 299 (*S.c.g.* II, 38, 1143, in reply to n. 1135; and *S. th.* I, 46, 2, ad 1); two others use the argument to prove some other doctrine (*De subst. sep.* c. 9, nn. 93, 100; *Comp. theol.* 99, n. 189); and one text shows both the argument and the reply in a unique form (*S.c.g.* II, 38, 1137, replied in n. 1144). The somewhat different but classic formulation of Thomas' reply is in *De pot.* 3, 14, ad 8 in oppositum: de ratione aeterni est non habere durationis principium; de ratione vero creationis habere principium originis, non autem durationis; nisi accipiendo creationem ut accipit fides.

123. Speaking as a theologian of the error of holding eternal creation to be a fact, Thomas remarks, Est etiam hoc contra fidem Ecclesiae et ideo ad hoc removendum dicitur: "Factorem coeli et terrae." *Si enim fuerunt facta, constat quod non semper fuerunt.* (*In Symb. Ap.* art. 1, n. 880.)

124. Thomas calls the first Bonaventurean argument *debile* (*S.c.g.* II, 38, 1146), although it is much stronger than the fourth. On the other hand, he did use some extremely weak arguments, *e.g., S. th.* I, 46, 2, 4a and *Quodlib.* III, 14, 2, 1a, 2a, which two he termed ridiculous (ridiculum: *S. th.* I, 46, 2, ad 4; derisibile: *Quodlib.* III, 14, 2, ad 2).

125. *In II. Sent.* 1, 1, 5, ad 3 in opp. Cf. *Quodlib.* III, 14, 2, ad 2.

ber of a series; a supposedly beginningless world has no first day (member); therefore, the objection does not apply to the world *if* it is eternal.[126] Bonaventure is dissatisfied with such answers, and pointedly asks, "Has a single past revolution infinitely preceded today's revolution?" For, he reasons, if none did, the world is temporal; and if at least one did, an absurdity follows. Thomas' position seems to be that the entire series of revolutions is infinitely distant from the present day with respect to the *past*,[127] while any given single past revolution is of a finite distance from the present.[128] This reply, it may be argued, is perfectly consistent with Thomas' view that the series of past revolutions or days is potentially infinite: infinite *ex parte anteriori*; finite, *ex parte posteriori*. In fact, the Neothomist Esser charges Bonaventure with having the wrong idea (*verkehrten Begriff*) about the infinity of days Thomas has in mind because, in Esser's opinion, Bonaventure fails to realize that only the beginningless succession is infinite, while all individual days are of a finite distance from each other.[129] In other words, Bonaventure's above mentioned pointed question "rests on a false premise" (*beruht auf einer falschen Voraussetzung*) and, as such, leads necessarily to a false conclusion by way of the fallacy of composition.[130]

Some critics are satisfied neither with Thomas' reply nor with Esser's defense of it. L. Roy and C. Vollert, for instance, charge Thomas' reply with question-begging,[131] whereas E. Rolfes endeavors to show that Esser's criticism of Bonaventure is unjustified. For, Rolfes argues, no fallacy of composition is committed by maintaining the finitude of the whole past of the world as long as no single past day in Thomas' own admission is of infinite distance from the present, because in the absence of any such day there is simply nothing that would make the

126. *S.c.g.* II, 38, 1145; *S. th.* I, 46, 2, ad 6.

127. *In II. Sent.* 1, 1, 5, ad 3 in opp.

128. *S. th.* I, 46, 2, ad 6.

129. "Nur die end- oder vielmehr anfangs-lose Aufeinanderfolge ist unendlich, wie wir sagten, während alle einzelnen aufeinanderfolgenden Tage endlich sind, in a. W. nicht das, was aufeinander folgt, ist unendlich, sondern das Aufeinanderfolgen selbst." Thomas Esser, *Die Lehre des hl. Thomas von Aquino über die Möglichkeit einer anfangslosen Schöpfung* (Münster: Verlag der Aschendorffschen Buchhandlung, 1895), pp. 128–29.

130. *Op. cit.*, p. 129.

131. "Not all are satisfied with this reply. L. Roy, 'Note philosophique sur l'idee' de commencement dans la création', *Sciences Ecclésiastiques*, II (1949), 224, complains that St. Thomas fixes a point of departure, and precisely this is in question; to resolve the problem, one must not fix an initial day." *St. Thomas Aquinas, Siger of Brabant, St. Bonaventure, On the Eternity of the World.* Vollert, Kendzierski, Burne, trs. (Milwaukee: Marquette University Press, 1964), p. 67 n. 42.

whole past series infinite.[132] If this seems to be sound reasoning, Rolfes' last argument is apparently devastating: To maintain that, in the past, there was no first revolution is to hold that *all* days are preceded by others; but this is the same as to hold that there were days in addition to all days. Therefore, one past day must have been without a preceding one—the first day.[133]

This reasoning seems to accomplish what so many temporalist arguments do not; truly showing the impossibility of an eternal world at the level of the philosophy of nature or, to use Thomas' terminology, on the part of the creature.

2. Having critically analyzed the two cosmogonic theories at the cosmological level, i.e., on the part of the creature, we must begin to analyze these theories at the metaphysical level, i.e., on the part of God and, more specifically, from the point of view of divine eternity.

Thomas himself, as so many before him, is fully aware of the relevance of divine eternity to this issue. He expresses this awareness by repeatedly employing an Augustinian argument against the eternity of the world, on grounds of divine eternity: both the world and God cannot be eternal because the finite world cannot be coequal with the infinite God.[134] The other and incomparably more important expression of Thomas' awareness of the relevance of divine eternity to the metaphysical possibility of eternal creation is found in the numerous texts in which Thomas critically interprets and evaluates many of his own temporalist doctrines (statements) in the light of divine eternity.

By studying these critical texts in Thomas, one is given invaluable clues to facilitate the comparative evaluation of eternalist and temporalist creationism as advocated by Thomas and Bonaventure, respectively. To proceed systematically in the utilization of these clues offered by St. Thomas himself, let us consider, first, Thomas' evaluative statement in question and, next, apply the principles employed in those critical statements to the generic issue of eternal *versus* temporal creation.

132. "Denn wenn kein einziger Tag unendlich weit zurückliegt, was liegt dann unendlich weit zurück?" Rolfes, *art. cit.* p. 11.

133. *Art. cit.*, p. 12.

134. Thomas, *In II. Sent.* 1, 1, 5, sed contra 7; *S. th.* I, 46, 2, 5a; *De pot.* 3, 14, sed contra 1 et 2. *Cf.* Philo, *De opif. mundi,* LXI, 171 (Loeb-ed. I, 135); Tertullian, *Adv. Hermog.* c. 4 (PL 2, 225); Ambrose, *De Hexaem.* I, 3, 11 (PL 14, 138f.); Augustine, *De civ. Dei,* XII, 15, 2 (PL 41, 369); *In Gen. ad litt.* VIII, 23 (PL 34, 389f.); Anselm, *Monol.* c. 24 (PL 158, 178); Richard of St. Victor, *De Trin.* II, 6–8 (PL 196, 904f.); Alexander of Hales, *Summa theol.* I, i. 1 tr. 2 q. 4 c. 4, 3a, n. 64 (I, 93a). Thomas' reply rests on Boethius' distinction between divine eternity, which is *tota simul,* and the eternity of the world, which is successive (*see* n. 91).

Thomas' critical statements in question are as follows:

(1) The doctrines that God has not willed the world to be from eternity or always (*ab aeterno, semper*) and that the world has not so existed do not refer to an infinite time preceding creation; instead, they signify that God created the world after it was not.[135]

(2) On the other hand, to say that the world began to exist after nonbeing or after it was not is itself not more than a metaphorical expression, and it certainly does not mean that there was a time when the world was not in existence,[136] or that the creature exists, once created, *after* it existed in another manner.[137] What it does mean is merely that the causality of the eternal God was involved in the creation of the contingent world.[138]

(3) Similarly, the statement, "the world did not exist before," and the phrase "the beginning of time" refer not to any real time which actually preceded the world but to an imaginary time.[139] Thus, the only being that truly preceded the world is God, and even God did so only by the priority of His nature and the duration of His eternity rather than by priority of time.[140] It is precisely this priority of divine nature and divine power that justifies the conclusion that, before it existed, the world was possible.[141]

(4) Moreover, the saying that God may have a new effect as well as

135. Cum enim dicimus res non semper fuisse a Deo productas, . . . intelligimus . . . quod Deus tempus et res simul in esse produxerit postquam non fuerant. (*In VIII. Phys.* 2, 989.) Cf. *In II. Sent.* 1, 1, 5, ad 13. For the two interpreted texts, see nn. 54f., 58 and 59.

136. Nam prius quod dicimus antequam tempus esset, non ponit aliquam temporis partem in re, sed solum in imaginatione. Cum enim dicimus quod tempus habet esse post non esse, intelligimus quod non fuit aliqua pars temporis ante hoc nunc signatum. (*S.c.g.* II, 36, 1126.) For the two interpreted doctrines, see nn. 56, 57 and 61 above.

137. Nam creatio mutatio dici non potest nisi secundum metaphoram, prout creatum consideratur habere esse post non esse . . . nam quod nullo modo est, non se habet aliquo modo; ut possit concludi quod, quando incipit esse, alio modo se habeat nunc et prius. (*S.c.g.* II, 37, 1131.)

138. Oportet enim hoc modo exprimi in ipsis rebus causalitatem divinam ut res ab eo productae esse inciperent postquam non fuerant. Hoc enim evidenter et manifeste ostendit eas non a se ipsis esse, sed ab aeterno auctore. (*Comp. theol.* c. 99, n. 190.)

139. Nam prius quod dicimus antequam tempus esset, non ponit aliquam temporis partem in re sed solum in imaginatione. (*S.c.g.* II, 36, 1126.) For the interpreted doctrine, see n. 62; for additional texts interpreting the doctrine, see *De pot.* 3, 17, ad 20; *Comp. theol.* 98, n. 188; *In XII. Met.* 6, 2498; *In VIII. Phys.* 2, 989; *In II. Sent.* 1, 1, 5, ad 13.

140. *In II. Sent.* 1, 1, 5, ad 7; *De pot.* 3, 17, ad 20.

141. *Comp. theol.* 99, n. 190.

the novelty of the effect signifies not any succession in God himself but the fact that God knows and wills that effect not to be eternally but to begin after nonbeing[142]—a phrase which, as seen above,[143] ultimately means no more than the divine causality involved in the production of the world.

The end result of this textual analysis is that all the evaluated texts are metaphorical and metaphysically amount to this simple causal doctrine: God is the free cause of the world—a doctrine that is *per se* neither eternalist nor temporalist and, as such, acceptable to the advocates of both eternal creation and temporal creation.

But Thomas leads us even further on this path of metaphysical criticism by suggesting that, in place of the question, "Why did God create the world when He did rather than earlier?" one should rather ask either "Why did not God will the world to be eternal?" or "Why did God appoint the measure of time which He did to the world rather than another measure?"[144] Two questions need to be raised here: (1) Why does Thomas disapprove of the question, "Why then and not before?" and, (2) Are the two questions which Thomas recommends in place of the original question more proper or reasonable?

Aquinas disapproves of the original question not only because it, like the above evaluated statements, presupposes imaginary time[145] and, as such, has only a metaphorical value, but also and mainly because that original question presupposes a metaphysical absurdity: succession in God's eternal duration. For, Thomas argues, the phrase "before" in the question at hand refers to a successive duration, and that duration cannot be a nondivine successive duration. The reason for this is that before the conceivable or actual beginning of the created world there is no time at all; indeed, there is nothing contingent in existence, and *nothing* has neither measure nor duration.[146] Thus, the question, "Why

142. *S.c.g.* II, 36, 1123; *De pot.* 3, 17, ad 12; *In lib. De causis,* pr. 11, n. 271. For the two interpreted statements, *see* nn. 64, 66.

143. *See* the text of *Comp. theol.* 99, n. 190 in n. 138 above.

144. Non est igitur ratio quare nunc et non prius in hoc consideranda: sed solum, quare non semper. (*S.c.g.* II, 35, 1116.) (Non) est quaerendum, quare nunc et non prius, sed quare huius temporis voluit esse mensuram. (*Comp. theol.* 98, n. 187.) Cf. *De pot.* 3, 17c. fin.

145. (Cum) de exitu universi esse a Deo loquimur, non est considerandum, quod tunc et non prius fecerit . . . Ista enim consideratio tempus praesupponit ad factionem, non autem subiicit factioni. (*De pot.* 3, 17c. fin.) Dicendum, quod Deus est prior mundo duratione. Sed *ly* prius non designat prioritatem temporis, sed aeternitatis. Vel dicendum, quod designat aeternitatem imaginati. (*S. th.* I, 46, 1, ad 8.) Cf. *In II. Sent.* 1, 1, 5, ad 7.

146. Non est autem ante totius creaturae inchoationem diversitatem aliquam

then and not before?" refers to God's own duration. But this duration has absolutely no diverse parts or moments, that is, no succession or
time, by reason of God's immutability.[147] Here we are at the heart of
the matter: divine eternity is the principle that precludes the question,
"Why then and not before?"

3. Having been guided this far by Thomas himself, we can now ask
ourselves, Are the questions which Thomas suggests in place of the
original question—which implies a metaphysical absurdity—better?

Thomas' reasoning behind the suggested two questions, "Why not
always?" and "Why that measure of time?" is quite obvious. Strictly
logically or, rather, according to our imagination, *if* God decides to
create the world then He has two fundamental *sets* of alternatives: to
let or not to let the world always exist; and, in the latter case, to let the
world have no beginning but an end, or a beginning but no end, or both
a beginning and an end—three alternatives each of which can be re-
duced to the question, "How much time to allot the world?" Reflecting
upon these two sets of alternatives and, with them, upon Thomas' two
suggested replacements of the original question, it seems evident that
God is free to decide that the world be not eternal *only if* God can
decide not to create the world "immediately," i.e., at the moment when
He considers the issue of creation, but to *postpone* creation to a later
moment in His eternal life. But, evidently, this is absolutely impossible
because "now" and "later," as Thomas himself teaches, are completely
meaningless in the eternal duration of God for the simple reason that in
His duration there are absolutely no diverse moments and thus no succession.[148] This being so, willing the world always to exist and not willing it always to exist are simply no alternatives at all. Consequently, as
long as one cannot choose between two impossible or meaningless
(absurd) alternatives, God cannot or is not free to choose between an
always and a not always existing world.

Two objections can be expected here immediately. One is that this
argumentation is nothing but the age-old eternalist argument that,

partium alicuius durationis accipere . . . Nam *nihil* mensuram non habet nec dura-
tionem. (*S.c.g.* II, 35, 1116.)

147. Dei autem duratio, quae est aeternitas, non habet partes, sed est simplex
omino, non habens prius et posterius, cum Deus sit immobilis. (*S.c.g.* II, 35, 1116.)
(Ipsa) aeternitas successione caret, tota simul existens. (*S. th.* I, 10, 1c.) (Esse)
divinum est esse totum simul, absque successione. (*S. th.* I, 46, 2, ad 5.) Sic ergo
tempus habet prius et posterius . . . aeternitas autem non habet prius et posterius,
neque ea compatitur. (*S. th.* I, 10, 5c.) Cf. *ibid.*, art. 1, ad 3; art. 2, ad 4; art. 4c.

148. Deus non aliter se habet nunc quam prius, non magis nunc res producit
quam prius (*In VIII. Phys.* 2, 988.) *See also* n. 147 above and *In lib. De causis*,
pr. 11, n. 271.

since God's act of willing the world is eternal, the world itself is necessarily eternal—an argument to which Thomas repeatedly replied that from the eternity of the act the eternity of the effect does not necessarily follow.[149] The proper answer to this objection seems to be that the eternalist argument, to which the objection refers, is quite different from the above reasoning. For, unlike that argument, the above reasoning is explicitly based on the meaninglessness or absurdity to God's intellect of the alleged alternatives "always" and "not always" (as they stand for "now" and "later" in the successionless duration of God) *and* on the consequent impossibility of God's willing or choosing the absolutely unintelligible.

Another objection may be that, if God can understand temporal things, He can also produce new, i.e., noneternal effects, even though God Himself is eternal.[150] The answer is, again, clear: God certainly can understand temporal things; but from this it does not follow that He can choose between creating them eternally or not eternally. For, from *God's* point of view, to will noneternal things, God would have to differentiate between diverse moments in His own eternal duration, and this is exactly what is impossible in respect to His immutable eternity and unintelligible to His intellect.

The first question suggested by Thomas as a substitute, then, is metaphysically not only not better but not even less absurd than the original, "Why then and not before?" Let us consider next the second substitute question, "Why this rather than that measure?" Of the three specific alternatives which this question entails, no metaphysical impossibility is implied in God's willing an ending or a nonending world. For even apart from creation or in the absence of any created being, indeed, even if God decided not to create at all, the idea of terminating or not terminating, continuing or not continuing, the successive duration of the created world is perfectly intelligible. This is so for the obvious reason that it does not imply any succession in God's own duration, but only in the duration of the world which, if it exists, exists successively. Consequently, it is entirely reasonable to speak of God as being free to choose between an ending and a neverending world.

Different, however, is the case with a divine choice between a be-

---

149. *S. th.* I, 46, 1, ad 10; *In II. Sent.* 1, 1, 5, ad 11; *S.c.g.* II, 35, 1113, in reply to cap. 32, n. 1089; *De pot.* 3, 17, ad 9, ad 7, ad 14. *Cf.* Augustine, *Conf.* XI, 10, and 11–12 (*PL* 32, 814f.).

150. Et . . . ita, quamvis sit esse suum aeternum et immutabile, potest tamen intelligere aliquod esse temporale et mobile. Et ideo, etsi suum intelligere sit sempiternum, per ipsum tamen producere potest effectum novum in tempore. (*In lib. De causis*, pr. 11, n. 269.)

ginning and a beginningless world. For, as shown above, if God wills the world in His successionless eternity, the world receives the act of existing, i.e., *becomes*—neither eternally nor noneternally, neither then nor later, but *simply* becomes. To the world this means that, being willed by God, the changing world necessarily begins to exist or begins to have its successive duration in such a way that, at the first moment of its existence, time in the incomplete sense begins; and, at the second moment of its existence, time in the complete sense begins.[151] To the predictable Thomistic criticism, that the *beginning* of the world does not follow from its being *willed* by God (since God may will it to exist without a beginning), the proper answer is obvious: This criticism postulates exactly what has been just shown to be metaphysically impossible, *viz.*, the choice between willing and not willing the world always to exist. Thus, it remains true that, by the sole reason that God wills it to be, the world becomes; and that the existence of the world being successive, by the becoming of the world, time begins. Consequently, it is true to say that the world begins to be or that the world is temporal.

From this analysis at least four conclusions follow. First, that, while God has a choice between an ending and a neverending world, God has no choice between a beginning and a beginningless world. Second, that God is not free with respect to the measure of time He may allot the world *ex parte anteriori*, i.e., as to when the world should begin. Third, that God is free to decide whether the beginning world should or should not cease to exist. Fourth, that God is also free to decide after how much time of existence it should cease to exist *if* He decides that it should cease to be at all.

Putting these conclusions together, we find that, by reason of divine eternity, the first substitute question recommended by Thomas ("Why not always?") is simply improper, while the second substitute question is proper with certain qualifications only.

However, the above reflection on St. Thomas' substitute questions from the point of view of divine eternity has led to a realization incomparably more important than the partial impropriety of a temporalist question which Thomas suggests in place of another. For this other realization directly affects Thomas' cosmogonic theory at its roots: the metaphysical absurdity of the alleged alternatives "creating an eternal world" and "creating a temporal world" means no less than that Aquinas' cosmogonic theory is left without its epistemological foundation at the factual level, and without its metaphysical foundation at the

151. *De pot.* 3, 17, ad 5 and ad 15; *In VIII. Phys.* 2, 982f., 989; *S. th.* 46, 1, ad 7; *In II. Sent.* 1, 1, 5, ad 5.

level of possibility. For Aquinas, cosmogonic agnosticism at the level of fact rests on the principle that we cannot know whether God, in His absolute freedom, has chosen eternal or temporal creation,[152] and his position at the level of possibility is that both eternal and temporal creation are possible,[153] whereas divine eternity, as shown, renders both of these alternatives, in the sense St. Thomas understands them, meaningless and absurd. All that is true, instead, is what is true about the temporalist statements which Thomas himself evaluated: that the eternal God is free to decide whether or not He should create the world.

In this light, the question arises whether this conclusion is simply temporalist so as to justify St. Bonaventure's temporalism. This conclusion definitely seems to confirm Bonaventure's position, but to say simply that it does so would be an oversimplification. Instead, the proper reply seems to be that, if taken exclusively, the above conclusion favors neither the temporalist nor the eternalist position; if taken inclusively, but from two different points of view, it favors both positions in some fashion.

To explain this thesis, we must go back again for a moment to the immutable and eternal God freely deciding to create. This decision, just as the decision not to create, is an act eternally reached in God's own, incomprehensible eternity. Correspondingly, the world is necessarily eternal in the sense of its being eternally willed and eternally created. This is to say, the world is eternal *ex parte Dei*, from the point of view of the eternal God.[154] On the other hand, as Thomas himself once explicitly and formally admitted, inasmuch as the world's being created means simply the world's becoming or beginning to be, the world is necessarily temporal—temporal in virtue of its becoming, *ex parte creaturae*.[155] (Undoubtedly, this eternalist-temporalist view bears

152. Sed aeternus mundus est, quatenus Deus vult esse . . . Non est igitur necessarium mundum semper esse. Unde nec demonstrative probari potest. (*S. th.* I, 46, 1c.) Unde patet quod ex simplici Dei voluntate dependet, quod praefiguratur universo determinata quantitas durationis . . . Unde non potest necessario concludi aliquid de universi duratione, ut per hoc ostendi possit demonstrative mundum semper fuisse. (*De pot.* 3, 17c.) Dicendum, quod ea, quae simplici voluntati divinae subsunt, demonstrative probari non possunt . . . Creatio autem mundi non dependet ex alia causa nisi ex sola Dei voluntate. (*Quodlib.* III, 14, 2c.)

153. *See* nn. 78, 79 and 104 above.

154. *Cf.* Thomas, Dei actio est aeterna, cum sit sua substantia (*De pot.* 3, 17, ad 12); (Suum) velle est sua actio; et sicut suum velle est aeternum, ita et actio (*In II. Sent.* 1, 1, 5, ad 11); and *In lib. De causis*, pr. 11, n. 269, as quoted in n. 150 above. For Bonaventure, see *In I. Sent.* d. 20, art. un. q. 1, sol. opp. 3 (I, 369b); and d. 30, art. un. q. 1, concl. (I, 522b).

155. *See* the text in n. 123 above. This is the point made by Bonaventure in his principal, *ex nihilo* argument, *In II. Sent.* d. 1 p. 1 a. 1 q. 2, arg. 6 in contr. (II, 22a.)

some resemblance to the cosmogonic theories of Meister Eckhart as well as Nicholas of Cusa.[156] However, it radically differs from those views in obviously avoiding their pitfalls: the pantheistic tendency, their ambiguities,[157] and their inconsistencies.[158])

This thesis with its premises may seem to limit God's knowledge, or God's power, or even God's eternity. It may appear to limit divine knowledge because it seems to imply that God does not comprehend alternatives which man comprehends, or that God needs the world to understand time. It may also seem to limit divine power or omnipotence because it seems to imply that God cannot create successively one crea-

156. Meister Eckhart: (Deus) unica scilicet et eadem simplici operatione, et in aeternitate et in tempore operatur, sic temporalia ipse intemporaliter sicut aeterna. *Expos. in ev. Ioan.* c. 1, v. 38, n. 216; *Die lateinische Werke* (henceforth: *LW*), III, Christ, Koch, eds. (Stuttgart: W. Kohlhammer, 1965), 182. (Deus) nec ante nec prius poterat mundum facere. *Sermones,* sermo 45, n. 458, *LW* IV, Benz, Decker, Koch, eds. (*ibid.* 1956), 380. For Nicholas of Cusa, see *De visione Dei,* c. 10, nn. 41 f., *Werke,* I (*Quellen und Studien zur Geschichte der Philosophie,* V) Paul Wilpert, ed. (Berlin: W. de Gruyter, 1967), 308f.; and *De dato patris luminum,* c. 3, n. 106, *Opera omnia,* IV, P. Wilpert, ed. (Hamburgii: F. Meiner, 1959), 78. An additional point of similarity is the identification of the *createdness* with the *beginning* (temporality) of the world. *See* Eckhart, *Liber parabolarum Genesis,* II:18, n. 109, *LW* I, Weiss, I, K., ed. (Stuttgart: Kohlhammer, 1964), 575; *In ev. Ioan.* I: 12, n. 152, *ed. cit.* p. 126; and Nicholas, *De Genesi,* c. 2, n. 156, *Opera omnia,* IV, 113.

157. A classic instance of Eckhart's ambiguities is the expression of the doctrine that God did not exist before the world: Unde cum quaereretur a me aliquando, quare deus prius mundum non creasset, respondi quod non potuit, eo quod non esset. Non fuerat prius, antequam esset mundus. (*Expos. lib. Gen.* I:1, n. 7, *ed. cit.* I, 190.) (Deus) nec ante nec prius poterat mundum facere, quia nec ante nec prius erat, quando mundus non erat. (*Sermones,* sermo 45, n. 458, *LW* IV, 380)—a doctrine the formulation of which was undoubtedly influenced by Erigena: Deus ergo non erat, priusquam omnia faceret (*De divisione naturae,* I, 72, PL 122, 517C; cf. III, 7, col. 639 BC.) Insofar as Eckhart means here only that one cannot speak of God's *temporal priority* to the creation of the world, he conforms to both Augustine ("ante principium temporis non erat tempus. Deus enim fecit et tempora . . . Non ergo possumus dicere fuisse aliquod tempus, quando Deus nondum aliquod fecerat, *De Gen. contra Manich.* I, 2, 3, PL 34, 175; cf. *De civ. Dei,* XI, 6, PL 41, 321f.) and Thomas (*see* nn. 145–147 above). This favorable interpretation is justified by Eckhart's Thomistic insistence that any succession attributed to divine eternity is the product of the imagination. (*Sermones,* sermo 45, n. 458, *LW* IV, 380; *In ev. Ioan.* I: 38, n. 216, *LW* III, 181; *Expos. libri Gen.* I:1, n. 7, *LW* I, 190.) However, this is not the only conceivable interpretation. For another, *see* nn. 158, 159.

158. The most flagrant inconsistency in Eckhart's cosmogonic theory is the teaching that once, or as soon as, God was, He created the world: Simul enim et semel quo deus fuit . . . etiam mundum creavit. (*Expos. lib. Gen.* I: 1, n. 7, *LW* I, 190.) In this statement Eckhart evidently reads succession into divine eternity, despite his own repeated warning that doing so is due to the imagination. (*See n.* 157.)

ture *after* another, but only simultaneously—which is absurd. And, finally, it may seem to limit even divine eternity, because it appears to imply that, before the beginning of the world, God Himself did not exist; or, even worse, that God is as old as the world—one of the ecclesiastic charges raised against Meister Eckhart's eternalism.[159] However, the above thesis implies none of these propositions.

First of all, the proposed thesis does not imply that God does not comprehend alternative courses of action which we do understand, for two reasons. One of these reasons is that, unless the world exists, "always" and "not always" or "eternally" and "temporally" as genuine alternatives mean *nothing* in God's own eternal reality (because there are no diverse moments in the *tota simul* duration of God), and not comprehending *nothing* is not a limitation of divine knowledge. The other reason is that these so-called alternatives in reference to divine eternity are actually meaningless and unintelligible to the human intellect, too: only the imagination makes us think that we do understand them. Furthermore, the proposed thesis does not imply that God needs the world to understand succession or time; because, knowing Himself, God knows all possible creatures and everything about them, such as succession and time.[160] Second, the above conclusion does not imply any limitation of the divine power either. For diverse moments and succession are intelligible to God in reference *to the created world* and, thus, God can freely decide when to create a creature *after* the first or any subsequent creature—just as He can freely decide, once He created the world, whether and when to end the existence of the world. Third, the suggested thesis does not limit divine eternity either, and, especially, it does not mean that God is as old as the world. For any talk about God and the world being "of the same age" is not merely a metaphorical expression but also, and more importantly, the unmistakable sign of conceiving divine duration as being successive.

4. *If* the above analysis concerning the eternity and the temporality of

159. "Et secundum hoc, tunc Deus non fuit, antequam Deus creavit mundum, et ita, cum Deus non creavit mundum ante VII milia annorum, Deus non fuit ante VII milia annorum, vel ante illud tempus, quo Deus mundum creavit." *Votum Avenoinense*, a. 1, in F. Pelster, "Ein Gutachten aus dem Eckhart-Prozess in Avignon," *Aus der Geisteswelt des Mittelalters*, Grabmann Festschrift, *Beiträge*, Suppl. III, 2 (Münster, 1935), 1109. This interpretation and the consequent condemnation of Eckhart's view in question are the direct and regrettable results of the ambiguity and inconsistency in such texts as *Expositio libri Genesis*, I, n. 7 (*see* nn. 157 and 158).

160. *Cf.* Thomas: (Quamvis) sit esse suum aeternum et immobile, potest tamen (sc. Deus) intelligere aliquod esse temporale et mobile. (*In lib. De causis*, pr. 11, n. 269.)

184

the world be right, the following conclusions with regard to the two cosmogonic theories in question are also true:

(1) Thomas' doctrine, that creation can be either eternal or temporal, is, as it stands without qualification, metaphysically untenable by reason of divine eternity in which there are no diverse moments; and should be rephrased as follows: The world is both eternal and temporal—eternal, from God's point of view, as it is eternally willed and created by God, and temporal, from the creature's point of view, as its being created is, as such, becoming, and its becoming gives rise to the beginning of time.

(2) Bonaventure's teaching that the world is necessarily temporal, or that it necessarily has a beginning, needs a distinction: The world is necessarily temporal from the point of view of the creature, in virtue of its createdness, but it is also necessarily eternal or impossibly temporal from God's point of view, insofar as the world cannot be created at one rather than at another moment in the divine eternity but simply in the divine eternity—i.e., eternally.

(3) Bonaventure shares Thomas' inconsistency in once reading succession into divine eternity, which he considers to be absolutely without succession.[161]

(Comparing the needed and suggested changes in (1) and (2), Bonaventure fares much better than Thomas. For the suggested rephrasing constitutes a radical change in the Thomistic position, whereas the distinction added to Bonaventure's view is only a matter of formulation.[162])

Moreover, *if* the presented critical analysis be right, the following conclusions concerning the *defense* of the cosmogonic theories in question are also true:

(1) Thomas fails to demonstrate the possibility of eternal creation because he does not consider the issue either from the point of view of divine eternity as it lacks diverse moments or from the point of view of the notion of eternal creation as it apparently leads to an absurdity.[163]

161. In reply to the fifth eternalist argument, Bonaventure first compares God with a free agent who need not act once he exists (*non oportet quod statim cum est operetur*). Next, he compares God as willing to create the world in time rather than from eternity with a priest as willing *now* to hear Mass *tomorrow*: Ab aeterno enim voluit producere tunc, quando produxit; sicut ego nunc volo cras audire missam. (*In II. Sent.* d. 1 p. 1 a. 1 q. 2, ad 5; II, 23b.) For the text expressing the succession-lessness of divine eternity, *see* n. 91 above. *Cf.* Albert, who also terms eternal creation "inconvenient," and states that God eternally willed the world to become "at the congruous time" (*voluit ut congruo tempore fieret*). See Albert, *Summa theol.* II, tr. 1 q. 4 m. 2 a. 5 p. 1, quaest. incidens I, ad 5 (XXXII, 106a).

162. *See* n. 154 above.

163. *See* Rolfes' criticism in n. 133 above, and also Constantin Gutberlet, *Allgemeine Metaphysik*, Kap. 11, § 5, vierte Auflage (Münster: Theissingsche Buchhandlung, 1906), pp. 316–19.

(2) Bonaventure fails to demonstrate the impossibility of eternal creation because his principal argument is vulnerable, and because he did not use the metaphysically decisive argument against eternal creation, *viz.*, the argument taken from the absolute impossibility of God's choosing between nonexistent moments in His eternal duration for the creation of the world.

(3) Thomas' position on the possibility of eternal creation is indemonstrable; thus, his failure to demonstrate his theory is objectively grounded. Bonaventure's position on the necessity of temporal creation is demonstrable, and thus Bonaventure's failure to demonstrate his position lacks objective foundation.

(With regard to (1) and (2), neither Bonaventure nor Thomas fares better than his opponent, because each displays a twofold weakness in defending his own cosmogonic theory. But in regard to (3), Thomas fares better than Bonaventure, because one cannot be expected to prove the impossible to be true, whereas one can be expected to prove the necessary to be true.)

* * *

This critical evaluation is offered here by no means as a final judgment on the respective values of the cosmogonic theories of Bonaventure and Thomas, but merely as a challenge to present-day philosophers. And it is so offered in the hope that it will lead to further discussions on the question of the eternity of the world, and that it will deepen general interest in the thought of St. Bonaventure and St. Thomas Aquinas. This end has special significance this year, as philosophers all over the world find reason to extend appreciation to the genius of both *doctor seraphicus* and *doctor angelicus*.

Contributors

Brady, (Rev.) Ignatius, O.F.M. Professor of Philosophy, Duns Scotus College (1942–52) and Catholic University of America (1959–61). Lector Generalis OFM (1952). Member of the editorial staff of the Editors of Quaracchi (1956–59); of Commissio Internationalis Bonaventuriana (1971–   ). Prefect of the Theological Commission (editorial staff), Quaracchi (1961–71); Grottaferrata (1971–   ). Translator and editor of *The Marrow of the Gospel, A Study of the Rule of St. Francis of Assisi*. (Co-)Editor of *Liber de Anima* of Wm. of Vaurouillon; *Rogeri Marston Quodlibeta Quatuor; Petri Lombardi lib. I–II Sententiarum;* and *Fr. Mathei Aquasparta Quaestiones de Ieiunio*. Co-author of *Prolegomena in Rogeri Marston Quodlibeta Quatuor*. Author of *A History of Ancient Philosophy; Conferences on St. Clare of Assisi,* and *Prolegomena in libr. I–II Sententiarum Petri Lombardi;* and of numerous articles in journals and books, including *Archivum Franciscanum Historicum, Dictionnaire de Spiritualité, Franciscan Studies, Incontri Bonaventuriani, La Sacra Scrittura e i Francescani, Lexicon für Theologie und Kirche, Miscellanea Mediaevalia de Pobladura, The New Scholasticism, Proceedings of the American Catholic Philosophical Association, Recherches de Theologie ancienne et médiévale, S. Bonaventurae Opera theologica selecta, S. Bonaventura 1274–1974, Studia Mediaevalia et Mariologica P. C. Balic dicata,* and *Studies in Philosophy and the History of Philosophy.*

Cousins, Ewert H. Professor of Philosophy, Fordham University, New York City. Ph.D. *honoris causa* from Siena College (1974); research scholar at the Ecumenical Institute for Advanced Theological Studies at Jerusalem (1972–73); member of the Teilhard de Chardin Research Institute of Fordham University (and of the Executive Committee, 1964–68), and of the American Teilhard de Chardin Association (being its president in 1971–72), as well as of the Metaphysical Society, Mediaeval Academy of America, Société Internationale pour l'Étude de la Philosophie Médiévale and the American Catholic Philosophical Association. Author of one book (*Bonaventure and the Coincidence of Opposites*) and 31 articles (17 of which are on St. Bonaventure) in various American, Canadian, French, Italian, and Spanish journals and proceedings. Editor of two books (*Process Theology* and *Hope and the Future of Man*) and member of the editorial commission of *S. Bonaventura 1274–1974*, 4 vols.

Kovach, Francis J. Professor of Philosophy, University of Oklahoma, Norman, Oklahoma. Member of American Catholic Philosophical Association, American Society for Aesthetics, British Society for Aesthetics, Societas Internationalis Scotistica, Société Internationale pour l'Étude de la Philosophie Médiévale, and Southwestern Philosophical Society. Author of two books (*Die Aesthetik des Thomas von Aquin, eine genetische und systematische Analyse* and *Philosophy of Beauty*); and 20 articles in the journals *American Benedictine Review, American Journal of Jurisprudence, Archiv für Geschichte der Philosophie, Benedictine Review, Revista Portuguesa de Filosofia, Review of Metaphysics*, and *Southwestern Journal of Philosophy*; and in the books *Actes du IV et V Congres Internationale d'Esthétique, Art Liberaux et Philosophie au Moyen Age, Deus et Homo ad mentem I. Duns Scoti, Die Metaphysik im Mittelalter, La Filosofia della Natura nel Medioevo, New Catholic Encyclopedia*, and *Proceedings of the American Catholic Philosophical Association*.

Kreyche, Robert J. Professor of Philosophy, University of Arizona, Tucson, Arizona. President, American Catholic Philosophical Association, 1967–68. President and Founder, Thomas More Institute, 1970–. Christian Culture Award Medallist, 1974. Member of American Catholic Philosophical Association, American Philosophical Association, Metaphysical Society of America, and Southwestern Philosophical Society. Co-author of *Reflections on Man*. Author of seven books (*Logic; The Critical Realism of Roy Wood Sellars; First Philosophy; God and Contemporary Man; God and Reality; The Making of a Saint*; and *The Betrayal of Wisdom*); and of 12 articles in *Akten des XIV. Internationalen Kongresses für Philosophie, The Catholic Mind, Center Magazine, Proceedings of the American Catholic Philosophical Association, Reflections on Man, Prophets of the West; New Dynamics and Sexual Love; Religion and Society; Ensign*; and *The Salesianum*.

McInerny, Ralph M. Professor of Philosophy, University of Notre Dame, Notre Dame, Indiana. Associate editor of *The New Scholasti-*

cism. President of American Catholic Philosophical Association (1972). Member of American Philosophical Association, American Catholic Philosophical Association, Metaphysical Society of America, Author's Guild, and Sören Kierkegaard Society. Author of seven books (*Logic of Analogy, History of Western Philosophy, Studies in Analogy, Thomism in an Age of Renewal, New Themes in Christian Philosophy*, and *Marx*); three novels (*Jolly Rogerson, A Narrow Time*, and *The Priest*); and 33 articles in journals and books, including the Acts of the 1955 and 1959 International Thomistic Congresses, *La Filosofia della Natura nel Medioevo, Laval Théologique et Philosophique, The Modern Schoolman, New Scholasticism, Proceedings of the American Catholic Philosophical Association, Revista di Filosofia Neoscolastica, Revue Philosophique de Louvain, Science Ecclésiastique, Studies in Honor of Charles De Koninck, Studies in Medieval Philosophy*, and *The Thomist*.

Owens, (Rev.) Joseph, C. Ss. R. Professor of Philosophy, Pontifical Institute of Mediaeval Studies, Toronto, Ontario, Canada. Professor of Philosophy, School of Graduate Studies, University of Toronto. President, American Catholic Philosophical Association, 1955–56; Metaphysical Society of America, 1971–72; Society for Ancient Greek Philosophy, 1969–1972. Member of the Editorial Board, *The Monist*, 1961–. Secretary, Section II, Royal Society of Canada, 1969–1972. Chairman, PIMS Department of Publications, 1969–73. Author of *The Doctrine of Being in the Aristotelian Metaphysics; St. Thomas and the Future of Metaphysics; A History of Ancient Western Philosophy; An Elementary Christian Metaphysics; The Wisdom and Ideas of St. Thomas Aquinas; An Interpretation of Existence*; and of 29 articles in *American Philosophical Quarterly, Analecta Gregoriana, Gregorianum, International Philosophical Quarterly, Mediaeval Studies, The Modern Schoolman, Mind, Monist, New Scholasticism, Philosophical Interrogations, Proceedings of the ACPA, Proceedings of the American Philosophical Association, Proceedings of the 7th Inter-American Congress of Philosophy, Readings in Metaphysics, Review of Metaphysics*, and *Transactions of the Royal Societies of Canada*.

Quinn, (Rev.) John Francis, C.S.B. Secretary, Fellow, and Professor of Philosophy, Pontifical Institute of Mediaeval Studies, Toronto, Ontario, Canada. Associate Professor of Philosophy, Mediaeval Centre, School of Graduate Studies and Department of Philosophy, University of St. Michael's College, in the University of Toronto, Ontario, Canada. Served on the Editorial Boards of *S. Bonaventura 1274–1974*, a five-volume septemcentennial series (Rome) and *St. Thomas Aquinas 1274–1974*, a two-volume septemcentennial study (Toronto). His publications include *Charles Reade; The Historical Constitution of St. Bonaventure's Philosophy;* "Chronology of St. Bonaventure," *Franciscan Studies;* "St. Bonaventure's Fundamental Conception of Natural Law," *S. Bonaventura 1274–1974;* and "Certitude of Reason and Faith in St. Bonaventure and St. Thomas," *St. Thomas Aquinas 1274–1974.* Member of Société Internationale pour l'Étude de la Philosophie Médiévale, American Catholic Historical Association, and North American Patristic Society. Elected a lifetime Fellow of Società Internazionale di Studi Francescani.

Sweeney, (Rev.) Leo, S. J. Visiting Professor of Philosophy, Loyola University of Chicago; previously, Creighton University, Omaha, and Catholic University of America. Secretary (1960–63) and President (1965–66) of Jesuit Philosophical Association of America. Member of Executive Council, American Catholic Philosophic Association (1969–71). Editor of four books and *The Modern Schoolman.* Author of *A Metaphysics of Authentic Existentialism* and *Infinity in the Presocratics;* and of 28 articles in the journals *Gregorianum, Journal of History of Philosophy, Manuscripta, Mediaeval Studies, The Modern Schoolman, New Scholasticism, Revue philosophique de Louvain,* and *Speculum;* in *Collier's Encyclopedia, Encyclopedia Americana, Encyclopedia Dictionary of Christian Doctrine, New Catholic Encyclopedia;* and in the books *Arts Liberaux et Philosophie au Moyen Age, Etienne Gilson Tribute, Great Events from History, Miscellanea Mediaevalia, Proceedings of Jesuit Philosophical Association, Proceedings of the American Catholic Philosophical Association, Studia Patristica,* and *Wisdom in Depth.*

Index

B. in the entries stands for St. Bonaventure; T., for St. Thomas.

counsel, judgment, and desire, 42ff.;
on virtues, 45ff.; on subsidiary
sciences, 45, 51; on Christ, 47; on
errors of philosophers, 47, 50ff., 55;
on intellectual virtues, 48; on judicial
virtues, 48–50; on worship, 49; on
natural piety, 49ff.; on politics, 51; on
moral virtues, 51; on cardinal virtues,
52–54; and moral philosophy, 54ff.;
on illumination, 57, 59, 60; on the
divine name, 71; on knowledge and
belief, 127ff.; on infinity, 133ff.,
143–48; temporalist arguments of,
criticized by T., 171–76; *see also
Eternity of the World*
Bondi, H.: 157
Bongerol, J. G.: 134
Bonnefoy, J. F.: 134
Brady, I. C.: 16, 62, 134, 141
Broome, J. H.: 127
Brown, P.: 133
Brunner, J.: 62

Cajetan, Cardinal: 156, 161
Cantor, G.: 133
Capreolus: 160, 161, 166
Cartesianism: 65
Casara, S.: 66, 67
Catania, F. J.: 139
Chalcidius: 157
Chenu, M. D.: 136
Chrysostomus, St.: 158, 159
Cicero, M. T.: 48, 49, 53, 56
Comte, A.: 88
Contenson, P. M. de: 136, 139, 143
Cousins, E. H.: 15
Critolaus: 157
Cross, F. L.: 71

David of Dinant: 143, 144
Davies, T.: 156
Democritus: 157
D'Entreves, A. P.: 110
Denzinger, H.: 146, 159
Descartes, R.: 117
De Vogel, C. J.: 71
De Wulf, M.: 105, 108, 109
Diogenes of Apollonia: 157
Divine infinity: 134–40
Donat, J.: 159
Dondaine, H. F.: 136, 138, 139
Doucet, V.: 141
Dubrule, D. E.: 140
Duns Scotus, J.: 57, 64, 156, 161, 167
Durandus a S. Portiano: 161, 166, 167,
175

Eddington, A.: 159
Emmen, A.: 141
Enuma elish: 155
Epicurus: 158
Erigena, John Scotus: 158, 170, 183
Ermatinger, C. J.: 139, 140
Esser, T.: 175
Eternity of the World: views on, 7, 21,
155–62; views of B. and T. on, 162–
67, 171–84; points of agreement be-
tween B. and T. on, 168f.; points of
disagreement between B. and T. on,
169–71; summarized, 185–86
Eustace of Arras: 62

Fairweather, E. R.: 59
Fidelis, Fr.: 65
Fischacre, R.: 139, 140, 145
Francis of Assisi, St.: 60

Galen: 156
Gardeil, H. D.: 161, 166
Gelinas, E. T.: 109
Gerard of Abbeville: 140
Gilbert of Poitiers: 69
Giles of Rome: 158, 159
Gils, P. M.: 135
Gilson, E.: 64, 131
Gioberti, V.: 65
Gnostics: 158
Gorgias of Leontini: 69, 156
Gredt, J.: 156
Greek Fathers: 7, 8, 17, 19, 20, 65, 146
Gregory Nazianzenus, St.: 71
Gregory of Nyssa, St.: 153
Guardini, R.: 127
Guerric of Saint-Quentin: 136–39, 143,
146, 150
Gutberlet, C.: 185
Guyot, B. G.: 136, 138, 139

Hartshorne, C.: 16
Hasselbach, R. E.: 59
Hebraic (Semitic) heritage: 7, 20
Hegel, G. W. F.: 18, 89, 101
Heidegger, M.: 80
Henry of Ghent: 57, 64
Heraclitus: 157
Hermogenes: 158
Hervaeus Natalis: 156, 161
Hesiod: 159
Hinnebusch, W. A.: 145
Hoyle, F.: 157
Hugh of St. Cher: 135, 136
Hugh of St. Victor: 10
Human subjectivity: 5–7

Immortality of soul: 7, 21
Irenaeus, St.: 158, 159
Islamic problematic: 5–7, 20–23

Jansen, B.: 64
Jeiler, I.: 66, 67
Joannes Climacus: 124
John Damascene, St.: 10, 34, 70–72, 79, 137, 138, 142, 146
John of Rochelle: 141
John of St. Thomas: 162, 165, 167
John Scotus Erigena: see John Scotus Erigena
Journet, C.: 83
Jungmann, B.: 157
Justinus, St.: 158

Kant, I.: 12, 14, 117, 156
Kierkegaard, S.: 130, 131
Kirk, G. S.: 157
Klubertanz, G. P.: 145, 152
Krause, J.: 65
Kreyche, R. J.: 104
Kurdzialek, M.: 143f.

Ladner, G. B.: 71
Langton, S.: 160
Leibnitz, G. F.: 89
Lemaitre, G.: 156
Lemmens, L.: 134
Leonine edition: 5
Leucippus: 157
Leverrier, U. J. J.: 85
Locke, J.: 159
Lovergan, B.: 14
Long, R. J.: 140
Longpré, E.: 62
Lovejoy, A.: 16, 18
Lucretius: 158

McCaslin, R.: 135
McInerny, R. M.: 124, 128, 131
McKeon, C. K.: 160
Magill, F. N.: 153
Magrini, E.: 133
Malebranche, N. de: 65
Manicheists: 158
Marcus Aurelius: 158
Mareshal, J.: 14
Margerie, A. de: 57
Maritain, J.: 87f., 106, 107
Marston, Roger: 62, 63
Matthew of Aquasparta: 62, 63
Meister Eckhart: 14, 160, 183, 184
Melani, G.: 62
Meneghin, V.: 66, 67

Morall, J. B.: 110
Moses Maimonides: 156, 159, 160
Mühlenberg, E.: 153
Muslims: 6, 7, 21
Mutakallimun: 158, 159

Neo-Platonism: 70
Neo-scholastic revival: 5
Neo-Thomism: 5–7
Nicolas of Cuse: 160, 183
Nietzsche, F.: 157

Oates, W. J.: 158
O'Connor, D. J.: 109
Olivi, P. J.: 64
Öpik, E. J.: 156
Origen: 158, 171
Ortoleva, G.: 65
Owens, J.: 75, 134

Pagus, J.: 139
Parmenides: 69, 70, 78, 85
Pascal, B.: 126f., 128
Peckam, John: 62, 63, 160
Pelster, F.: 184
Peter de Chanter: 59
Peter Lombard: 77, 128, 131, 134, 135, 137, 158, 159
Peterne, M. B.: 133
Phelan, G. B.: 70, 109, 113
Philo of Alexandria: 52, 157, 159, 176
Philoponus: 160
Plato: 48–50, 65, 69, 89, 92, 98, 113, 115, 117, 158; see also Platonism
Platonism: 13, 21, 34, 52; see also Plato
Plotinus: 52, 65, 69, 89, 137, 153, 158, 171
Ponferrada, G. E.: 135
Porphyrian tree: 73
Pouillon, H.: 77
Pseudo-Dionysianism: 6, 17
Pseudo-Dionysius: 7, 8, 15, 69, 83
Pseudo-Grosseteste: 160
Prather, J.: 134, 143
Preller, V.: 23

Quaracchi edition (editors): 5, 57, 58
Quinn, J. F.: 134

Radhakrishnan, S.: 71
Rahner, K.: 14
Ratzinger, J.: 131
Raven, J. E.: 157
Reese, W. L.: 16
Regnon, T. de: 15
Reinstadler, S.: 159

Richard of Mediavilla: 63, 64
Richard of Middleton: 160
Richard of St. Victor: 176
Robert Grosseteste: 135, 159, 160
Rolfes, E.: 161, 172f., 185
Rosmini, A.: 66
Rosminianism: 55, 66
Rossi, G. F.: 135
Roy, L.: 115
Rucher, P.: 64

Sartre, J. P.: 13
Schlegel, R.: 156
Schönmetzer, A.: 146
Scriven, M.: 156
Sextus Empiricus: 156
Sharp, D. E.: 159, 160
Siger of Brabant: 43
Simplicius: 157, 158, 171
Socrates: 48, 49, 51
Sokolowski, R.: 152
Soto, D.: 161
Spencer, H.: 157
Spinoza, B.: 89
Steenberghen, F. Von: 131, 133
Stohr, A.: 16
Stoics: 89, 100
Strauss, L.: 109
Suarez, F.: 161, 167
Sweeney, L.: 71, 135, 137ff., 139, 140, 142, 143, 149, 152, 153

Tempier, S.: 159
Tertullian: 158, 159, 176
Thales: 157
Themistius: 157
Theophrastus: 157
Theories of Being: 69
Theran, G. H. M.: 133
Thierry of Chartres: 69
Thirteenth-century thought, areas of: 5–7
Thomas Aquinas, St.: epistemology of, 8; interpreters of, 14; theistic proofs of, 15; works of, 20, 61, 62, 70, 71, 73–75, 78–81, 90, 92, 105, 108, 110–13, 116, 118, 131, 132, 167, 172, 173; on darkness of ignorance (state of confusion) concerning God, 69, 70, 79–86; on "ways of removal," 70ff.; on name of God, 70, 71; on "he who is," 72, 78, 80–83; on process of abstracting notion of God, 73–85; on transcendentality of goodness, 76ff.; on wisdom, 77ff.; on transcendental

properties, 77, 78; on being, 79ff.; on process of conceiving "being," 80ff.; world view of, 88–92; on divine and human practical knowledge, 90; on providence, 91ff.; on natural law, 91, 115, 116, 128; on moral virtues, 92–101; on power and habit, 93ff.; on need for virtues, 94–99; on eternal law, 98ff., 111; on virtue and passion, 100ff.; on prudence, 101, 105, 115; on man, social and political, 105–109; on common good, 106ff., 116; on teleology of society, 107; on *bonum honestum* and *utile*, 107ff.; on politics and government, 110–15; on preambles of faith, 118, 125ff., 129ff.; on existence of God, 118ff., 127; on thinking and knowing, 119–21; on believing *vs.* knowing, 119, 121–23; on religious belief, 121–24; on eternity of world, 128, 155, 163–67, 177–84; on divine infinity, 148–53
Thomas of York: 160
Tolman, R.: 156
Tongiorgi, S.: 160
Transcendental Thomism: 8, 14, 15

Ubaghs, G. C.: 65
University of Paris: 9, 21, 60, 131, 135
Urráburu, J. J.: 159, 162
Ussher, J.: 159

Vasquez, G.: 161, 167
Vaux Saint-Cyr, B. C. de: 141
Vignaux, P.: 59
Vollert, C.: 175

Wackerzapp, H.: 160
Wallace, W. A. 135
Walter of Bruges, 62
"Wayfaring state": 71
Weisheipl, J. A.: 134, 135
Weltin, E. G.: 153
Whitehead, A. N.: 16, 18
Whitrow, G. J.: 159
William of Auvergne: 136
William of Baglione: 62
Wilpert, P.: 183
Wippel, J. F.: 59
Wolter, A. B.: 59, 64, 134
Works of B. and T., chronology of: 134ff.

Zigliara, F. T. M.: 161
Zorzoli, E.: 67